IRISH ART

IRISH ART
in the Early Christian Period
(to 800 A.D.)

by
FRANÇOISE HENRY

METHUEN & CO LTD · LONDON

Irish Art in the Early Christian Period first published 1940. Second edition 1947
This completely revised edition first published in Great Britain 1965 by
Methuen & Co Ltd, 11 New Fetter Lane London EC4
Copyright © 1965 Françoise Henry
Text printed in Great Britain by Robert MacLehose & Co Ltd, The University
Press, Glasgow
Colour and monochrome plates printed by Les Presses Monastique and
L'Imprimerie Darantière, Dijon, France
Monochrome gravure plates printed by L'Imprimerie Braun, Mulhouse,
France

Contents

ABBREVIATIONS USED IN THE TEXT

Bel. M.   *Ulster Museum, Belfast*
Br. M.   *British Museum, London*
N.M.D.   *National Museum of Ireland, Dublin*
R.I.A.   *Royal Irish Academy*
T.C.D.   *Trinity College, Dublin*
Ashm. M.   *Ashmolean Museum, Oxford*
Bodl. Libr. *Bodleian Library, Oxford*

List of Maps and Drawings

List of Colour Plates

The colour photographs are by P. Belzeaux-Zodiaque, except two which are by J. Dieuzaide-Zodiaque.

Captions to individual colour plates may be found at the foot of each facing page

PRINCIPAL SITES

Iona

ISLAY

Candi
Ca

Fahan

DOOEY

AILEACH Derry

Bann

LOUGH RAVEL

LISNACROGHERA

Bangor
Moville

U L S T E R

Inismurray

Nendrum

Devenish

EMAIN Armagh

LOUGH
GARA

CONNACHT CRUACHAN

MEATH

ARDAKILLAN

Fore

Boyne

Roscommon

Kells

TARA

UISNEACH

LAGORE

BALLINDERRY

Clonard

Clonmacnois

Durrow

Finglas

Clonfert

Rahan

Kildare

Liffey

Tallaght

CAHERCOMMAUN

Lorrha

DUN AILINN

ARAN

Terryglass

Clonenagh

Glendalough

Inis Cealtra

Roscrea

Mona
Incha

LEINSTER

Barrow

Shannon

CARRAIG AILLE

CASHEL

M U N S T E R

Suir

Blackwater

Lismore

GARRYDUFF

GARRANES

St Davi

0   50 miles

0   100 km.

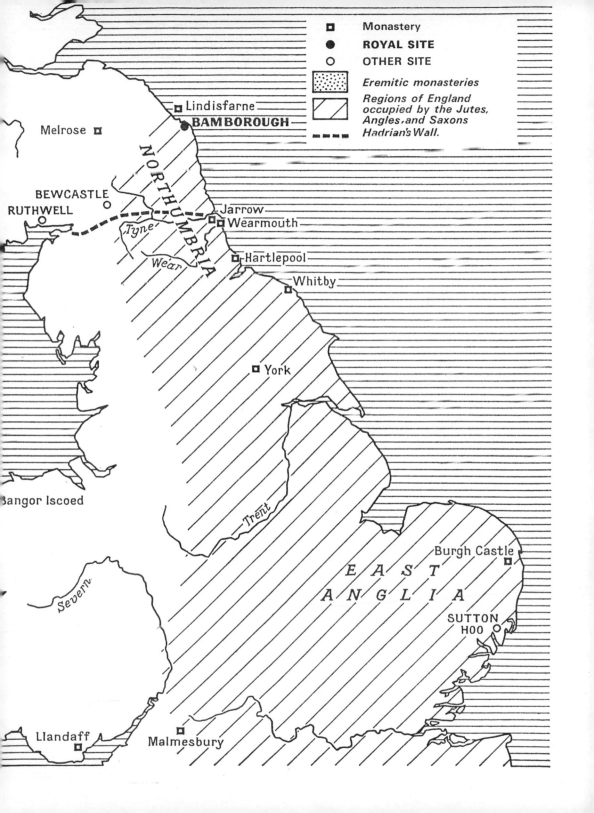

Monastery

ROYAL SITE

OTHER SITE

Eremitic monasteries

Regions of England occupied by the Jutes, Angles, and Saxons

Hadrian's Wall.

Melrose

Lindisfarne

BAMBOROUGH

NORTHUMBRIA

BEWCASTLE
RUTHWELL

Jarrow
Wearmouth

Tyne

Wear

Hartlepool

Whitby

York

Bangor Iscoed

Trent

E A S T

A N G L I A

Burgh Castle

Severn

SUTTON
HOO

Llandaff

Malmesbury

DONEGAL

DERRY

ANTRIM

L. Neagh

Bann

TYRONE

DOWN

LEITRIM

FERMANAGH

L. Erne

MONAGHAN

ARMAGH

LOUTH

SLIGO

CAVAN

MAYO

ROSCOMMON

LONGFORD

L. Ree

MEATH

L. Mask

L. Corrib

WESTMEATH

Boyne

DUBLIN

GALWAY

Shannon

OFFALY

KILDARE

Liffey

Aran

LEIX

WICKLOW

L. Derg

CLARE

TIPPERARY

KILKENNY

CARLOW

Barrow

WEXFORD

LIMERICK

Suir

Blackwater

WATERFORD

KERRY

CORK

0   50 miles

0   50   100 km.

Preface

IT MUST always be a strange experience to attempt to bring a book up to date after an interval of twenty-five years; in the case of the present volume perhaps even stranger than usual. The first edition was written at a time when everything with which it was concerned was still at the stage of discovery and when the main outlines of the picture were only beginning to emerge. Now the whole situation is altered. Some manuscripts which were nearly inaccessible to the ordinary reader are now widely known through complete or partial facsimiles, and E. A. Lowe's *Corpus* supplies a guide to the others. The metalwork from the Viking graves is gathered in a publication and excavation reports have helped to give some idea of the kind of settlements in which chance finds exhibited for a long time in museum cases were originally made and used.

But although this makes the handling of the material easier and lightens the task of explaining and describing—since most readers can check easily any general statement—recent controversies as to the part played by England in the elaboration of Irish art have tended to blur some aspects of the subject. They represent probably a passing phase and it would be dangerous to give them too much importance, so that they have only been dealt with when it was absolutely essential. As in the first edition it is necessary to emphasize the fact that this book attempts to give as coherent a picture as possible of works of Irish *style*, whether they were actually made in Ireland or in some of the Irish extensions abroad. Strangely enough, whilst some writers were attaching more and more importance to Lindisfarne and were trying to make it a sort of centre of elaboration of the Irish style, my own views on the subject, determined by a more detailed study of the material available, were evolving in the opposite direction. Hence the suppression of an independent chapter on Lindisfarne which existed in the first edition. It seemed also that a more continuous treatment of the historical background was needed. It would be, however, a deplorable mistake to consider the second chapter of this book as a 'history' of Ireland from the fifth century to the coming of the Vikings. It is in no way intended as such but should be taken only as an outline of those historical circumstances which were directly connected with art development.

The method of illustration has been changed completely, the emphasis being put on the definition of detail. This means that fewer objects are represented, but thanks to the publications now available, which can be easily consulted, this does not in fact constitute a drawback, and the excellent photographs of Belzeaux-Zodiaque taken specially for this book and its French edition will help the reader to see the objects nearly as well as if he were holding them in his hands.

The scope of this volume has been slightly altered. It stops with the coming of the Vikings to Ireland around A.D. 800. A second book will deal with the period from the coming of the Vikings to their defeat in the beginning of the eleventh century, and a third one will carry the story of Irish art to the arrival of the Normans at the end of the twelfth century.

The acknowledgments in the preface of the first edition now make melancholy reading because of the many names of departed friends which they include. And the debts of gratitude owed to Gerard Murphy and Seán P. Ó Ríordáin in regard to that first publication have been made more acutely obvious by the constantly recurring regret at being now deprived of their advice.

The preparation of this extended and revised version would have been impossible without the understanding of Dr Tierney, President of University College, Dublin, and the facilities which he has made available to me, and also without the help given to me by the Centre de la Recherche Scientifique. It has been made specially pleasant by the friendly collaboration of all the members of the Department of Archaeology of University College, Dublin, and by the untiring assistance of some friends, Geneviève L. Marsh-Micheli, William and Áine O'Sullivan, Máirín O Daly, and above all, Maureen Murphy.

I am very grateful for the way in which my work has always been facilitated by all the staff of the National Museum of Ireland, and especially by the Director, Dr Lucas, and the Keeper of Irish Antiquities, Dr Raftery; by Dr Parke, and all the staff of the Library of Trinity College, Dublin; by Mr P. Le Clerc, Inspector of National Monuments and his staff; by Dr R. Hayes, Director of the National Library of Ireland; by Professor O'Kelly in Cork and Mr L. Flanagan in Belfast. In research in the British Museum, I have been greatly helped by Mr R. Bruce-Mitford, Keeper of British Antiquities, by Dr Werner, Director of the Laboratory and by Mr J. Brown, then on the staff of the Department of Manuscripts. I want also to thank the Dean of Lichfield, who made all arrangements for the taking of photographs in colour of the Lichfield Gospels, and Mr R. Powell who facilitated in every way the study of the manuscript whilst it was in his care for re-binding. I am indebted to M. René Crozet, Directeur du Centre d'Etudes médiévales of the University of Poitiers, for much encouragement and information as to comparative material.

For all the care and hard work which have gone into the taking of the Belzeaux-Zodiaque photographs, the courage and spirit of enterprise of Dom Angelico Surchamp, O.S.B., and the technical skill of M. Belzeaux are essentially responsible. All the other photographs come from the Photographic Archives of the Department of Archaeology of University College, Dublin. We are glad to thank, for authorizations to take or use some of these photographs : the National Museum of Ireland, the Commissioners of Public Works in Ireland, the Vice-Provost and Librarian of Trinity College, Dublin, the President and Council of the Royal Irish Academy, the Director of Belfast Museum, the Trustees of the British Museum, the Director of the Victoria and Albert Museum, the Dean and Chapter of the Cathedral of Lichfield, the Dean and Chapter of the Cathedral of Durham, Dr Hunt, Keeper of Western Manuscripts in the Bodleian Library, the Director of the Ashmolean Museum, the Director of the Musée des Antiquités nationales, M. Porcher, Curator of the Manuscripts in the Bibliothèque nationale, the Prefect of the Ambrosian Library, the Director of the Laurentian Library, the Directors of the Museums of Stockholm, Copenhagen, Oslo, Bergen and Trondheim, the Librarian of the Library of Saint-Gall, Mrs Marsh-Micheli, Mrs 1. Crosier and Mr L. de Paor; and for authorizing the reproduction of drawings Mr T. Burckhardt, Dr H. G. Leask and the Museums of Oslo and Stavanger.

It is perhaps necessary to remind the reader that *Scotus* or *Scottus* in texts of the Early Christian period always means Irish, and also to introduce some apologies : it is nearly unavoidable to use sometime the word Saxon where Angle would be more apt (in reference to Northumbria, for example), and it is practically impossible to be consistent in the spelling of Irish words, some occuring in quotations, others deformed by custom. Thus, for example, Inish (island) and Lough (lake) will be found frequently, besides the more correct forms Inis and Loch. For this I can only beg the greatest indulgence from the reader.

Topographical indications in brackets refer to the Irish counties of which a map is given on p. xii.[1]

[1] The French version of this book, published by the Editions Zodiaque, has appeared in September 1963.

xvi

1. Irish Art in Pagan Times

A REMARKABLE continuity is one of the most striking aspects of Irish art. For centuries, during the Early Middle Ages, Irish artists were nearly always satisfied to combine abstract patterns according to very strict and elaborate rules. Influences from outside gave new impulses from time to time, but never altered very deeply the appearance and fundamental spirit of Irish decoration. Only if we realize that a long pagan tradition supplied the first elements and the essential decorative principles of the art which flourished in the monasteries after the fifth century, will we see the reason for this persistence of outlook.

Already in prehistoric times,[1] during the megalithic period, Ireland had an art of remarkable quality of which the firmly carved spirals of the threshold stone of New Grange (Pl. 1), as well as the delicate chevron and circle decoration of some gold objects give us an idea. But the civilization from which this art sprang withered slowly into an indigent late Bronze Age which seems, in spite of a few importations, to linger on without any deep changes during part of the period which corresponds to the Continental Iron Age.

We know very little about the population of Ireland at that time. Its origin, the race to which it belonged, the language it spoke, are so many interrogation marks to which very varied answers have been given.[2] Ireland will emerge, in the first texts concerning her, speaking a Celtic language and inhabited in part by people who bear Celtic names. But we do not know at what time Celts first made their appearance in the

---

[1] Macalister, *Arch. Ir.*, Raftery, *Preh. Ir.*, A. Mahr, 'New Aspects and problems of Irish Pre-History', *P.P.S.*, 1937, pp. 262 sqq., Seán P. Ó Ríordáin, 'Prehistory in Ireland, 1937–46', *P.P.S.*, 1946, pp. 142 sqq.

[2] See : MacNeill, *Phases*, O'Rahilly, *Hist. and Myth.*, H. Hubert, *Les Celtes* (Paris, 1932). T. G. Powell, *The Celts* (London, 1958), Id., 'The Celtic Settlement of Ireland', *H. M. Chadwick Memorial Studies* (Cambridge, 1950), pp. 171 sqq.

country, from where they came, and whether they landed in several successive waves.

One of the few fixed points in this incertitude is that the 'La Tène' civilization, that of the Continental Celts during the second Iron Age, was introduced into Ireland during the centuries immediately preceding the birth of Christ.[1] Though there were close links with England from which objects were exported into Ireland, the most important contacts seem to have been directly with the Continent. In many cases, no doubt, they are only due to the journeys of a few merchants or to the travelling of wandering craftsmen. This is the most superficial aspect of the problem. But there have also been found in Ireland stones carved with Celtic patterns and statues which are obviously religious monuments. These have a very different significance. They imply a background of cult and myth (Pls. 2, 3, Fig. 1). Visible signs of a belief, they can only have been introduced by invaders coming with their priests, their art, probably their poetic tradition. Gaulish refugees fleeing before Caesar's conquests have been suggested several times,[2] and it sounds certainly the most plausible hypothesis. The old trade route of the tin and gold between Gaul and the mines of Cornwall and Ireland had been known to seafarers for centuries. They probably availed themselves of it. They may have come in rather small numbers, and it is probable that the bulk of the population was at first only very superficially affected by the

[1] On La Tène art in Ireland, see Allen, *Celtic Art*; E. C. R. Armstrong, 'The Early Iron Age or Hallstatt Period in Ireland', *J.R.S.A.I.*, 1924, pp. 1 sqq.; Id., 'The La Tène Period in Ireland', *J.R.S.A.I.*, 1923, pp. 1 sqq.; Raftery, *Preh. Ir.*; Id., 'Zur Zeitbestimmung der irischen Eisenzeit', *Marburg Studien*, 1938, pp. 202 sqq.; Id. 'A suggested Chronology of the Irish Iron Age', *F.-S. M. Néill*, pp. 272 sqq.; Stuart Piggott, 'The Carnyx in Early Iron Age Britain', *Ant. J.*, 1959, pp. 19 sqq.; R. J. C. Atkinson – Stuart Piggott, 'The Torrs Chamfrein', *Archaeologia*, 1955, pp. 197 sqq.; E. M. Jope, 'The Keshcarrigan Bowl and a bronze Mirror-Handle from Ballymoney, Co. Antrim', *U.J.A.*, 1954, pp. 92 sqq.; Id. 'Two Iron Age Bridle-Bits from the North of Ireland', *U.J.A.*, 1950, pp. 58 sqq., E. Rynne, in; Acts of the 5th Prehistoric Congress Hamburg (Berlin 1961), pp. 705 sqq.

[2] Cf. the hypothesis by T. F. O'Rahilly of a flight of the Helvetii to Ireland, T. F. O'Rahilly, *The Goidels and their predecessors* (London, 1936), and MacNeill's suggestion that the Eoghanachta were the Eburovices who would have come to Ireland after being defeated by Caesar, *An Reult*, I, No. 2 (1922); See also O'Rahilly, *Hist. and Myth., passim.*

change and clung for a long time to its old semi-megalithic customs. But in the course of time the new culture seems to have permeated the whole country and to have coloured all its ways of thinking and its artistic notions.

The progress of the Romans first in Gaul, then in Britain, brought them in the first century A.D. to the shores of the Irish Sea. Agricola contemplated the possibilities of a conquest of Ireland. But other cares made him change his mind and during the following centuries the Roman Legions never attempted to cross the ill-famed Irish Sea which Solinus in the third century A.D. describes as 'billowy and restless and navigable only during a very few days in the whole year'.[1] Still, Irish boats crossed occasionally, and the Irish, by trade or plunder, came to know many aspects of the civilization of their neighbours.[2] They imitated them in many ways. The 'Black Pig's Dyke', that enormous earthen rampart which the Ulstermen raised against the invasions of their neighbours, was probably an imitation of the wall of Hadrian,[3] and the first system of writing ever used in Ireland, the ogham alphabet, is a clumsy transcription into a rectilinear script of the Latin alphabet.[4]

When the Imperial power weakened the wealth of Britain, developed during centuries of Roman peace, became such an attraction that the fourth-century historians record constant raids of the 'Scotti' (Irish). These raids enabled them to share in some of the fantastic accumulation of silver plate and trinkets which were swooped upon by the plunderers of towns and churches everywhere in the Empire. They also carried away slaves. It was during one of these looting expeditions that the young boy who was to become Saint Patrick was taken from the village

[1] *Collectanea rerum memorabilium*, XII.

[2] In fact, there was also direct trading between Ireland and the Continent, as Tacitus remarks that 'the ports and landing places of Hibernia are better known than those of Britain, through the frequency of commerce and merchants' (*Agricola.*, ch. 24).

[3] MacNeill, *Phases*, pp. 131, 151; *contra*: O. Davies, 'The Black Pig's Dyke', *U.J.A.*, 1955, pp. 29 sqq. See also: W. F. Kane, *P.R.I.A.*, (C), 1908–9, pp. 301 sqq., Ibid., 1916–17, (C), pp. 539 sqq.

[4] J. MacNeill, 'Notes on the Distribution, History, Grammar and Import of the Irish Ogham Inscriptions', *P.R.I.A.*, 1907 (C), pp. 329 sqq.; K. Jackson, 'Notes on Ogam Inscriptions of Southern Britain', *The Early Cultures of North-West Europe* (Cambridge, 1950); E. MacWhite, 'Contribution to a Study of Ogam Memorial Stones', *Z.C.P.*, 1961, pp. 294 sqq.

where he had spent his childhood and brought as a captive to Ireland.[1]

The collapse of the Empire resulted in an Irish expansion on the coasts of Britain – in Wales and Scotland – which culminated, during the last years of the fifth century, in the 'migration of the Sons of Erc' and the establishment of the Scottish kingdom of Dál Riada. Henceforward, the Irish world was not only Ireland itself, but included also an ever-increasing part of the West of Scotland, first Kintyre, then Argyll, and finally, about the early seventh century, the coasts and islands up to Skye. The similar incursions which took place on the coast of Wales are less well known and do not seem to have resulted in such organized settlements.

What can be gathered of life in Ireland during the six or seven centuries preceding the introduction of Christianity in the fifth century, shows a scattered population, living mostly in farm buildings protected by circular palisades or dry-stone walls on the slopes of the hills, or in small artificial islands erected on the edge of the lakes and of the marshes which seem to have covered a good deal of the centre of the country. The rath (fortified farm) and the crannog (artificial island) are the most common types of habitation in Ireland at that time[2] and will remain so until late in the Middle Ages.[3] Larger hilltop enclosures may be the equivalents of the oppida of the Continental Celts.

The country was divided into several kingdoms. In the constant struggle between them the power of Connacht rose, threatening its rival, Ulster. The Cúchulainn saga recalls the legendary version of one phase of that struggle.[4] Though it started being written down as an organized epic only in the sixth or seventh centuries it embodies so much of older material that it gives precious indications of the life of that early period. Its descriptions agree with the text of the Greek and Latin writers who show us a society where cattle was the essential source of wealth and war and plunder the chief occupations.

[1] See pp. 18–19. [2] Ó Ríordáin, *Antiquities*.

[3] For the late use of crannogs, see *inter alia*: Wood-Martin, *Lake Dwellings*, pp. 164–5; W. Reeves, 'An Account of the Crannog of Inishrush and its Ancient Occupants', *U.J.A.*, 1911, pp. 3 sqq.

[4] Thurneysen, *Helden und Königsage*; M. Dillon, *The Cycles of the Kings* (London–New York, 1946); *Irish Sagas*.

The names of places from which kings ruled have been preserved: Cruachan in Connacht, Emain (near Armagh) in Ulster, Uisneach, Tara, Dun Ailinn, Dinn Ríg. In Emain and in Cruachan there remain circular enclosures and tumuli. Tara, a long, low hill above the plain of Meath, to the north of Dublin, has similar remains.

Uisneach was partially excavated in 1929 by R. A. S. Macalister and R. L. Praeger[1] who found there, upset by more recent constructions, circular rock-cut ditches belonging to the early occupation.

One of the sites on the hill of Tara, the Rath of the Synods, was excavated in 1952–4 by S. P. Ó Ríordáin[2]. The findings justified the descriptions of the epics which mention large wooden constructions: wooden houses surrounded by several concentric palisades standing above deep rock-cut trenches, had been re-built several times. They may have had up to a point a ritual purpose, but they were certainly lived in and, as in many other later sites, remains attesting the activity of smiths and enamellers were found there. The period of occupation is dated by Roman importations to the first and second centuries A.D. These importations reveal contacts not only with England, but also with the Continent.[3]

The excavations of the Mound of the Hostages,[4] a tumulus about 50 yards away from the Rath of the Synods, begun in 1956 by S. P. Ó Ríordáin, were terminated after his death by Ruaidhrí de Valéra. They introduce us to a much more remote past in the occupation of Tara : the mound covered a megalithic tomb in whose tumulus forty or so burials of the Middle Bronze Age had been inserted. These discoveries give to Tara the background of a prehistoric necropolis and sanctuary later adapted by the Celts to new needs and turned into a royal residence still keeping a religious aura.

As for the religious carvings, we have no data to enable us to recon-

---

[1] R. A. S. Macalister–R. L. Praeger, 'Report on the Excavation of Uisneach', *P.R.I.A.*, 1928, pp. 69 sqq.

[2] S. P. Ó Ríordáin, *Tara, The Monuments on the Hill* (Dundalk, 2nd ed., 1957), pp. 22–3.

[3] Though it has to be remembered that Continental objects such as *terra sigillata* vases could arrive in Ireland through England.

[4] Ibid. pp. 23–4.

struct the monumental frame into which they may have fitted. They are
of two kinds: stones covered with ornaments, and human or animal
figurations. This corresponds to the main categories of carvings of the
Continental Celts.[1] Chance may play an important part in the distribution of those which have come down to us. But it is nevertheless a
remarkable fact that they all belong to the West or North of Ireland, the
two kingdoms at war in the Cúchulainn epic. The distribution of those of the
Irish La Tène objects which are localized is on the whole very similar,
so that one feels tempted to think that these regions are those where the
Gaulish invaders of the time of Caesar established their most prosperous
kingdoms and the area where their religion became most deeply rooted.

All these stones are massive blocks, scarcely shaped. On the Turoe
stone (Fig. 1),[2] which is four feet high, curvilinear motifs are carved in
low relief, arranged without any thought of symmetry: discs and foliage
are strung together in a continuous pattern, limited only by a rectilinear border. The treatment of relief is strongly reminiscent of that of
the Rhenish pyramid from Pfalzfeld which is in the Museum at Bonn,[3]
one of the great monuments of carving of the Continental Celts. The
stone at Castlestrange (Roscommon)[4] has an even more formless
design covering its surface in deeply cut lines. Another similar monument of larger size is found at Killycluggin (Cavan) (Fig. 1).[5] Its

[1] It is now an acknowledged fact that the Continental Celts carved representations of their gods and heroes, so that the detailed treatment of this subject in the
first edition has been omitted. See: Raymond Lantier, in Marcel Aubert's *Histoire
de l'Art*, I (Paris, 1922), pp. 1 sqq.; Id. 'Le dieu celtique de Bouray', *Monuments
Piot*, 1934, pp. 34 sqq.; Jacobsthal, *C.A.* (1945); R. Lantier–J. Hubert, *Les origines
de l'art français* (Paris, 1947); Varagnac–Fabre, *Art gaulois* (1956); see also:
R. Lambrechts, *L'exaltation de la tête dans la pensée et dans l'art des celtes* (Bruges,
1954).

[2] J. Raftery, 'The Turoe Stone and the Rath of Feerwore', *J.R.S.A.I.*, 1944,
pp. 39 sqq.

[3] Jacobsthal, *C.A.*, Pls. 9–12.

[4] Armstrong, 'La Tène', op. cit.; Champneys, *Ir. Eccl. Arch.*, p. 67, Pl. XXX.

[5] R. A. S. Macalister, 'On a stone with La Tène decoration recently discovered
in Co. Cavan', *J.R.S.A.I.*, 1922, pp. 113 sqq.; Id., *Arch. Ir*, p. 145; for another
fragment, see: S. P. Ó. Ríordáin, *J.R.S.A.I.*, 1954 (Miscellanea), p. 68. A stone
found at Mullaghmast (Kildare; N.M.D.) may belong to this series, but is more
likely to be of later date.

Fig. 1. Turoe stone (Galway);
Killycluggin stone (Cavan).

pattern, very elegant, obeys more closely a rhythm of composition than that on the two other monuments. It consists of finely drawn curves ending in tightly coiled spirals.

The statues are all of a strange, rough style, which simplifies volumes and accentuates violently the features of the face. They have more in common with such inhuman and abstract Celtic monuments as the double statue from Holzgerlingen or the fragment from Echterdingen, both in Stuttgart Museum,[1] than with the Gaulish statues from Provence and Languedoc, carved under Mediterranean influence.[2] Two of them have been found on islands of Lough Erne (Fermanagh).[3] One has the same double-statue structure as the monument from Holzgerlingen (Pl. 3),

[1] Jacobsthal, *C.A.*, Pls. 13 and 15.
[2] F. Benoît, *L'art primitif méditerranéen de la vallée du Rhone* (Paris, 1956).
[3] D. Lowry-Corry, 'The Stones carved with Human Effigies on Boa Island and on Lustymore Island, in Lower Loch Erne', *P.R.I.A.*, 1933(C), pp. 200 sqq.

7

whilst the position of the arms which is characteristic of this German statue is found on a bust which was kept for a long time in a rock-garden at Tanderagee (Armagh)[1] (Pl. 2) and is now in the cathedral of Armagh. It shows a clumsy creature with a thick neck, wearing a horned helmet similar to those in the Gaulish trophies carved on the Roman arch at Orange,[2] or to that worn by the Gaulish figure from La Celle-Mont-Saint-Jean (Sarthe).[3] Its mouth is wide open as in a shriek, its moustache stands up and it seems to hold its left shoulder with a right hand which is only a kind of stunted paw. Other statues of men and beasts are now collected around this one in the chapter-house of the cathedral of Armagh. They are not all of the same age, but the animal carvings may go back also to pagan times. They may be fragments from a sanctuary which the foundation in the fifth century of the cathedral of Armagh was intended to supersede.

As for the metal objects from this period, their study is extremely difficult. First of all, we lack a corpus, or even lists of objects; also many of them have no precise location, or have such a vague origin as to be of little help. Only a very small number of sites from that time have been scientifically explored. Robber excavations like those carried out in the nineteenth century in the crannog of Lisnacroghera (Antrim),[4] which was no doubt inhabited over a fairly long period, leave us rather helpless.

We are thrown back on typological and stylistic considerations to try and put some order into this material which covers a span of five or six centuries. Typology is not as helpful here, however, as one might expect. This chiefly because no sooner were imported objects introduced into Ireland than they were, as Joseph Raftery has very rightly pointed

[1] A. Kingsley Porter, 'A Sculpture at Tanderagee', *Burlington Magazine*, Nov. 1934, p. 227; R. A. S. Macalister, 'A Sculptured Figure Stone from Tanderagee', *J.R.S.A.I.*, 1935, pp. 156 sqq.; the carving was probably found in a bog near Newry; see also: G. F. Patterson–O. Davies, 'The Churches of Armagh', *U.J.A.*, 1940, pp. 82 sqq.; and Anne Ross, 'The Horned God of the Brigantes', *Arch. Aeliana*, 1961, pp. 63 sqq.

[2] P. Coussin, 'Les frises de l'Arc d'Orange', *R.A.*, 1927, *passim*.

[3] Varagnac–Fabre, *Art gaulois*, pls. 38–9.

[4] Wood-Martin, *Lake-Dwellings*, pp. 173 sqq.; Macalister, *Arch. Ir.*, p. 153; *J.R.S.A.I.*, 1891, pp. 542 sqq.

out, imitated with the utmost fancy, the imitations losing rapidly any likeness to their model. The most striking examples of this process are given by the brooches or fibulae of which Ireland supplies a remarkably erratic series.

On the other hand, one would be entitled to expect some result from stylistic considerations, given the high proportion of decorated objects. But in this case two elements are at work to defeat us: first the individualistic tendency already mentioned, second the limitations of the decorative repertoire. La Tène artists had derived from palmettes and scrolls a system of curvilinear patterns which did not allow for endless variations.[1] This art, in addition, reached Ireland under a semi-geometrical guise which adds even more to its limitations. The same compositions recur over and over again: three curves arranged triskele fashion in a circle, combinations or associations of non-concentric circles, circles or curves combined with a foliage motif. It would be dangerous to ascribe any one of them to a single definite period. It is tempting to try to group these objects, to compare them with Continental or English objects, but it remains, except in a few well-defined cases, only a game of chance. In consequence, various and contradictory attempts have been made to establish a chronology. A tendency to believe that Celtic patterns have disappeared from Ireland at the time when they stopped being used in England is implicit in several of them. In fact it seems obvious that, on the contrary, curvilinear patterns which withstood the impact of classical themes in Roman England until well into the second century A.D. had an infinitely better chance of survival in Ireland. It is consequently very likely that no 'hiatus' ever existed in Ireland between late La Tène objects and the first enamelled penannular brooches which may appear already in the fourth century and were certainly currently in use in the fifth and sixth centuries.[2]

Indeed, there are some facts which may give ample food for reflection on the persistency of these patterns. Nils Åberg is probably perfectly right when he attributes to the seventh century[3] two similar objects, one Irish – the brooch found in the Ardakillin crannog (Roscommon)

[1] Smith, *Guide Iron Age*, pp. 18 sqq.; Coffey, *Guide*, pp. 1 sqq.
[2] See p. 14. [3] Åberg, *Occident–Orient*, I, p. 25.

9

(Pl. 10) which belongs to a well known Merovingian type[1] – and the other Scottish – the silver repoussé plaque from the Norries Law hoard found with sixth-seventh centuries objects and with coins of which the latest is from A.D. 680.[2] These two objects have in common, beside the repoussé technique, the use of very high relief curves falling abruptly on the background on one side; they are very similar to a series of very large Irish discs in repoussé bronze which are in the Dublin Museum and the British Museum. We shall in consequence adopt a late dating for all these objects, some of which have been occasionally attributed to an early period. The kinship of their decorative themes with much earlier ones which are fairly dateable is so striking that the continuity of this art is thus demonstrated.

So, in spite of the difficulties outlined above, it remains possible to establish a few fixed points. Let us examine some others.

Six bronze scabbards engraved with very elegant patterns have been found in Ulster, to the north of Lough Neagh, not very far from each other: some are from Lisnacroghera (Antrim) and the others were found in the Bann at Toome and at Coleraine (Antrim-Derry).[3] Treated with various degrees of skill, their patterns are all variations on motifs which are used on the Continent in the decoration of third- and second-century scabbards and which appear also on the English scabbards from Bugthorpe and Hunsbury. But the Irish swords are curiously small. Their scabbards are very peculiar in outline and have completely aberrant chapes. We may have to allow time for such changes. But even if they are later than their Continental parallels, they still have to be dated to the last centuries before Christ. It looks as if they came from an isolated group of craftsmen, as so far no other scabbard of this type

---

[1] That which E. Salin calls 'fibules ansées symétriques' (Salin, *C.M.*, II, pp. 299–300). He dates an elaborate example from Charnay (Saône-et-Loire) to the eighth century, but the more current type belongs to the seventh. Several examples were found in the Hypogeum of Mellebaude, at Poitiers (C. de la Croix, *Hypogée-Martyrium*, Pl. XVIII). They are different in general shape from the equal-armed brooches found in Saxon graves which are probably of Continental Germanic origin.

[2] Allen–Anderson, I, pp. LXXXIII sqq.

[3] Raftery, *Preh. Ir.*; E. M. Jope, 'An Iron Age decorated sword-scabbard from the River Bann at Toome', *U.J.A.*, 1954, pp. 92 sqq.; Smith, *Guide Iron Age*, p. 160.

has been found in other parts of Ireland, and they allow us a glimpse into a workshop where La Tène art was known not as a few novel patterns, but in its very spirit. The scrolls are produced very skilfully (Pls. 6, 7) by work which is more than simple engraving and includes depressed zones with serrated edges and tightly coiled spirals whose curves are finely rounded. The insertion of these spirals which occur also on the Killycluggin stone and which strangely call to mind the megalithic ones raises a problem. Right through the history of art in Ireland in the first centuries A.D. there are facts which show a contact with megalithic patterns: for the early period (second–fourth century) the workshop of carved bones established in one of the cairns of Lough Crew (Meath);[1] later, the presence of fragments of megalithic carvings in the Rath of Togherstown near Uisneach (seventh–eighth century) and in the crannog No. 1 of Ballinderry (ninth–tenth century); all this shows over a long period, contacts with prehistoric art which opens up the way for imitations, more likely on the whole than simple survivals though these can never be ruled out altogether.

Other curvilinear patterns of very simple tracery and much nearer to the true spirit of La Tène art are exemplified by the horse-trappings found at Attymon (Galway) (Pl. 4). These are not easy to date and are interesting chiefly as examples of the very sensitive feeling for line and modelling characteristic of the work of the Celtic craftsmen in Ireland.[2]

From this early period, enamelling, an essential technique of Celtic art, was known and practised with great skill. A small object from

[1] E. A. Conwell, *The Tomb of Ollamh Fodhla* (Dublin, 1873), p. 54; H. S. Crawford, 'The engraved bone objects found at Lough Crew', *J.R.S.A.I.*, 1925, pp. 15 sqq. These objects were lost for a number of years, but are available again in the National Museum, Dublin. J. Raftery has re-excavated the megalith and found more bone fragments, some complementary to those found by Conwell (such as part of the stag hunt, Pl. 7); I am grateful for the information he gave me on the subject.

[2] I am leaving out of this discussion the gold collar from Broighter (Antrim) (R. L. Praeger, 'The Broighter gold Ornaments', *J.R.S.A.I.*, 1942, pp. 29 sqq.). The so-called 'Broighter hoard' was a collection of miscellaneous objects which probably came from a private collection (G. Little, *Irish Press*, Nov. 1959). This does not necessarily mean that the collar was not found in Ireland. But a doubt remains.

11

Lisnacroghera (Pl. 1) shows two little bronze ducks sitting over a band of red enamel through which run wavy lines of bronze. Another object in Belfast Museum is enamelled in the same way. These zig-zags running through a narrow field of enamel are found at Mont Beuvray, near Autun,[1] on objects practically contemporary with the conquest of Caesar and this helps to give an approximate date to the Irish objects.

Another enamelled object of great importance was found in 1959 at Somerset, near Ballinasloe (Galway),[2] together with several objects which may not be all of exactly the same date, but which go back to about the time of Christ or a slightly earlier period. It is a small bronze relief and openwork disc meant probably to be mounted on a flat surface of bronze, wood or leather (Fig. 6). It still holds a filling of red opaque glass which shows through the openings of the bronze grille. Its decoration was made by a technique found also on a series of La Tène objects of various dates both in England and on the Continent (Bouzonville œnochoés, Cuperly disc, Battersea shield, Hod Hill boss). This process consists in placing in a clay mould into which it fits exactly a little boss of openwork bronze. Enamel or molten glass is then introduced in the cavities formed by the cuts in the bronze surface and is often held in place by a small ball of clay. This was probably a way of avoiding the difficulties of enamelling a rounded surface. On some of the English bosses a polychrome effect has been obtained by putting discs of blue glass in a few of the apertures of the bronze; red molten glass is then applied on the whole surface and backed with clay; it holds the blue glass in position and is only to be seen in those of the openings which have not been filled with blue. The Somerset boss was made by a similar method : a substance now vanished had been inserted in the compartments of the perimeter; a thick blob of viscous glass was then let down into the boss lying upside down in its mould; the glass filled the top opening where it is still flush with the outer bronze surface; in the other openings where it was only holding the vanished substance, it remains everywhere on a level with the inner surface of the bronze. Many centuries later, the bosses of the Ardagh chalice were made by a nearly identical method.

[1] Henry, *Em. Occ.*, Figs. 6 and 10.
[2] J. Raftery, 'A Hoard of the Early Iron Age', *J.R.S.A.I.*, 1960, pp. 2 sqq.

A slightly later stage of the evolution of the Irish La Tène objects is supplied by the cemetery on Lambay island,[1] to the north of Dublin Bay. A few tombs were discovered in 1927, when the landing quay was being rebuilt. The objects have survived, but unfortunately very little record was kept of their associations in the tombs. We find there, in the first century A.D., a massive influx of Roman and Brito-Roman objects; an iron mirror, military fibulae, etc. One tomb yielded openwork bronze objects with La Tène patterns, another a repoussé bronze disc which gives a well-dated example of that oft-repeated pattern, the three curves inscribed in a circle. A curious indication is supplied by the presence both of a Roman brooch and of its exact copy by a local craftsman who cast it in one piece, so that the pin holds to the catch and cannot be used.

This massive importation of Roman objects goes on during the whole of the Empire.[2] We have seen that there were some in the Rath of the Synods. Many others have been found here and there in Ireland. And the survival to a late date of Roman forms shows how overpowering these models had been. One may quote in this respect a little bronze scratcher of the sixth century of a type frequently found in the Roman 'toilet sets', but here enamelled with a definitely Irish pattern (Dublin Museum).[3] A belt buckle found in Lagore carries right into the seventh or eighth century the outline and ornament of the buckles worn by Roman legionaries.[4] The vogue, in the sixth and seventh centuries, of hanging-bowls derived from Roman models is another manifestation of the same tendency. Techniques also have been introduced. One of the most striking is the manufacture of sticks of millefiori glass whose segments were combined with champlevé in Gallo-Roman enamelling and which reappear, used in a similar way, in Irish metalwork. Another is the preparation of purple dye, an industry the Romans learned from the Phoenicians and which became prosperous on the coasts of Ireland and England during the Early Middle Ages.[5] Irish craftsmen had also

[1] R. A. S. Macalister, 'On some Antiquities discovered upon Lambay', *P.R.I.A.*, 1929 (C), pp. 240 sqq.

[2] S. P. Ó Ríordáin, 'Roman material in Ireland', *P.R.I.A.*, 1947, pp. 35 sqq.

[3] *C.A.A.I.*, I, Pl. 41, 5.   [4] Henry, *Ir. enam.*, Pl. IX.

[5] See pp. 48–9. It is mentioned by Bede (*H.E.*, I, 1), as one of the sources of wealth of Britain.

perhaps learned at that time the delicate soldering which goes into the making of very fine filigree work such as Greek craftsmen had introduced into Italy.[1]

In this, we are not dealing only with direct importations. Via Scotland and Wales came Roman types of objects already partly altered, such as the penannular brooch which was to enjoy a wide popularity in Ireland. H. Kilbride-Jones,[2] relying on striking similarities which exist between Irish examples and those found in the border regions between Scotland and the Roman world, attributed to the third century A.D. the appearance of the first enamelled brooches. Some of the dates on which he based this assertion may need revising,[3] and a slightly later date would allow better for the transmission of shapes and their adaptation to enamelled decoration. It still remains likely, however, that the Irish enamelled brooches were being made towards the end of the Empire. Their decoration consists of a new version of curvilinear design with thin lines of red enamel. Sometimes, little discs of millefiori glass are combined with the champlevé work or replace it.

The principles ruling the decoration of this period of which, so far, we have only indicated the general appearance, deserve a more thorough examination. They are based on an extraordinary virtuosity in the use of the compasses. The premiss of this method may have been stated elsewhere than in Ireland[4] – on the Continent or in Britain, perhaps in Wales or in Cornwall – and a few of the objects found in Ireland where it is applied may be importations. It matters little. The essential fact is that in Ireland it survived, whilst it was gradually vanishing in England under the impact of classical art.

A close examination of some objects may give a key to the way it works. First, the 'box' from the Somerset hoard (Pl. 5). The use of compasses has left clear marks there. But it does not lead to a rigid balance. From a centre which has left no visible trace two concentric circles have been drawn of which one is the outline of the object while the other

[1] See p. 74.   [2] Kilbride-Jones, *Brooches*.
[3] H. N. Savory, 'Some Sub-Romano-British Brooches from South Wales', *Dark Age Britain*, pp. 40 sqq.
[4] See pp. 216 sqq.

limits the decorated area. Another centre, slightly apart from this one, which can be seen clearly, has been used to draw a series of incomplete circles. The space included between the widest of these circles and the limit of the decorated area – an off-centre ring – has been divided into two uneven zones, one in relief, the other covered with stippling. A low relief disc encroaching on the engraved circles completes this strange abstract composition based on compass drawn arcs, which is both regular and asymmetrical. It is infinitely pleasing, partly because of its puzzling enigma which cannot be resolved at a glance.

Even from what might well be a dull combination of circles, the artist will draw surprising effects. A pair of Irish spoons or castanets, of a type which is known from various parts of Britain as well as from Irish finds, gives a good example of this: the circles are drawn from a series of centres scattered along a vertical line and from one which is slightly away from that line, and simply by variations in the diameter, the draughtsman succeeds in producing a series of combinations of curved shapes (Fig. 27).

There is a still more complex exercise: the bone slips from Lough Crew (Pl. 8) give a whole gamut of designs made by combining arcs in continuous or opposed patterns which produce a balanced rhythm. As the centres have left a clear mark on the surface of the bone, it is possible to reconstruct the whole process (Fig. 31).[1] It requires great experience of all possible combinations of curves which accord and can be made to flow into a continuous line. From this, one can pass without transition to the combination of curves of the Bann disc which E. M. Jope has reconstructed (Fig. 30).

This system at first sight purely mathematical, is in fact neither mechanical nor inhuman. It constitutes a means of expression both elastic and crisp, very close to music and using, as music does, numeral elements as units which the human mind can organize. It represents one of the greatest feats of abstract art, an abstract art which involves enough geometry to make of the building of its patterns an intricate problem, while at the same time avoiding it just enough to keep intact the flavour of a human choice. To anybody giving a cursory glance at

[1] See p. 220.

15

the five centuries which precede the introduction of Christianity, it may seem that nothing happens over all those years, that one just meets here and there some objects which have always roughly the same type of design, a poverty-stricken tangle of curves and spirals. In reality this is the time when the strange method which will be the backbone of all the art of Christian times is being slowly elaborated.

2. Irish Christian Art: the historical background

As WE have just seen, the picture we are able to draw, from the very scanty documents at our disposal, of the Ireland of the first four centuries of our era is that of a country living in a strange seclusion, on the fringe of the Roman Empire, but outside its grip, free to foster and develop the age-old prehistoric tradition which had been handed down to her. She did not have the Roman conceptions of law, state and organization stamped on her mind, nor the cold rectitude of Latin thought. She was to preserve to the Middle Ages a prehistoric fluidity of mind. She was to be spared the violent clashes of opposed outlooks, the difficult adjustments which resulted in the Gallo-Roman and Brito-Roman civilizations. Unlike the other Celts, the Irish of the Roman period were not to be made ashamed of an old culture, they were not awkwardly to bend their minds to foreign ways of thinking, they were not to be the colonized people aping even the worst aspects of a well-organized, well-fed, industrialized, and matter-of-fact civilization. But at the same time, the Roman sense of order and discipline which remained the dream of the once Romanized countries all through the Middle Ages, Ireland was only to know at second hand.

In the same way she escaped the effects of the Germanic storm, which, for all its catastrophic appearance, brought a new life wherever it raged. Secluded from these conflicts and catastrophies, hardly conscious of them, the Irish developed slowly to their ultimate consequences the possibilities of a culture extinct everywhere else in Europe. It was and remained a typical North European culture, foreign to Mediterranean concepts and to Latin discipline.

We shall come soon to the study of the transformations undergone by Irish pagan art when it had to adapt itself to the framework of a Christian way of life. But before that it is necessary to outline the background against which this transformation and the subsequent development took place.[1]

First of all, what do we know of social conditions at the beginning of this story – that is to say in the fifth century A.D.?[2] Although much escapes us the main features can be filled in. The basis of Irish society was an extended form of the family which established very close links between the various members of the 'derbfine' and provided at the same time the basis of the rules of royal succession. The country was divided into a great number of 'tuatha', each ruled by its own king. The petty king ruling a tuath was the subject, in a very loose way, of a more powerful king, who in his turn might be the subject of another king. All these chieftains played an essential part in the social and cultural life of the country. They were the patrons of the artists. Their efforts to boost up their prestige and assert their importance were at the root of the power wielded by the poets, dispensers of praise and satire; the necessity of always keeping up to date the genealogies which were the basis of claims to successions had brought about the formation of a class of 'historians'. In addition to this, an order of jurists ('brehons') were the guardians of the laws and saw to their proper application. Of religion, very little is known, but in it druids played a fundamental role; they kept schools in which the teaching seems to have been essentially oral and entrusted to the memory of their pupils without the help of writing.

Into this society, Christianity was introduced about the time when the Roman Empire was collapsing. The south-east of the country probably felt the influence of the churches of Britain as early as the end of the fourth century. It is only a little later, however, when the Legions had already left Britain (A.D. 410), that organized missions appeared. Of one, that of Palladius, Prosper of Aquitaine tells us that it was sent in 431 by Pope Celestine I. As for the missionary labours of Saint Patrick, we know of them mostly through his own writings, the *Confessio*, and the *Epistle to Coroticus*:[3] he tells of his captivity in pagan Ireland, his

---

[1] The essential reference for most of the events discussed in this chapter is: Kenney, *Sources of Irish History*.

[2] *Early Ir. Society*.

[3] N. J. D. White, *The Latin Writings of St. Patrick* (Dublin, 1905); L. Bieler, *Libri Sancti Patricii* (Dublin, 1952); J. B. Bury, *The Life of St Patrick and his Place in History* (London, 1905); L. Bieler, *St Patrick, his writings and Life* (London, 1920).

18

escape, then of his return to preach the Gospel. A missionary animated by the burning faith which emanates from his writings, who in addition had already lived in the country and knew its language and its ways, was well equipped to succeed.[1] Towards the end of the century Christianity was certainly firmly implanted in Ireland and Armagh, the future metropolis of the Irish Church, had been founded.

It had become established without any violent disturbance. Legends of Saint Patrick's contests with the druids and of his destruction of the idol Crom Cruach suggest that the religious system of which the early sculptures were a manifestation was still alive. But it yielded surprisingly quickly. There were no martyrs and no persecutions. The Irish seem to have accepted the new faith impulsively, while Saint Patrick and his followers showed no undue intolerance, accepting and adapting what could be kept of old beliefs and secular customs. His policy seems to have been the same as that which Pope Gregory the Great outlined two centuries later to Mellitus when sending him to preach to the Saxons: keep the old temples, and, after destroying the idols they contain, turn them into churches. Keep the old festivals and allow the people to kill oxen as usual, but dedicate the feast to the Holy Martyrs whose relics are in the church.[2] The result was a happy compromise between the old Celtic tradition, which was not asked to die a violent death, and the new faith, the new ideal, the new organization which in a short period changed the life of the country so deeply and gave it a new orientation.

This is why the old Celtic art does not disappear with the coming of Saint Patrick. He and his companions had grown up in Roman environments. They obviously brought with them books and sacred objects, chalices, patens, bells; they may even have had metalworkers and masons

[1] On the controversies about various aspects of the life of Saint Patrick, and the possible existence of two missionaries called Patrick, see: T. F. O'Rahilly, *The two Patricks* (Dublin, 1942), M. Esposito, 'The Patrician Problem and a possible Solution', *Ir. Hist. Studies*, 1956, pp. 131 sqq.; *Saint Patrick* (Thomas Davies Lectures, ed. by Rev John Ryan, Dublin, 1958); J. Carney, *The Problem of Saint Patrick* (Dublin, 1961); D. Binchy, 'Patrick and his Biographers, Ancient and Modern', *Studia Hibernica*, 1962, pp. 1 sqq.; F. Shaw, S.J., 'Post-Mortem on the Second Patrick', *Studies*, 1962, pp. 237 sqq.

[2] Bede, *H.E.*, I, 30.

with them. New shapes of objects, new types of buildings made their appearance, but there was no reason why the traditional patterns of Celtic art should not be displayed on these objects and monuments.

This blending of old and new ways was made easier by circumstances. With the coming of Saint Patrick it appeared as if Ireland was about to become part of the Roman world, from the spiritual point of view at any rate. But at that very moment the Empire collapsed, swept in all directions by the Germanic invasions, and the conquest of England by the Saxons left the Christian communities of the West – Wales, Ireland, Strathclyde – isolated from the rest of Europe. During a century and a half intercourse with the Continent was rare. In this new seclusion, much more complete than that of Roman times, an Irish Christian civilization was slowly evolved.

Its coming did not entail the upsetting of the old social order. The tribal system remained the backbone of Irish society. The royal successions were still ruled by the same complicated methods which were frequently the occasion of assassination and warfare. Many of the laws and customs of the pagan period persisted. However the foraying expeditions across the Irish Sea were stopped and this may well have brought about a change in the mode of life of kings who for centuries had derived their wealth from plunder. The royal enclosures of pagan times were deserted one after the other and gradually a new political balance was established. Whilst the South seems to have enjoyed great prosperity and probably comparative peace in the orbit of the kingdom of Cashel, the leadership of Connacht gave way in the rest of Ireland to that of two groups of families both descended from King Niall of the Nine Hostages (end of the fourth century): the Northern Uí Néill whose territory more or less corresponded to the present Donegal, with gradual extensions towards the east and south, and the Southern Uí Néill who ruled vast territories extending from Meath to Offaly.[1]

It seems in fact that gradually the court of chieftains, surrounded by poets and historians, lost a good deal of its glamour, whilst the Church was assuming more and more the function of leader of intellectual and

[1] MacNeill, *Phases*, pp. 184–6.

artistic activities. One of the most important factors of this transformation was the appearance of monasteries throughout the island.[1] Saint Patrick may have been a monk and it is possible that the monastic element played its part already in the Church which he founded. But it is in the sixth century, probably under the influence of the monastery of Candida Casa in Strathclyde[2] and the Welsh foundations of Gildas and David that monasticism spread through the whole of Ireland. It is said to be on his return from Candida Casa that Saint Enda established the first important Irish monastery on Aran. Then his disciples, Saint Finnian and Saint Ciaran founded respectively the abbeys of Clonard and Clonmacnois, and soon Ireland was dotted with innumerable monasteries. They became the essential element in the structure of the Irish Church which for centuries had no territorial dioceses but was governed by the abbots of the great religious houses.

The new institution fitted into the existing social system. The monastery very often gives the impression of being a concern of the tuath. Its land was given by a local king. Sometimes it was established in a royal rath. Abbatial successions have a tendency to follow a pattern very similar to that ruling the king's succession,[3] and to keep within the limits of a family group. And if the king protects the monastery, he expects also some support for it, if only that of presence. It was not until the beginning of the ninth century that ecclesiastics were officially excused from the obligation of accompanying the armies.[4]

[1] See: Gougaud, *Christianity*; Ryan, *Monasticism*; W. Delius, *Geschichte der irischen Kirche von ihren Anfängen bis zum 12. Jahrhundert* (Munich, 1954); Bieler, *Ireland*.

[2] The Christian community of Strathclyde developed around Candida Casa, the monastery founded in the fifth century by Saint Ninian in Wigtownshire, the Rosnat or Magnum Monasterium of Irish tradition. See: Bede, *H.E.*, III, 4; Ryan, *Monasticism*, p. 106; J. Macqueen, *St Nynia* (Edinburgh–London, 1961).

[3] For example at Iona (Reeves, *St Columba*, pp. 269 sqq.); for some others, see N. K. Chadwick, *The Age of the Saints in the Early Celtic Church* (London, 1961), pp. 63 sqq.; some monasteries, however, do not follow this pattern: J. Ryan, S.J., 'The Abbatial Succession of Clonmacnois', *F.-S. M. Néill*, pp. 490 sqq.

[4] *A.F.M.*, 799 (*recte* 804); for the significance of that law, see J. Ryan, S.J., 'The Cáin Adomnáin', in: *Studies in Early Irish Law* (Dublin, 1936), pp. 269 sqq. (see p. 274).

Towards the middle of the sixth century, Saint Columba,[1] who belonged to one of the branches of the Northern Uí Néill, began his foundations, Derry in the north, Durrow in the central plain. His establishment in Iona, on the coast of Scotland, about 563–5, and the evangelizing of Scotland which followed it, mark the beginning of an expansion of the Irish Church which was to go on for centuries. In this special case it was only in fact an establishment in an Irish overseas territory, the kingdom of Dál Riada which had been colonized by Irish settlers in the fifth century on the opposite shore of the sort of inland sea which extends from the Hebrides to the north coast of Ireland. The monasteries founded by Saint Columba in Ireland and in Scotland remained closely united. During the last period of his life, it was from Iona that Saint Columba governed them and for centuries afterwards, Iona, which possessed the tomb of the founder and whose abbots – his 'coarbs' or successors – were still drawn from his kin, remained the centre of the order. It became in the course of time the head of a 'paruchia' which extended from the kingdom of Dál Riada, through the Western Pictish territory, probably as far as the Orkneys and Shetlands to the north and the Firth of Forth to the south.

This expansion into Scotland is only one aspect of a movement which drew the Irish 'peregrini' out of Ireland. Legend has got hold of the departure of Saint Columba and shows him stopping only when the faint line of the Irish coast had disappeared over the horizon, summing up in this journey what was to be the mainspring of so many others: the determination to break with everything that was known and loved, sometimes as a penance for a definite fault, but more often out of a deliberate seeking for mortification.[2] In a world where each individual was strongly integrated in a social unit, to forego this support, this normal framework of life, meant divesting oneself of everything. Very often these departures are not prompted by an evangelizing purpose, but sprang rather, as Bede says when speaking of Saint Fursa, from a

---

[1] On Saint Columba, see Kenney, *Sources*, pp. 422 sqq.; Reeves, *St Columba*, *passim*; Anderson. *Adomnan*, preface.

[2] K. Hughes, 'The Changing Theory and Practice of Irish Pilgrimage', *Journ. Eccles. Studies*, 1960, pp. 143 sqq.

heart 'desiring the wandering life (peregrinatio) for the love of the Lord'.[1] It means, as they often recall, leading the same life as Abraham, to whom God had said: 'Go forth out of thy country and from thy kindred and out of thy father's house and come into the land which I shall show thee.'[2] It is what the author of a sermon in Irish of the eighth century calls 'the white martyrdom'.[3] This deliberate seeking of a break with original surroundings, this effort to put oneself totally in the hand of God are in several cases the initial motive of journeys which, however, often end in preaching and sometimes in 'red martyrdom'.

So the peregrinatio is one of the aspects of their asceticism, that asceticism which is the distinctive mark of the Irish monk, in the eyes of their contemporaries. Even if we consign to the realm of legend some of its fiercest aspects, there remains a longing for a life stripped of all but bare essentials. This is an aspect which we find mentioned in all accounts of them and which at times appeared to their contemporaries as too harsh, too inhuman. It leads also to that attenuated form of the peregrinatio, the seeking of solitude in remote places. The life of the Desert Fathers was for ever haunting the mind of the Irish monks. 'Quis mihi locum avium poterit ostendere?'[4] asked Saint Anthony the hermit; Saint Columba speaks of his brethren who have gone to seek 'desertum in pelago intransmeabili'.[5] If some of the sixth-century foundations, Bangor, Derry, Clonard, Durrow, were situated on rich land, many others were deliberately erected in desolate spots: Clonmacnois lost in its vast solitude of bogs and marshes, the monastery of Saint Enda on the bare crags of Aran, Nendrum, Devenish, Inis Cealtra on islands in lakes and estuaries. Tradition attributes to Saint Brendan

[1] Bede, *H.E.*, III, 19.

[2] See for example the *Life of Saint Brendan*, where Abraham is quoted: 'Illius vero precenti quod dictum Abrahe: "Exi de terra tua et cognatione tua", non immemor effectus, peregre proficisci ardenti volebat desiderio' (Plummer, *VV. SS. Hib.*, I, 'Vita Prima Sancti Brendani', pp. 103–4). The same quotation is given, with a fuller commentary, in the *Old Irish Life of Saint Columba*. (See: W. Stokes, *Three Irish Homilies* (Calcutta, 1877), pp. 91, 97.)

[3] See p. 153.

[4] 'Who could show me a solitude (a place without roads)', *Vita Beati Antonii*, 14; Migne, *P.L.*, LXXIII.

[5] 'A desert (a solitude) in the trackless sea' (an island), *Vit. Col.*, II, 42.

23

hermitages on that summit of the Dingle peninsula which is constantly swept by passing clouds, and on one of the most forbidding of the sea pyramids of the Blaskets. He is supposed to have settled at the end of his life on Inishglora, that little flat island off Erris whose western end is ploughed bare by western breakers, and in every one of these places ruins are there to testify to the past presence of hermits. Saint Columba is associated with the wildest parts of the coasts of Donegal and Mayo, before he finally settled on Iona, a bleak island a few miles long, isolated from the mainland of Scotland by the mountains of Mull. And Saint Aidan, when he came to Northumbria, refusing to settle on the mainland, established his see on the windswept island of Lindisfarne.[1] The description given by Bede of the foundation of the monastery of Lastingham by Cedd, a pupil of Lindisfarne, could easily apply to some of these sites : 'The Bishop chose himself a place whereon to build a monastery among steep and distant mountains which looked more like lurking places for robbers and dens of wild beasts than dwellings for men.'[2]

As well as the love of solitude and the desire for mortification, for reducing the material amenities of life to the strict minimum, a preference for the open spaces of the sea and for bare mountains may have played its part in such a choice. The Columban monks, as described to us by Adamnan, seem to have been nearly amphibious creatures, always coming out of a boat or seeking one. Adamnan's writings give the impression of a life where the blowing of the wind in a sail, the bird cast ashore by the tempest,[3] the 'loathsome and very dangerous creatures' of the sea,[4] were everyday reality; of a life whose ultimate dream – or achievement – were the sea-wanderings of Saint Brendan. And the words put in the mouth of Saint Columba by a twelfth-century poet are probably a true description of their feelings :

> 'Delightful I think it is to be in the bosom of an isle,
> On the crest of a rock
> That I may look there on the manifold
> Face of the sea

---

[1] Bede, *H.E.*, III, 3. [2] Bede, *H.E.*, III, 23.
[3] Like 'our stranger guest the crane', *Vit. Col.*, II, 48.
[4] *Vit. Col.*, II, 42; also : I, 19.

That I may see its heavy waves
Over the glittering ocean
As they chant a melody to their Father
On their eternal course. . . .'[1]

Still the Irish monks did not carry renunciation to the point of the suppression of artistic or intellectual activities. A life of studies was one of the essential features of the organization of monasteries and the intellectual level seems to have remained very high amidst the general cultural decay of the time. This is all the more striking because it involves a complete revolution in Irish habits. First of all there was the introduction of writing in a country where teaching so far had been in the usual Celtic manner, completely oral, and where the only known alphabet was the Oghamic, totally impractical for anything more elaborate than a short inscription. Then there was the establishment of Latin in one of the few countries of Western Europe where it was not at the time a spoken language, of Latin placed from the start in that position of scholarly language which it will hold everywhere during the latter part of the Middle Ages. It may well be the reason why the Latin used in Ireland escapes to a great extent the debasement which resulted everywhere else from the contamination of the spoken language.[2] It is essentially a literary, erudite language based on scriptural and classical models and very different from the awkward, provincial Latin spoken by Saint Patrick. The firm and occasionally pedantic style used by Columbanus from the time he arrived on the Continent gives a fairly clear idea of the results of a century of such teaching.[3]

The Irish language, however, had not been superseded. It remained the only language used in secular life and was not banished from the monasteries. One of the oldest surviving texts in Irish is a sermon, and when an Irish scholar annotated a text he used Irish half the time, which suggests that part of the teaching was given in the vernacular.

[1] Jackson, *Nature Poetry*, p. 9.
[2] M. Roger, *L'enseignement des lettres classiques d'Ausone à Alcuin* (Paris, 1905), pp. 236 sqq.
[3] Walker, *S. Columbani Op.*, pp. lxvi sqq., and Bieler in the same book, pp. lxxviii sqq.

25

At a very early date, texts in Irish will be copied in monasteries. Latin poems and Irish poems appear side by side and the metrical system of the first influences the second. Everything gives the impression of an intellectual life rich and full in creative power, perhaps indeed because of this extensive use of the mother tongue beside Latin.

We shall never know, assuredly, how much survived in these monastic schools of the teaching of the druidic schools of which they were up to a point the heirs. Continuity and change are indicated by a text in the Introduction to the Irish Laws : 'Until the coming of Patrick, three only had a right to raise their voice : a historian telling tales of old, a poet bestowing praise and satire, and a judge (brehon) delivering a judgment according to tradition. But since the coming of Patrick, all their speeches are tied up by the men of the holy tongue, of the Scriptures.'[1] The poet will go on versifying, sometimes meeting violent opposition because of his exactions, of the praise blackmailing from which he derives his substance. But the 'historian telling tales of old' is absorbed to a great extent by the monastery. It seems that already some texts of the Irish epics were written down, sometimes with an attempt to give them a Christian tone.[2] At the same time there is a first effort to insert Irish history into those vast comparative charts of world events established by Eusebius of Caesarea which were known to the West in the translation of Saint Jerome enlarged by the additions of Prosper of Aquitaine. The result was a chronicle of Irish affairs which was used later by the Irish Annalists of the eleventh and twelfth centuries. In spite of the erratic contacts with the Continent, some at least of Jerome's biblical translations had reached Ireland and were being copied in the sixth century by the Irish scribes.[3] There seems to be enough to amply justify the tone in which Columbanus, writing to Gregory the Great, speaks of 'our masters and the ancient Irish philosophers'. The basis of the brilliant middle seventh- and eighth-century development has been laid during this earlier period.

In the beginning of the seventh century the barrier constituted by

---

[1] *Ancient Laws of Ir.*, I, p. 18.

[2] Thurneysen, *Helden und Königsage*, pp. 357–71.

[3] Such as the text of the psalms found in the Cathach. See p. 60 and pp. 171–3.

pagan England disappears and the secluded atmosphere of the sixth century gives place to a renewed intercourse with the Continent and with England itself.

The first of these contacts occurred in fact before the conversion of the Saxons. About 590, Columbanus, a monk of the abbey of Bangor[1] which had been founded a short time before on the shore of Loch Laíg (Belfast Lough), decided to depart for the Continent.[2] He was a man of remarkable ability, endowed with a steely will. He was probably lector in the monastery, but he began, as Jonas his biographer puts it, 'to desire the pilgrimage.' He left with twelve companions and arrived in Gaul where he preached before King Sigebert of Austrasia; then he reached the Vosges where he established a hermitage in an old Roman fort, at Annegray. Shortly afterwards, the community having increased in numbers, he built a monastery at Luxeuil out of the ruins of a Roman spa. The monastery prospered and became an important spiritual centre in the east of Gaul. The uncompromising manner of Columbanus brought about increasing difficulties with Brunhilda and her son Theuderic, King of the Burgunds with the result that Columbanus was eventually expelled and had to depart with his Irish companions, leaving in Luxeuil the native monks whom he had trained. An attempt at embarking for Ireland from Nantes fell through. Columbanus then remained for a while not very far from Paris, a stay which paved the way for future foundations which were to follow his rule for a while, Jouarre, Faremoutiers, Rebais. Then came a journey on the Rhine to which we owe a boat-song composed by the saint, punctuated every three verses by a refrain marking the dipping of the oars :

'Heia, viri! nostrum roboans echo sonet heia!'[3]

After some time in Switzerland where he left Gall, one of his companions, over whose tomb a celebrated abbey was soon to rise, he crossed the Alps and founded in the foothills of the Apennines, south of Milan, the monastery of Bobbio where he died in 615.

---

[1] Kenney, *Sources*, pp. 395 sqq.

[2] Jonas, *Vita Columbani*; Walker, *S. Columbani Op.*, 'Introduction', pp. xvii sqq.

[3] 'Ho, lads, let the booming echo repeat : Ho!' Walker, op. cit., p. 190.

The civilizing influence of this twenty-five years' journey through Western Europe was tremendous. Luxeuil, Bobbio, were amongst the most important cultural centres of the Early Middle Ages. In those troubled times when Barbarian and Romanized populations were hardly amalgamated, when Arianism was only beginning to recede, Columbanus, drawing on the experience of the Irish monasteries where he had been brought up, managed to create havens of peace, balance and sanctity.[1] And for the Irish travelling on the Continent in the following centuries, as pilgrims or missionaries, Saint Gall and Bobbio long remained rallying centres. We shall see the important place they hold in the history of Irish illumination.

Still another aspect of this journey deserves to hold our attention: it is in a way a first episode of what will be called 'the Easter controversy'. Saint Columbanus soon discovered that the methods still used in Ireland to fix the date of Easter had become obsolete on the Continent.[2] Still he found it difficult to believe that they were not the only efficient ones. Hence all sorts of difficulties arose and he was accused quite gratuitously of being tainted with the 'quartodeciman' heresy. To this we owe a series of letters to several successive popes. If he addresses them practically on a footing of equality and does not hesitate occasionally to scold them in his usual outspoken way, his attitude towards the Holy See is nonetheless well defined. In one letter he says: 'Nos enim . . . devincti sumus cathedrae Sancti Petri.'[3] Elsewhere: 'We, all the Irish who live at the ends of the world, are disciples of Saint Peter and Saint Paul . . . and we have kept intact the evangelic and apostolic doctrine, none of us being either a heretic . . . or a schismatic; but the catholic faith which we have received from you, that is to say from the successor of the holy apostles, has remained unchanged.'[4] There is some point in recalling these texts in which the attachment to archaic customs is combined with an absolutely clear acknowledgment of the papal supremacy, as a good deal of the history of the controversy has been warped by the

[1] P. Riché, *Education et culture dans l'Occident barbare* (Paris, 1962), pp. 371 sqq.; Bieler, *Ireland*, pp. 85–94.

[2] P. Grosjean, S.J., 'Recherches sur les débuts de la controverse pascale chez les Celtes', *An. Boll.*, 1946, pp. 200 sqq.; Kenney, *Sources*, pp. 210 sqq.

[3] Walker, op. cit., p. 49.   [4] Ibid., p. 38.

habit many historians have taken of opposing the 'Celtic party' to the 'Roman' one. The problem is much more complex and it is necessary to stress that it was possible to be sincerely both 'Celtic' and 'Roman'.[1]

The same difficulties arose in the course of the conversion of England. In 597 Gregory the Great sent Augustine with a few companions to preach the Gospel to the Saxons.[2] Augustine settled in Canterbury and started exploring a territory which held all sorts of surprises. There also the question of the calculation of Easter was quick to arise. When Augustine met some of the Welsh bishops, he discovered how much their ecclesiastical customs had come, in isolation, to differ from those of the rest of the world. Shortly after his death the controversy reached Ireland where the reaction was a pained indignation. The Irish were not far from thinking that the rest of the world was in error, that their monasteries alone protected from all upheavals had preserved tradition intact. Wilfrid, at the Synod of Whitby, was to bring them back roughly to a true sense of proportions : 'Though your fathers [i.e. Saint Columba and the other Irish saints] were holy, do you think that those few men in a corner of the remotest island, are to be preferred before the universal Church of Christ throughout the world ?'[3]

We know the early episodes of the controversy partly through Bede,[4] partly through a text of Irish origin.[5] After a letter from the Archbishop of Canterbury and the bishops of London and of Rochester, followed a few years later by a letter from Pope Honorius I, came a crisis soon after 630. Cummian, abbot of a monastery of the centre of Ireland, gathered together some of the abbots of the chief monasteries in his neighbourhood.[6] They decided to send envoys to Rome to clear up the question of the various Easter computations. Three years later the travellers returned to declare themselves convinced that the Irish were wrong. To the weight of what they had seen at Eastertide in Rome they were

---

[1] J. Ryan, S.J., 'The Early Irish Church and the See of Peter', *Medieval Studies presented to Aubrey Gwynn, S.J.* (Dublin, 1961), pp. 3 sqq.

[2] Bede, *H.E.*, I, 23.   [3] Bede, *H.E.*, III, 25.

[4] Bede, *H.E.*, II, 4; II, 19; III, 25; Kenney, *Sources*, No. 56, p. 218.

[5] The letter of Cummian to Segene, Abbot of Iona (Ussher, *Sylloge*, p. 432); Kenney, *Sources*, No. 57, p. 220.

[6] Emly, Clonmacnois, Birr, Mungret and Clonfert Molua.

able to add the testimony of a Greek, a Hebrew, a Scythian and an Egyptian, who were staying in the same house with them and who told them that they all celebrated Easter at the same date; contacts which, incidentally, have to be borne in mind for further reference. The greater part of Ireland seems to have accepted their testimony and to have rallied to the Roman computation shortly after 630. But the Abbot of Iona to whom the letter of Cummian is addressed was not convinced by it and for years Iona and some of its subordinate monasteries, such as Lindisfarne, the Columban monasteries in Scotland and a few of those in the north of Ireland, still held to their archaic customs.

All this forms the background to what we can guess of the activities of the Irish schools at that time. The controversies and the contacts with the Continent which they brought about, probably had a stimulating effect both through the intellectual activities they fostered and through the new texts which reached Ireland at that time. Towards the middle of the century works of exegesis appear. Father Grosjean has given back two of them to a group of churches founded around 630–40 by Mo-Chuta or Carthach (in Latin Carthagus) – Rahan, Lismore and various churches under its sway.[1] They are a *Commentary on the Catholic Epistles* and the *De Mirabilibus Sacrae Scripturae* attributed in various recensions to Saint Augustine of Hippo. This false ascription arose originally because its author (whom several details of the text easily identify as Irish) takes as a literary conceit the name of Augustine and dedicates his work to the 'monasterii Carthaginenses'. In this context they are obviously those founded by Saint Carthagus and not those of the African Carthage of the time of Saint Augustine. We are obviously dealing with an erudite circle whose members affect well-known names, as will the scholars gathered around Charlemagne in the time of Alcuin; some of them also are called by their Irish names and can be identified. This treatise reveals a thorough knowledge of patristic literature and also a rather original approach to biblical criticism. It can be dated to 655. This makes it practically contemporary with two works which are not much more than compilations, the abridged version of Gregory the Great's *Commentary*

---

[1] P. Grosjean, S.J., 'Sur quelques exégètes irlandais', *Sacris Erudiri*, 1955, pp. 67 sqq.

on the Book of Job (Moralia in Job), dating from about half a century earlier, by Laid-cend, a monk of Clonfert-Molua (Leix), and an adaptation of the *Treatise on Hebrew names* of Saint Jerome, by Aileran, a scholar of Clonard.

Beside these purely erudite works there appear already in the middle of the century, if not earlier, Latin lives of saints which may have been preceded by compilations in Irish. One of the earliest is probably the *Life of Saint Brigid of Kildare* by a hagiographer who affects the name of 'Cogitosus';[1] it probably goes back to around 650 and is likely to emanate from Kildare. This is a collection of miraculous facts, more interesting for what it tells of life in Ireland in the seventh century and for its archaeological information than as a document on the saint of whom it hardly tells us anything. Muirchú, the author of one of the oldest lives of Saint Patrick,[2] written towards the end of the century, claims to have been inspired by the example of Cogitosus, whom he calls his 'father'. About the same time saw the writing of the oldest Latin *Life of Saint Fursa*[3] which Bede used in his *Historia Ecclesiastica*.[4] Finally, about 685, the most remarkable of these Lives, that of Saint Columba, was written in Iona by his successor, Adamnan.[5]

All these works are to a great extent inspired by models well known at the time such as the *Life of Saint Benedict* by Gregory the Great, the *Life of Saint Martin* by Sulpicius Severus (which will be copied into the Book of Armagh), the *Life of Germanus of Auxerre* by Constantius (which inspired an episode of the *Vita Columbae*).[6] They do not aim for the most part at giving an exact and consecutive narrative of events, but an impressive idea of the sanctity of the man concerned. They have to be judged from that angle and appreciated as a series of disconnected episodes. The *Life of Saint Columba* and some parts of the *Life of Saint Fursa* take on then an extraordinary vividness, by the adequacy of details and the animated quality of the narrative. Thus, for example, a short paragraph of the *Life of Saint Columba* where a young brother stops in front of the cell where the saint is engaged in writing, to ask

---

[1] *AA. SS. Boll.*, Febr. 1 (1658), 135.
[2] *An. Boll.*, 1882, pp. 531 sqq.
[3] Kenney, *Sources*, No. 296, I (pp. 501–2).
[4] Bede, *H.E.*, III, 19.
[5] See note, p. 166.
[6] *Vit. Col.*, II, 34.

him to bless the pail of new milk which he carries on his back.[1] Or the long chapter where the saint is shown spending what he knows to be his last day on earth visiting the various buildings, checking that there is an abundant supply of wheat for the following winter, then copying a page of a psalter in his cell, finally to collapse in the dark when arriving in the chapel for the night office.[2] Saint Fursa's vision is so described that it haunts the mind. All this, like the work of the exegetes is written in a Latin which is not only fairly correct but sometimes elegant, and with great variety of style ranging from the limpidity of Adamnan to the flamboyant rhetoric of Muirchú.[3]

From other pursuits of the students in the Irish schools of this time we know little. Manuscripts of a later date will testify to an interest in Latin grammar which is in no way surprising; of profane studies the *Commentary on the Bucolics and the Georgics* attributed to Adamnan[4] may be an indication, confirmed in fact by the numerous classical reminiscences in the Latin of Columbanus.[5] Geometry mentioned by Aldhelm amongst the subjects of study in the Irish schools[6] has left no traces in texts of that time. Music, the study of which is also well attested, escapes us in the same way, and the texts of hymns copied in the Antiphonary of Bangor are unfortunately devoid of any notation.[7]

Holiness of life and a great love of study, this is what made the reputation of the Irish masters who worked to shape the Saxon converts into good Christians. They were numerous, and if some of them are to us little more than mere names, like the Máeldubh or Máeldun who was the founder of the monastery of Malmesbury and the master of Aldhelm,[8] there are others whom we can get to know very well, such

---

[1] 'Concerning the expulsion of a demon that lurked in a milk-pail', *Vit. Col.*, II, 16.

[2] 'Of the passing away to the Lord of our holy patron, Columba', *Vit. Col.*, III, 23.

[3] L. Bieler, 'Studies on the text of Muirchú', *P.R.I.A.*, 1950, pp. 179 sqq.

[4] Kenney, *Sources*, pp. 286–7.

[5] Walker, *S. Columbani Op.*, pp. lxvi; L. Bieler, 'The Humanism of St Columbanus', *Mélanges colombaniens* (1950) pp. 95 sqq.

[6] See p. 35.   [7] Warren, *Antiphonary of Bangor*.

[8] Kenney, *Sources*, p. 32; G. F. Browne, *St Aldhelm, his Life and Times* (London, 1903).

as Fursa of whom Bede speaks at length, and of whom there exists also, as we have seen, *Lives* written in Ireland. He was a hermit for a while on an island in Lough Corrib, and he became very celebrated through his vision of the Other World re-told at length by Bede and of momentous consequence for medieval literature and thought. He came to East Anglia,[1] called perhaps by King Sigebert who was trying to perfect the conversion of his people. He was accompanied by several other Irishmen amongst them his brothers Foillan and Ultán. Sigebert gave them Cnobesborough (Burgh Castle, Suffolk), one of the shore forts of Roman times whose ruins he probably used as a quarry to build his monastery. He arrived shortly after 630 and a few years later left his brothers in England and went on the Continent. He died in 649 or 650 when on his way back to his English monastery which seems to have been wrecked only a few years later. So that it existed, with varied fortunes, but certainly under the patronage of the kings of East Anglia and playing an important part in the kingdom, for at least twenty years.[2] During that period it contributed to the contacts between Irish and Saxon arts.[3] As no conflict about the calculation of Easter is ever mentioned in relation to it, we are entitled to assume that Fursa – like Máeldubh – was one of the Irish who rallied very early to the Roman computation.

About the time when Fursa was being called to East Anglia, similar events were taking place in the north of England. A first attempt to convert Northumbria, made by Paulinus, one of the Canterbury missionaries, ended in catastrophy and Paulinus had to flee before the hostility of a pagan king.[4] In 635, however, Oswald, who had been baptized whilst he was living in exile in Iona,[5] had hardly become king

---

[1] Bede, *H.E.*, III, 19. Traube, *Perrona Scottorum*; Bieler, *Ireland*.

[2] F. M. Stenton, *Anglo-Saxon England* (Oxford, 1943), pp. 116–17.

[3] See p. 74–5; also: Henry, *Ir. enam.*, pp. 81–2.   [4] Bede, *H.E.*, II, 20.

[5] From the accession of Edwin to the throne of Northumbria (A.D. 617), the sons of Ethelfrid, among them Oswald and Oswy, went into exile (*A.S.Chr.*, A.D. 617, p. 16). They seem to have gone to Iona and perhaps to Ireland. Bede (*H.E.*, II, 1) says that 'all the time that Edwin reigned, the sons . . . of Ethelfrid . . . , with many of the younger nobility, lived in banishment among the Scots or Picts and were renewed with the grace of baptism'. They came back at the death of Edwin

when he sent to the 'Ancients of the Scotti' asking for a bishop who could instruct his subjects. Aidan was sent to him and settled in the island of Lindisfarne, nearly opposite to the royal residence of Bamborough.[1] The monastery he founded remained closely united to Iona to which it was connected through the monastery of Melrose, in the south of Scotland. Finan, the successor of Aidan, came from there also. Around them were gathered Irish monks who had come to help in the conversion of Northumbria and English monks they had trained to the Irish way of ecclesiastical life, so that the monastery of Lindisfarne soon became as much a fragment of Ireland abroad as Iona itself. It, in turn, became a centre around which gravitated new foundations, first in Northumbria (Hartlepool, Whitby, etc.)[2] then, when the king of the Middle Angles (Leicestershire) had been baptized by Finan, in this new kingdom of which an Irishman, Diuma, became the first bishop.[3] Finally, the king of the East Saxons having been also baptized by Finan, the Lindisfarne missionaries reached the Thames.[4]

The period which goes from 635 (arrival of Aidan) to 663–4 (Synod of Whitby), a period of nearly thirty years, is a time when Irish influence shone very brightly in England. Bede is shaken out of his usual matter-of-factness when he recalls its memory. His profound piety, hostile to all pretence and shamming, finds a perfectly congenial turn of mind in a man like Aidan who 'strained with all his strength to practise everything which he had seen prescribed in the Gospels.'[5]

As was only natural, the missionaries did send their pupils to be taught in Irish monasteries. Bede tells us that at the time when the plague of 664 broke out 'many of the nobility and of the lower ranks of the English nation, were there (in Ireland) at that time who, in the

---

(A.D. 633) and Oswald became king in 635. So that they had spent about sixteen years in Iona or in Ireland. Of Oswald, Bede says that 'he had thoroughly learned the language of the Scots during his long banishment' (*H.E.*, III, 3), and he describes Oswy as 'instructed and baptized by the Scots, perfectly skilled in their language' (*H.E.*, II, 25).

[1] Bede, *H.E.*, III, 3.   [2] Bede, *H.E.*, III, 24.   [3] Bede, *H.E.*, III
[4] Bede, *H.E.*, III, 22.   [5] Bede, *H.E.*, III, 18.

days of the bishops Finan and Colman, forsaking their native island, retired thither, either for the sake of sacred studies, or of a more ascetic life; and some of them presently devoted themselves faithfully to a monastic life, others chose rather to apply themselves to study, going about from one master's cell to another. The Scotti willingly received them all, and took care to supply them with daily food without cost, as also to furnish them with books for their studies, and teaching free of charge'.[1] He even speaks in more detail of some of these English clerics, such as Egbert, who in 664 was stricken by the plague whilst he was still a young student in Ireland and made a vow, if he recovered, to live in exile all his life, so adapting to his own use the spirit of the Irish 'peregrinatio'.[2] Others left at a more mature age. The anonymous *History of the Abbots of Jarrow and Wearmouth* has preserved for us the memory of Cynefrid, the brother of Ceolfrid, who, probably around 660–5, gave up his abbacy and, leaving England, went to study and live a secluded life in Ireland.[3]

This trend of English students towards the Irish schools went on at least until the end of the seventh century, even at a time when schools of a quite comparable brilliance were opening up in England, at Canterbury, at Wearmouth, at Jarrow. We have proof of this in a letter written by Aldhelm of Malmsbury, who had himself been partly educated by an Irishman. He wrote, probably around 685, to a certain Eahfrid[4] who was coming back from a stay of six years in Ireland; he speaks of those boat-loads of young Englishmen who go to Ireland[5] to study grammar, geometry, the physical sciences[6] and the interpretation of texts by allegory and metaphor. All this, in his opinion, is rather ridiculous when these students could find in Canterbury masters like Theodore, the Greek

---

[1] Bede, *H.E.*, III, 27.   [2] Ibid.   [3] *H. Abb. a.*, 2.

[4] The letter was first published by Ussher, *Sylloge*, pp. 448 sqq.; see: R. Ehwald, *Aldhelmi Opera*, M.G.H., Auct. Ant., XV (1919), pp. 486–7. For a partial translation, see: G. F. Browne, op. cit., pp. 262 sqq. See: F. Henry, 'The Lindisfarne Gospels', *Antiquity*, 1963, pp. 100 sqq.

[5] 'The fields of Ireland are rich in learners and green with the pastoral numerosity of students.'

[6] These, Ehwald, using another text of Aldhelm for comparison, identifies as: arithmetic, music, astronomy, astrology, mechanics, medicine.

archbishop, and Hadrian the African who had been abbot of a monastery near Naples. Times are beginning to change. England, the nursling of the Irish, can now go its own way without help.

The first cause of the change was again the Easter controversy. Iona, as we have seen, had refused to accept the new computation. Lindisfarne, faithful disciple, had followed Iona and the conflict had soon become acute between the missionaries of Canterbury and those of Lindisfarne. It came to a head in 663 or 664 at the Synod of Whitby[1] where Colman, abbot-bishop of Lindisfarne, represented the Celtic party against Agilbertus, a Gaulish bishop who had studied for years in Ireland and after being bishop of the West Saxons, occupied the see of Paris; he deputed Wilfrid, Abbot of Ripon to speak for him as he spoke Saxon badly. On the final decision of the king, the Celts lost. Colman, soon afterwards, left Lindisfarne with the Irish monks and some thirty English and took refuge first in Iona and then in Ireland.

It is hard to evaluate exactly the consequences of this departure and to find out how far Irish influence waned in the north of England. Colman's successor, Tuda, was an Irishman who had accepted the Roman computation. But he died of the plague after a few months. He seems to have been the last Irish Abbot of Lindisfarne. But this does not mean that the atmosphere of the monastery changed very much with his death. Eata, Cuthbert, who were abbots after him, had been brought up from childhood by the monks from Iona. Nothing is known of their successor, Eadbert. But if, as has been said, Eadfrith (or Eadfrid), the abbot who wrote the Lindisfarne Gospels, is no other than this Eahfrid to whom Aldhelm wrote,[2] he had studied for six years in Ireland and we are again faced with somebody whose whole training was Irish. At this same time, Adamnan had become Abbot of Iona and the King of

---

[1] Bede, *H.E.*, III, 25; for the date and all dates in Bede, see: W. Levison, *England and the Continent in the eighth century* (Oxford, 1946), pp. 265 sqq. But see also: P. Grosjean, S.J., 'La date du synode de Whitby', *An. Boll.*, 1960, pp. 233 sqq. Bede who grew up amongst people still shaken by the controversy has probably overrated its importance. The *Saxon Chronicle* does not mention the Synod of Whitby and only makes an allusion to the departure of Colman (see: *A.-S. Chr.*, p. 21).

[2] See p. 35.

Northumbria, Aldfrid, in whom Irish tradition sees a son of Fina, a princess of the Northern Uí Néill,[1] had spent long years of studies 'in insulis Scottorum'. Twice Adamnan came to visit his 'friend, king Aldfrid',[2] in 686 and in 688 and when in 716 Iona finally accepted what Bede calls 'the rational and ecclesiastical manner of observing Easter',[3] relations again became very close.

Still, as was pointed out when discussing Aldhelm's letter, the situation had changed. It had changed from an official point of view. It is typical that there is not a single Irish name amongst those of holders of English sees enumerated by Bede in 731. It had changed from another point of view also : to the English, Ireland was no longer the only source of wisdom and scholarship. From 669 to 690, under the direction of Theodore and Hadrian, the school of Canterbury blossomed : 'As both of them were . . . fully instructed both in sacred and in secular letters, they gathered a crowd of disciples, and rivers of wholesome knowledge daily flowed from them to water the hearts of their hearers; and together with the books of Holy Scriptures, they also taught them the metrical art, astronomy, and ecclesiastical arithmetic.'[4] Bede says also that they taught them to speak Greek and Latin as well as their mother tongue.

Another factor played its part very strongly. A monk of Northumbrian origin, just back from some years in Lerins, Benedict Biscop, founded in 674 and 682 the twin monasteries of Wearmouth and Jarrow, to the south of the Tyne estuary.[5] In the following years he made several journeys. From Gaul he brought back masons and glaziers. From Italy he carried manuscripts. During his government and that of Ceolfrid, his monasteries became centres of studies permeated with Mediter-

---

[1] He was a son of Oswy, born during his exile in Ireland. He is known in Irish texts as Fland Fina and enjoys the reputation of a 'wise man' and a poet in Irish, though none of the poems attributed to him go back to his time. The Annals of Tigernach record his death at the year 704 : 'Alfrith mac Ossu – Fland Fina the Irish call him – Rex Saxon fuit.' Most of what is known about him is summed up in two notes : one in Reeves, *St Columba*, pp. 185–6, the other in Plummer's edition of Bede, vol. II, pp. 263–4.

[2] *Vit. Col.*, II, 46.   [3] Bede, *H.E.*, V, 15.
[4] Bede, *H.E.*, IV, 2.   [5] *H. Abb. a.*; Bede, *V. Abb.*

ranean culture, and they produced, in the early eighth century, the Codex Amiatinus, one of the most perfect of the texts of the Vulgate which have reached us, an enormous manuscript of imposing calligraphy, illustrated with a few miniatures of a style so completely Mediterranean that one of them has long been looked upon as borrowed from an Italian book.[1]

Though there remain in England classical tendencies which will live on in some of the details of the English high crosses, still, in a way, this is only an interlude, and a fairly brief one. The same year (A.D. 716) saw the death of Ceolfrid and the rallying of Iona to Roman methods, so that something of the atmosphere of the first years of Lindisfarne probably reappeared in Northumbria. Bede himself who spent all his life, since childhood, first in Wearmouth and then in Jarrow and who is the outstanding achievement of this 'Northumbrian Renaissance', shows, by the amount of space he devotes to the Irish missionaries in his *Historia Ecclesiastica,* how much their thought was still dominant in the country where they had laboured. He died in 735. Shortly after that date, Alcuin who was brought up in the north of England, had an Irish master, Colgu, to whom he was greatly attached, and an Irish fellow-student, Joseph, who accompanied him to France and died beside him. He was in contact with Lindisfarne, and probably also with Iona.

England, however, is not the only country where pupils of the Irish schools settled in the seventh and eighth centuries, some as 'pilgrims' like Columbanus before them, others as missionaries. They went much further afield.

There is first a whole series of English clerics who had come to study in Ireland and sometimes had stayed for years. Several of them seem to have settled around that Egbert who, having arrived in his youth, made a vow, at the time of the 664 epidemic of plague, not to go back to England and to spend the rest of his life in exile. It is impossible to know where he was established;[2] we do not even know whether he was

[1] *E.Q.C. Lindisfarnensis,* p. 147–9.

[2] Bede (*H.E.,* III, 27) mentions Rath Melsigi as the place where Egbert was at the time of the plague. This has been identified with Rath-maoil or with Rath-Maoilcath in Mayo by J. Healy (*Ireland's Ancient Schools and Scholars* (4th ed., Dublin, 1902, pp. 590 sqq.)). Rath Mesk, or Rath mesge (J. O'Laverty, *An*

living in an Irish monastery or in a foundation of his own. In any case his renown seems to have attracted other English 'pilgrims'. His ambition was to go like Wilfrid to preach the Gospel in Frisia, to the Continental Saxons, kin to those who had come to England. His attempts at departure did not succeed, but he inspired with his missionary dream a group of English and Irish whose leader was Willibrord,[1] a Northumbrian who had already spent twelve years in Ireland. Willibrord and his twelve companions succeeded where Egbert had failed and they sailed to Frisia in 690. Willibrord partly converted Frisia, founded the archbishopric of Utrecht and the monastery of Echternach (Luxembourg). He seems to have remained in contact with Ireland, as well as with his native Northumbria and we shall see that the manuscripts of Echternach bear the mark of this double origin.

About the same time, an Irish missionary of whom very little is known, Kilian, evangelized Franconia and Thuringia with eleven other Irishmen. In 698, he was massacred in Würzburg where his tomb remained for centuries a rallying centre for Irish pilgrims on their way to Rome or the Holy Land.[2]

Other Irish monks settled on the Continent in hermitages or monasteries. Fursa, when he left his English establishment around 638, passed some time first at Péronne,[3] staying with the palace mayor of

---

Historical Account of the Diocese of Down and Connor ancient and modern (Dublin, 1878–95), II, p. 267), in the Lagan valley, where a pillar-stone with crosses in circles has been found (E. Getty, *Notice of the Round Towers of Ulster*, pp. 28 sqq.) would also be a possibility. In any case, there is no proof whatsoever that Egbert remained at Rath Melsigi after the plague. The only thing which may be inferred from the story of his attempted departure is that he was living not very far from the sea or at least from a navigable river where his ship could be fitted.

[1] Bede, *H.E.*, V, 10; for the *Life of Willibrord* by Alcuin, see: Migne, *P.L.*, CI, 693–724.

[2] Kenney, *Sources*, pp. 512–13; his relics were transferred in 752 into the cathedral, and it is only from that time that the tomb of Kilian became a centre of attraction for wandering Irish clerics. That it still had Irish connections in the eleventh century is shown by the biography of Marianus Scottus of Mainz (Henry–Marsh–Micheli, *Illumination*, p. 127).

[3] Traube, *Perrona Scottorum*.

Neustria, Ercinwald, who started building a monastery for him. Fursa had with him relics of Irish saints which he may have left in Péronne; he seems in any case to have deposited there a manuscript of Saint Patrick of which Péronne diffused copies later.[1] Then, he went to Lagny near Paris, where he spent several years of retreat. He was on his way back to England when he died in 649 or 650. He was buried in Péronne, in the church of the monastery built by Ercinwald, of which the two brothers of Fursa, Foillan and Ultán were the first abbots. For more than a century their successors were Irishmen. One of them, Cellach or Cellanus exchanged letters with Aldhelm at the end of the seventh century.[2] In 774, the Annals of the Four Masters mention the death of Moenan 'abbot of the city of Fursa in France'. The Annals of Ulster (A.D. 779) call him 'Moinan mac Cormaic'. In the texts of the Early Middle Ages the monastery is called 'Perrona Scottorum'. The nearby monasteries of Saint Riquier and Corbie also took part in this Insular influx. Fursa's brothers and another Irish hermit, Fiachra (Saint Fiacre) scattered a series of Irish foundations across the north of France and Belgium. These, in their turn, attracted many 'peregrini Scotti'. The story of this Irish expansion on the Continent has been told often, in more detail than is possible here.[3] Through various allusions we can guess at the existence of Irish monasteries here or there. One of the most remarkable may be the monastery of Honau, built in an island of the Rhine near Strasbourg. Founded in 720, it is mentioned about 762–4 in a decree of Charlemagne and was probably in contact with Echternach at a slightly earlier date.[4] Hospices were built on the routes most often taken by travellers. Some of these, in fact, were only

[1] P. Grosjean, S.J., 'The Confession of Saint Patrick', in: *Saint Patrick* (Th. Davies Lectures, ed. by J. Ryan, S.J., Dublin, 1958).

[2] Ehwald, *Aldhelmi Opera*.

[3] Gougaud, *Christianity, passim*, Kenney, *Sources, passim*, Margaret Stokes, *Six Months in the Apennines* (London, 1892); Id., *Three Months in the Forests of France* (London, 1895); A. Tomasini, O.F.M., *Irish Saints in Italy* (trans.) (London, 1937); Bieler, *Ireland*.

[4] W. Reeves, 'On the Irish Abbey of Honau on the Rhine', *P.R.I.A.*, 1853–7, pp. 452 sqq. Kenney, *Sources*, pp. 528–9 and 784–5. There are charters concerning the Irish Monastery in Honau from 723 to 787. It was on the East bank of the Rhine, separated from the shore by marshes.

wanderers pretending to be pilgrims, and they did not come very far from throwing complete discredit on the authentic 'peregrini'. Others, such as Virgil of Salzburg, caused violent controversy by the boldness of the theories they expounded.[1] There can be very little doubt that this Irish element played its part in the shaping of Carolingian civilization; it was only strengthened by the presence of Alcuin whose ties with Irish teaching we have already seen.

All this wide movement of expansion of the Irish Church and the teaching obligations which it imposed on Irish monasteries brought many changes at home. The early hermitages or the abbeys where everything was reduced to the barest essentials, so admired by Bede, had been invaded by hordes of disciples. They had then to adapt themselves to new conditions. In the course of the eighth century, they continually increase in size. They turn into those 'monastic cities' which were in fact small universities. Life becomes organized there on a rather new basis. For that motley population of professors and students, lodgings are needed, and stores of various supplies. Agricultural labourers and craftsmen gravitate now around the monastery and constitute its 'familia'. Hence very material preoccupations. This sketch of the monastery of Toomregan, which appears incidentally in the story of Cenn Fealad the poet, is quite revealing: 'He was brought to the house of the abbot, where the three streets meet between the houses of the three professors, as there were three schools in that monastery, one school of Latin Studies, one of Irish Law, and one of Irish poetry.'

A text dating from the end of the century, the Introduction to the Calendar-Martyrology of Óengus-Céli-Dé,[2] gives a vivid idea of the transformations which had taken place in the course of the two preceding centuries. Óengus tells us: 'The little places where hermits settled two together, three together, are resorts of pilgrims, where hundreds, where thousands assemble.'[3] These new cities he compares to the fortresses of old: 'The old cities of the heathen, which men had devized for an enduring possession, are waste without worship. . . . Tara's mighty citadel

---

[1] On the present evaluation of the works of Virgil of Salzburg, see Bieler, *Ireland*, pp. 102-104.

[2] Stokes, *Martyr, Oengus*.   [3] Ibid., p. 26.

has perished with the passing of her princes; with a multitude of champions of wisdom great Armagh abides. . . . Now that victorious Aillil has departed, Rathcroghan is no more. But in Cluain's city is a glory beyond what kings attain. . . . And you who speak of Ciaran may tell of tuneful choirs that live on around him, and of all the rich tumult of Clonmacnois. . . . Emain's citadel has vanished save that its stones remain. Rome [or necropolis] of the Western World is multitudinous Glendalough.'[1]

Of these proud 'cities' one can guess that they get entangled up to a point in very mundane preoccupations. The Annals mention, in the course of the eighth and the beginning of the ninth century, the various 'familia' of monasteries which go warring against each other,[2] or against a neighbouring king. Some ambitions assert themselves, which are clearly of a worldly nature, such as the increasing insistence of Armagh on its Patrician origin which entailed the right of levying the 'tribute of Saint Patrick'. There is a whole side of the Irish Church of the eighth century which is organization, pomp and wealth. Art will not suffer from it – on the contrary – but it will derive from this aspect a slightly showy appearance.

This tendency has, however, hardly manifested itself when a movement of reaction appears. It may well be a natural continuation of all that activity of scriptural studies which we have seen at Lismore. A monastery on a small island in the estuary of the Blackwater, Dairinis,[3] which was dependent on Lismore, is partly responsible for the production of this collection of ecclesiastical prescriptions which, under the name of *Collectio Canonum Hibernensis* will enjoy such a popularity on the Continent.[4] This is a compilation which obviously aimed at supply-

---

[1] Ibid., pp. 24–6.   [2] Cf. *A.U.*, 759–60 and 763–4.
[3] Dairinis–Molana, a sixth century foundation, three miles north of Youghal. The channel separating it from the mainland has been reclaimed. The monastery was destroyed by the Vikings and was only re-established in Norman times. P. Power, 'The Abbey of Molana, Co. Waterford', *J.R.S.A.I.*, 1932, pp. 142 sqq.
[4] See Kenney, *Sources*, pp. 247–9; for the text: F. W. H. Wasserschleben, *Die irische Kanonsammlungen* (2nd ed., Leipzig, 1885); for the authorship: R. Thurneysen, 'Zur irischen Kanonsammlung', *Z.C.P.*, 1908, pp. 1 sqq.

ing precise data and rules for confessors. It is at the root of a movement which will produce several penitentials. Shortly after its redaction, the Abbot of Dairinis, whose nephew Máelrúain was to be the animator of the reform, had as a pupil this same Óengus whose poem has been quoted above. The movement spread in the centre of Ireland, to Clonenagh, Terryglass, Lorrha, Loch-Cré, and seems to have some links with Tech Moling in Leinster on the one hand and the neighbourhood of Cashel on the other. Finally it became centred on the twin monasteries of Finglas and Tallaght, near Dublin, which are called in contemporary texts 'the two eyes of Ireland'.[1] Máelrúain became abbot of Tallaght where, as well as in Clonenagh and Terryglass or Lorrha some of the most significant texts of the movement were written: the Tract on the Monastery of Tallaght,[2] the Martyrology and the Calendar of Óengus, and the Stowe Missal. The general tendencies of the reform led to a new development of asceticism, sometimes combined with a slightly puritanical tone, to a stricter observance of monastic hours, and their outcome was the reclusion either of a hermit living alone in a 'desert' or of a group of Céli-Dé (servants or companions of God) living together, sometimes on the outskirts of a large monastery. They brought about a new spate of activity in sacred studies. Robin Flower has very rightly commented on the tremendous amount of hagiographical studies which went as a preparation for the compilation of the Martyrology of Óengus. The subtle symbolism of the commentary on the Mass in the Stowe Missal presupposes researches on liturgy and deeply mystical preoccupations.

This is not all, and the texts concerning the reform of Tallaght have

---

[1] Flower, *The two Eyes of Ireland*.

[2] E. J. Gwynn–W. J. Purton, 'The Monastery of Tallaght', *P.R.I.A.*, 1911 (C), pp. 162 sqq. This gives an extraordinary picture of the way in which pagan elements still survived at that time. Between two paragraphs relating to practices of devotion, one finds a surprising mention of Máelruain indulging in the age-old custom of fasting against somebody and a no less surprising description of the results: 'Máelruain never fasted but thrice since he settled in Tallaght – namely against Antry, son of Fallmuire, about a business that arose between the monastery of Tallaght and him. After the first fasting, the king's leg broke in two; after the second the fire fell and burnt him from top to toe; after the third fasting the king died' (op. cit. p. 157).

come down to us surrounded by poems of a delightful limpidity.[1] We shall see that the movement is perhaps linked with the elaboration of a type of carved cross. It plays an essential part in the artistic and intellectual life of Ireland in the second half of the eighth century and the beginning of the ninth. Still it is not antagonistic to the big monasteries. Clonmacnois was certainly sympathetic to the reform and we have seen Óengus glorifying Armagh, Kildare, Glendalough and Clonmacnois. If there are here and there some sinister allusions to some other places we have to assume that they are aimed at monasteries whose discipline was completely relaxed, but not to the great schools, however noisy and agitated they may have become.

Schools and hermitages were all in fact, in these last years of the eighth century, threatened by an onslaught which was to shake the whole structure of Irish civilization to its roots. Towards the end of the century, the Annals begin to register the depredations of the 'Gentiles', the 'Foreigners', the pirates coming from Norway, the Vikings. Already in 793 rumours were abroad: all the islands of Britain have been laid waste, Lindisfarne has been attacked. In 801, possibly in 805, came the turn of Iona, where 'a great number of layfolks and ecclesiastics were massacred, that is to say sixty-eight' (A.Q.M.). The disaster seemed so final and the threat appeared so permanent that the transfer of the metropolis of the order of Saint Columba was decided, and in the following years the Annals tell us of the building of a 'monastic city' at Kells, south of Armagh, where the monks of the island monastery will take refuge with all their most precious possessions.

Soon, the fleets of the Vikings appeared also on the Irish coasts. The island monastery of Inismurray was destroyed in 802, never to rise again. In 822 or 824, Bangor was plundered, its wooden church was destroyed and 'the relics of Comgall were shaken out of their shrine'. Year after year, during that beginning of the ninth century, disasters follow each other, and the last pitch of horror is reached with the raid

[1] Meyer, *A. Irish Poetry*; Jackson, *Nature Poetry*; G. Murphy, *Early Irish Lyrics* (Oxford, 1956); R. Flower, *Poems and Translations* (London, 1931); Id., *The Irish Tradition* (Oxford, 1947).

of Turgeis in 836. It would lead us beyond the chronological limits of the present study to follow in detail the history of these invasions and of the struggle which went on until the beginning of the eleventh century. Suffice to point out the growing threat that weighed on these first years of the ninth century.

3. The Beginnings of Christian Art in Ireland

THE CHRISTIAN art which will develop in the framework of the complex and changing circumstances just outlined passes first through a phase of formation corresponding more or less with the time when Ireland was almost completely isolated from the Continent by pagan England and so approximately covers the end of the fifth century, the sixth and part of the seventh. This is an obscure period and difficult to handle, but it deserves to be examined in detail as it leads up to the adaptation of Celtic art to the new needs at the very time when, by a similar process, Irish epics and Irish laws were beginning to be written down and when the first attempts were made to put the historical traditions of the country in line with the world chronicles.

First let us see the setting in which these changes took place. Of the secular establishments of that time we can get some idea from excavations, chiefly those of two large raths[1] in County Cork, Garranes and Ballycatteen. Each of them was surrounded by three concentric rings of ramparts and ditches. Garranes,[2] excavated in 1941 by Séan Ó Ríordáin, is about 180 feet in diameter. Post-holes have been discovered but it is not possible to reconstruct the plan of a single hut. From the types of objects found it seems to have been occupied in the fifth and sixth centuries. The excavations have yielded a great quantity of fragments of Mediterranean pottery, of a type which was practically unknown at the time of the excavations but which has since been found in south-west Britain and a few Irish coastal sites.[3] The fragments are those

[1] On raths, see: V. B. Proudfoot, 'The Economy of the Irish Rath', *Med. Arch.*, 1961, pp. 94 sqq.

[2] S. P. Ó Ríordáin, 'The Excavation of a large Earthen Ring-fort at Garranes, Co. Cork', *P.R.I.A.*, 1924 (C), pp. 77 sqq.

[3] C. A. Ralegh Radford, 'Imported Pottery at Tintagel, Cornwall, an Aspect of British Trade with the Mediterranean in the Early Christian Period', in *Dark Age Britain*, pp. 59 sqq.; C. Thomas, 'Imported Pottery in Dark Age Western Britain', *Medieval Arch.*, 1959, pp. 89 sqq.

of large bowls of reddish pottery, generally associated with small amphorae having zones of horizontal ribbed decoration, which came probably as containers of wine or olive oil. Several fragments of bowls of this type found in Cornwall are stamped with a cross (generally a Greek cross with expanded arms). This has given rise to the hypothesis that we may have here an importation for liturgical needs. One may wonder if the forts, which are not very far from the sea, were not warehouses where goods landed nearby were stored (with the usual proportion of breakage). The importers lived no doubt in less well-protected houses which have left no visible traces on the surface of the ground. This would explain fairly well the absence of recognizable structures within the fort: inside the rampart there were probably only some shelters protecting heaped-up goods. Still, smiths and glaziers had worked in the less wind-beaten part of the rath, probably under lean-to roofs propped against the rampart. The ground was blackened by fragments of charcoal; there were numerous pieces of crucibles, stone and clay moulds for the casting of bronze objects, fragments of glass, some of them prepared for enamelling and one piece of champlevé enamel (Fig. 6, a) – remains of an industrial activity of which it is difficult to say who directed it and for whom it was made.

Ballycatteen,[1] a rath of the same type, of which the construction and the earliest occupation seem to go back to the end of the sixth century or the beginning of the seventh, was defended by three concentric rings of ramparts and ditches and also by a palisade built on the inside rampart. There were only very few traces of buildings in the lower level. But there also blackened earth and fragments of crucibles testified to a certain industrial activity.

Another rath in the same neighbourhood, Garryduff,[2] which had only one rampart, was probably built in the sixth century, but was occupied over a long period. The primary occupation of a rath of County Limerick, Carraig Aille No. 2,[3] which is on the top of a hill overlooking

[1] S. P. Ó Ríordáin–P. J. Hartnett, 'The Excavation of Ballycatteen Fort, Co. Cork', *P.R.I.A.*, 1943 (C), pp. 1 sqq.
[2] M. J. O'Kelly, 'Two Ring-Forts at Garryduff', *P.R.I.A.*, 1962 (C), pp. 17 sqq.
[3] S. P. Ó Ríordáin, 'Lough Gur Excavations, Carraig Aille and the "Spectacles"', *P.R.I.A.*, 1949 (C), pp. 39 sqq.

Lough Gur, is also likely to go back to the sixth century, given the type of hand-pin found in the excavations and the presence of an imitation of a Roman coin. It was a less ambitious construction, 90 feet in internal diameter, which was only protected by a stone wall 12 feet thick. There had been inside some round huts with central hearths. There were remains of houses outside the wall as well. This gives a good picture of the most common type of habitation at the time. The large establishments of the pagan period are being abandoned gradually, and it is only slightly later, about the middle of the seventh century, that it will be possible, thanks to the Lagore excavations, to form some idea of the appearance of a royal residence.

A considerable number of crannogs whose first occupation probably went back to the period we are dealing with, have been mercilessly plundered in the last century in the course of drainage schemes and drying-up operations.[1] But the crannog No. 2 of Lough Gara (Roscommon) excavated in 1957–9 by Joseph Raftery[2] and the crannog No. 2 excavated at Ballinderry (Offaly) in 1933 by Hugh Hencken[3] give some idea of their construction. Both had been built by the piling up of various materials on top of earlier settlements. The Ballinderry crannog was about 100 feet in diameter and was surrounded by a robust post-palisade. A layer of beams acted as the base of a hearth.

Other establishments in sand-dunes on the coasts of Mayo and Donegal seem to have been partly dedicated to the manufacture of purple dye, as they include enormous heaps of 'purpura lapillus', always broken in the same way. Some are on Inishkea North (Mayo)[4] where a large wooden hut with a central hearth seems to be dated to the sixth century or the beginning of the seventh by a penannular brooch and a small mirror-handle derived from a Roman prototype. A. B. Ó Ríordáin and Etienne Rynne excavated another one in 1960

[1] Wood-Martin, *Lake-Dwellings*.

[2] The report on the excavation of Lough Gara has not appeared yet. I am indebted to Dr Raftery for the information he gave me about it.

[3] H. O'Neill-Hencken, 'Ballinderry Crannog No 2', *P.R.I.A.*, 1942 (C), pp. 1 sqq.

[4] F. Henry, 'A Wooden Hut on Inishkea North, Co. Mayo', *J.R.S.A.I.*, 1952, pp. 163 sqq.

at Dooey, in Donegal,[1] which has yielded remains of the workshops of metalworkers and a great number of objects (Pl. 13).

What can we know of the appearance of churches and primitive monasteries? The masons of Saint Patrick may have built some stone churches in the fashion of those of Gaul and Britain. One of his biographers, Tirechán, writing in the seventh century, speaks of the 'daimliag' (stone church) built at Duleek by Saint Kenan, a bishop consecrated by Patrick himself. But nearly everywhere the native method of building walls of earth or wood is likely to have been retained. Tirechán also mentions a case when Patrick built a church in earth because there was no wood available. To this may be compared the text where Bede shows us Finan building at Lindisfarne, in the middle of the seventh century, a church 'made in the manner of the Scotti, not of stone, but entirely of hewn oak, and covered with reeds'.[2] Still, these churches were no mere huts. The 'great church' (Domnach mór) of Patrick in Meath is supposed to have been more than 60 feet long.

If we try to imagine the monasteries of Clonmacnois, Clonard and Durrow, or Bangor at the time when Columbanus left it, we have to conjure up a picture of wooden or earthen churches surrounded by wattle or wooden cells. In the present state of our knowledge, it is impossible to do more than evoke their appearance in very vague terms, as most of the large monasteries of the plain, too easily accessible to plunderers and built on land too rich and too desirable, have been completely wiped out. Even when ruins survive, as in Clonmacnois, centuries of fires and rebuildings have erased all traces of the primitive establishment. On the other hand, some of the monasteries of the wilderness have come down to us in an amazing state of preservation thanks to their position on nearly inaccessible islands or untilled land. In some cases the first buildings were wooden huts. This has been revealed clearly by the excavations of Church Island, near Valentia

[1] A. B. Ó Ríordáin–E. Rynne, 'A Settlement in the Sand-hills at Dooey, Co. Donegal', *J.R.S.A.I.*, 1961, pp. 58 sqq.
[2] Bede, *H.E.*, III, 25.

(Kerry).[1] But more permanent dry-stone buildings replaced them soon and their very simplicity of structure helped them to survive.

One of the most complete examples of such remains are the cells and oratories on Skellig Michael,[2] standing as fast on their dizzy platform of rock as in the days when the monks lived there (Pls. 18, 19). The Skelligs are giant pyramids of schist emerging from the Atlantic some ten miles from the Kerry coast. The smaller is the haunt of gannets which nest there in their thousands every spring. The other, dedicated to Saint Michael, is 714 feet high; the remains of the monastery, huddled on a narrow shelf of rock below one of its summits can only be reached by steep stone stairs (Pl. 17). Five huts are still standing; they are covered by corbelled domes made by an ageless method still used occasionally on the neighbouring coast; this was probably the usual way of building in that part of Ireland at the time when the monastery was first erected, that is to say about the sixth or seventh century. They are comparatively large, being from 9 to 15 feet in diameter; some are nearly 17 feet high and may have been divided in two stories by a wooden floor. They surround an oratory in the shape of an upturned boat beside which stands a large cross cut out of a slab. Another very small oratory has been built on an overhanging terrace on the extreme edge of the cliff. The huts have no decoration other than a cross of white stones above the door of some of them. The only ornaments are those engraved on the cross and on a few slabs in the little graveyard.

This monastery which has survived Norse raids and the assaults of the sea wind, seems, raised towards the sky on the top of a bare rock, surrounded only by the empty wilderness of the western ocean, to embody all the aspirations of the time. But other less spectacular remains are scattered all along the coast, some of them well enough preserved to be nearly as suggestive of the past. They all consist basically of a few cells and a very small oratory, with generally a cross-bearing slab or pillar beside it. These few buildings, sometimes im-

---

[1] M. J. O'Kelly, 'Church Island, near Valentia, Co. Kerry', *P.R.I.A.*, 1958 (C), pp. 57 sqq. The same was probably true on Inishkea.

[2] Henry, *Early Monasteries*, pp. 113 sqq.; L. de Paor, 'A Survey of Sceilg Mhichíl', *J.R.S.A.I.*, 1955, pp. 174 sqq.

pressive in their bareness, but in no way elaborate, correspond exactly with Bede's description of the monastery of Lindisfarne at the time of Colman's departure in 664 : 'The place which they governed shows how frugal and temperate he and his predecessors were, for there were very few houses, besides the church, found at their departure, indeed no more than were barely sufficient to make civilized life possible.'[1] There are ruins of that type on the islands or in the mountain valleys of Kerry, on Bishop's Island, off the coast of Clare, on Aran, on Ardillaun, Inishkea, Inishglora (Mayo), and Inismurray off the Sligo coast.[2] And if not much has survived of the early monastery of Iona, there are similar ruins on nearby islands of Scotland, and as far as the Orkneys and Shetlands.

Like all human settlements at a time when robbers and wild beasts were always at large most of the monasteries were enclosed by walls, generally more or less circular, of dry stones or of earth. Some of these walls, on Inismurray (Sligo) and in Kerry at Illaun-t-Senaig and Kildreelig, are enormous structures, 15 to 20 feet thick, or, as in the case of Saint Manchan's monastery in the Dingle promontory, great earthen banks surrounded by a ditch. These are likely to have been the defences of a rath abandoned to the monks by a local chieftain, a type of foundation mentioned in several texts.

In some cases, when that part of the ruins is sufficiently well preserved, it appears that the oratory and the tomb beside it, marked by a slab or pillar, are enclosed by a wall or isolated on a small terrace; this is the case on Duvillaun (Mayo) (Fig. 2) and at Loher (Fig. 2) and Killabuonia (Kerry). The oratories are usually built of carefully dressed stones. Their plan is rectangular, the two gables being slightly curved triangles, whilst the side walls, made by the corbelling of large flat stones join, at the top to form inside a narrow flagged ceiling surmounted on the outside by a sharp ridge. They are all oriented with a door in the middle of the west wall and a window in the east wall. The door was probably of wood or basketry and mounted in a wooden frame,

---

[1] Bede, *H.E.*, III, 26.

[2] *Handbook of the Islands and Coast of Ireland*, published by the R.S.A.I. (Dublin, 1904); Dunraven, *Notes*; Henry, *Early Monasteries*; Wakeman, *Inismurray*.

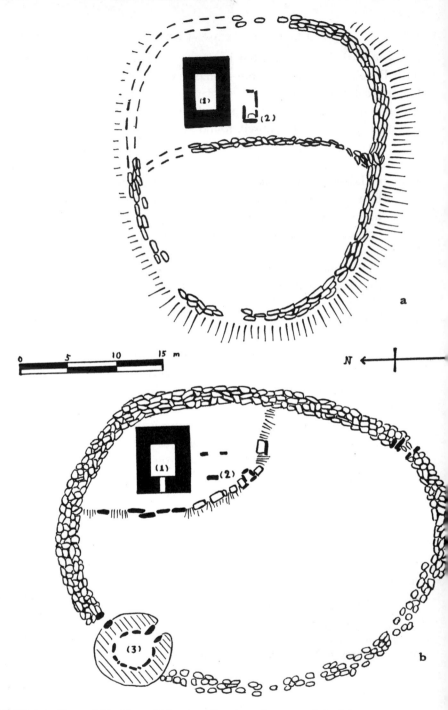

Fig. 2. a, plan of the hermitage of Duvillaun (Mayo): (1) ruins of oratory, (2) slab;
b, plan of the hermitage of Loher (Kerry): (1) ruins of oratory, (2) slab, (3) ruins of a hut.

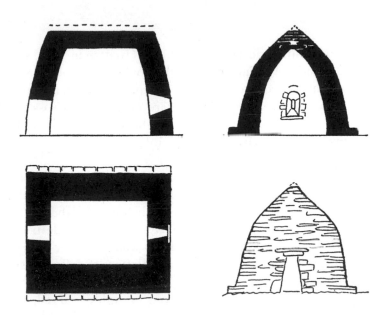

Fig. 3. Oratory of Gallerus (Kerry) :
section, plan and west front.

the two pierced stones which held it still in many cases protruding over
the lintel. The only one, apart from those of the Skellig, which survives
intact, is the oratory of Gallerus in the Dingle peninsula (Fig. 3), but
there remain a great number of ruins of buildings of the same type
(Pl. 19), at least thirty, scattered across the counties of Kerry, Clare and
Mayo. Their small size may seem disconcerting, even remembering
that they were meant for communities of a few hermits. Those which
have been measured (allowing for the fact that they are often half
buried), vary usually between 9 and 15 feet in length and only exceptionally exceed 19 feet (oratories of Church Island and of Caherciveen).
One may wonder if the altar was not sometimes raised in front of the
slab which usually stands beside the oratory, the latter, in this case
being used only as a sacristy and tabernacle, whilst the congregation
filled the whole enclosure, perhaps under a thatched roof. The slab in
most cases marks probably the tomb of the first hermit or of the saintly
founder of the monastery, which made it very suitable for this purpose.

A text in the *Life* of an English saint, Willibald (written in 754), shows also what part the cross-bearing slab or pillar could play in places where Christianity was introduced from Ireland. It says that in many English estates there was no chapel, but 'the standard of the Holy Cross, dedicated to Our Lord and reverenced with great honour, lifted up on high so as to be convenient for the frequency of daily prayer'[1]

These cross-bearing stones are found in varying numbers in nearly every one of the early monasteries. They range from engraved boulders or rocks, and rough pillars of a mere 2 feet in height, to elaborate slabs as much as 5 or 6 feet in height. Some also have survived the destruction of the buildings and stand alone in a field whose former religious dedication transpires only in the local appellation of killeen (small church) or cellurach.

They often bear simply a cross engraved or lightly carved, while some others have a much more elaborate decoration. But, however simple or complex their ornament, the same types are found in widely distant places, and they are of a perfectly uniform style, whether in Cork, Kerry, Mayo or Donegal.[2] Most of the types of crosses found in Ireland are universal to all Christendom at that time and have been brought to Ireland from Gaul, Italy or the Near East. Apart from the Greek cross, often made of arcs of a circle, and the Latin cross with expanded ends, which are the most common types, there are also simple Latin crosses and all sorts of varieties of crosses potent. Sometimes, as on Merovingian sarcophagi,[3] the three crosses are represented, or even a greater number of crosses. Various forms of the Chi-Rho monogram are used here and there, generally under the simplified and rather late shape where the curve of the Rho is simply added to the upper arm of the cross (Fig. 4, *b*). There is only one definite example, at Loher,

---

[1] *The Hodoeporicon of St Willibald* (Pal. Pilgr. Text Soc., vol. XVIII), p. 4.

[2] See H. S. Crawford, 'Descriptive List of Early Cross-Slabs and Pillars', *J.R.S.A.I.*, 1912, pp. 217 sqq.; 1913, pp. 151 sqq., 261 sqq., 326 sqq.; 1916, pp. 163 sqq.; also: Henry, *Slabs and Pillars*.

[3] Salin, *C.M.*, II, p. 167; for sarcophagi with multiple crosses, see same page; also D. Fossard, 'Répartition des sarcophages mérovingiens à décor en France', *Etudes mérov.*, pp. 117 sqq. (Pl. XII).

Fig. 4. Patterns on pillars and slabs:
    a, Caherlehillan (Kerry);
    b, Kilshannig (Kerry);
    c, d, e, Cloon Lough (Kerry);
    f, Dunfeeny (Mayo).

in Kerry (Pl. 16),[1] of a slab bearing the cross with the Alpha and Omega hanging from the arms, similar to Continental monuments such as the Merovingian slab from Challans (Vendée) (Nantes Museum)[2] or the lid of the sarcophagus of Boetius, Bishop of Carpentras, who died in 603 (Notre-Dame de Vie, Vaucluse),[3] but several slabs, at Church Island (Lough Currane, Kerry), on the Skellig, at Cloonlaur (Mayo), have debased forms of it.

Still, though the crosses are of a very universal type, the pillars bearing them pertain to local Irish and British tradition and may be in a way the heirs of standing stones erected prior to the introduction of Christianity. The first adaptation probably took place on the outskirts of the Roman world, in Wales and the south-west of Scotland (Strathclyde). The type of Christian funerary inscription usual towards the end of the Empire which, in Gaul and Italy in the fourth and fifth centuries is found written on stone tablets, is transferred in Britain on to more or less shaped monoliths in the fifth and sixth centuries. The most characteristic examples for Strathclyde are several pillars at Kirkmadrine (Wigtownshire)[4] and for Wales the Penmachno monument (Caernarvonshire).[5] There are also some examples in Cornwall.[6] This compromise between Continental Christian customs and semi-megalithic habits certainly had its influence in Ireland at the time when Candida Casa and the Welsh monasteries helped in the training of the Irish monks. In Ireland, however, the inscription is often omitted, and when it is present, it is generally written in oghams (Pl. 14). This is the case, for example, with a pillar which now lies at Arraglen (Kerry) on one of the slopes of Mount Brandon.[7] It has, on one side, a Greek cross inscribed in a circle, and on the other a Chi-Rho surrounded by the inscription (in oghams) 'Ronan the priest, son of Comgall'. The analogy is striking with one of the pillars of Kirkmadrine where, below a Chi-

[1] Henry, *Early Monasteries*, pp. 142–3.

[2] L. Coutil, *L'Art mérovingien et carolingien* (Bordeaux, 1930), fig. fac. p. 46.

[3] Salin, *C.M.*, II, p. 159.

[4] Allen–Anderson, III, pp. 494 sqq.; Macalister, *Corpus*, I, pp. 493–6.

[5] E. Nash-Williams, *Early Christian Monuments of Wales* (Cardiff, 1950), Pl. VIII, 101; Macalister, *Corpus*, I, pp. 369–70.

[6] Allen, *Celtic Art*, p. 163.   [7] Macalister, *Corpus*, I, p. 140.

Rho in a circle, is written in Latin characters : 'His jacent sci et praecipui sacerdotes id es . . . Viventius et Mavorius.'

In a few cases – probably on monuments dating from the end of the sixth or the beginning of the seventh century – inscriptions in an archaic form of Irish script accompany the cross; for example the contraction of the Nomina Sacra : D$\overline{N}$E, D$\overline{N}$I, etc. The first is inscribed on the side of the Reask pillar (Kerry) (Pl. 15). The slab which stands beside the ruins of an oratory at Kilfountain or Kilfinten (Kerry) (the church of Finten), bears the name of the saint: FINTEN, written vertically (Pl. 15).

On both these monuments the cross is surrounded by ornaments. To the quite simple crosses of their models the Irish soon added an elaborate decoration generally adapted from the repertoire of pre-Christian curvilinear ornament with which were combined here and there helix, swastika and fret patterns. Sometimes there is no more than spiral endings to the arms of the cross. This is not unknown on the Continent, but it seldom occurs there with the same exuberance; often a more elaborate spiral motif accompanies the cross as we have just seen on the Reask and Kilfountain pillars, and as occurs on the slab at Inishkea South (Mayo) (Fig. 14). These simple, but finely cut designs, form a surprising contrast to the coarse and little dressed surface of the stone; the firm composition, the bold lines of the cross, the certitude of the big circle surrounding it, combine with the uneven shape of the stone in a slightly jarring harmony which gives to these monuments a very particular charm. Even the simplest of them are infinitely pleasing. This refined elegance of purpose playing on an untamed background of rough material makes it an unforgettable experience to discover for the first time the Reask pillar or the big slab of Inishkea South, especially if an oblique sun brings out the delicacy of the modelling of the spirals and the subtlety of the relief.

The later of these monuments, made probably towards the middle or even the end of the seventh century, show an increasing tendency towards the regular shaping of the stone. But here an outside factor comes into play which we will have to study later in more detail.

This sensitiveness to the subtle tracery of a pattern or to the sharpness of a line is manifest also in the first attempts at decoration on vellum, very close, in their attractive hesitancy, to what is found on the early pillars.

Saint Patrick and his companions did certainly bring books with them, Gospels, psalters, etc. What was their appearance? It is possible to gain some idea of it from some of the fifth-century Latin manuscripts of Gaul and Italy which have come down to us. Some of them had probably, in the beginning of important paragraphs, enlarged letters, sometimes very sparsely decorated. The first Irish books were no doubt imitations of these models. Those of the fifth century and of the beginning of the sixth are lost and we are unable now to follow the first gropings of the Irish scribes and the way in which they altered the writing of their models to turn it slowly into that imposing Irish majuscule script which was to keep for centuries its distinctive character, and the slightly rounded minuscule which was used for the more ordinary books.

Only in the second half of the sixth century can we for the first time see them at work, in a few verses of the psalms engraved on wax tablets[1] and in the pages of a manuscript which tradition attributes to the pen of Saint Columba and which has reached us under the singular nickname of 'Cathach' ('battler' or 'champion').[2] Its history is strange. Already in fairly bad condition, with its pages partly worn at the edges, it was put, at the end of the eleventh century, in a tightly fitting wooden box covered with metal, made, probably in Kells, for Cathbarr O'Donnell, then chief of Cinel Conaill Gulban, the branch of the Northern Uí Néill to which Saint Columba had belonged. The box was repaired in the fourteenth century. In 1497 it was carried by its 'keeper' in front of the army of O'Donnell, which was, however, beaten. A few years later, Manus O'Donnell, another member of the family, when writing the *Life* of the saint, said, *à propos* of a famous battle: 'The Cathach is the name

[1] E. C. R. Armstrong–R. A. S. Macalister, 'Wooden Box with Leaves indented and waxed found near Springmount Bog, Co. Antrim', *J.R.S.A.I.*, 1920, pp. 160 sqq.

[2] W. Betham, *Irish Antiquarian Research* (Dublin, 1826), pp. 109 sqq.; H. J. Lawlor and W. M. Lindsay, 'The Cathach of St Columba', *P.R.I.A.*, 1916 (C), pp. 241 sqq.; Lowe, *C.L.A.*, II, 266; Nordenfalk, *Before the B. of Durrow*; Henry, *Débuts min. irl.*, pp. 19–20.

of the book which caused that battle. It is the chief relic of Saint Columba in the territory of Cinel Conaill Gulban. It is in a silver gilt box which must not be opened. And each time it has been carried three times, turning towards the right, around the army before a battle, the army came back victorious.'[1] The reliquary which nobody was to open went on being handed down in the O'Donnell family until one of its members, leaving Ireland after the Treaty of Limerick, took it to France. There a casket of silver was made to encase the old one. After being kept in France until 1802, it was brought back to Sir Neal O'Donel. In 1813 Sir William Betham,[2] Deputy Ulster King of Arms, being engaged in writing an account of the O'Donnell family, was lent the Cathach. Sir William, after many difficulties, opened the box and found in it a manuscript whose pages were stuck together by damp. He unstuck them. Later the manuscript was deposited in the Royal Irish Academy and its pages were remounted.

The Cathach was studied in detail in 1916 by Lawlor and Lindsay, and more recently by A. E. Lowe for the palaeography and by Carl Nordenfalk for the decoration. It is only a fragment of a psalter, consisting now of 58 folios in very bad condition. The beginning and the end are missing. The complete manuscript had probably about 110 folios. The damp has lost us also a binding, as Betham speaks of a wooden fragment covered with red leather which he found in the box and which is now lost. Originally it was about 9 by 6 in. It seems to be written entirely by the same hand, in a very archaic form of Irish majuscule. According to Lowe and Lindsay there is no palaeographical objection to the manuscript dating as far back as the time of Saint Columba. In fact, on its script alone, one would have to ascribe it to a very early date. Manus O'Donnell is certainly not an absolutely reliable authority, but the tradition which he hands down to us can not be wholly ignored. It fits in fact with everything which Adamnan tells us of the saint whom he shows several times writing in his cell. He speaks of a

[1] *Betha Colaim Chille, Life of Columcille, compiled by Manus O'Donnell in 1532*, ed. A. O'Kelleher and G. Schoepperle (Urbana, Ill., 1918), XIV, 178, pp. 182–3.
[2] See: P. B. Phair, 'Betham and the Older Irish Manuscripts', *J.R.S.A.I.*, 1962, pp. 75 sqq.

book 'written by the dear and holy fingers of Saint Columba',[1] of a book
of hymns for the week 'written by the hand of Saint Columba'[2] and he
shows the saint, on the last day of his life, sitting for a moment in his
hut, working at a transcript of the psalter which he was to leave unfinished. Whether this is, as Manus O'Donnell would have it, and as
Lawlor maintained, the very book which caused a battle and in consequence the exile of Saint Columba to Iona, is now impossible to know.
The story is in fact very confused and has come down to us wrapped up
in legends. One feels tempted to believe however that it holds some
truth, as that text which Columba copied without permission from a
book owned by his master Finnian, must have been in some way a great
novelty in Ireland. The Cathach being a fairly good recension of that
translation of the psalter by Saint Jerome generally called the 'gallican',
the whole story could be explained by the fact that Finnian, who is
supposed to have made a journey to Rome, had brought back with him
a Vulgate text so far unknown in Ireland[3] which Columba would have
been eager to copy. Under a web of fables, there is probably a real fact:
the introduction of the biblical translations of Saint Jerome into Ireland,
where slightly careless and too learned scribes were to mix them hopelessly in successive copies with the text of older translations which
they knew by heart, elaborating gradually the 'mixed Irish text' which
is to be found already well before the end of the seventh century in the
biblical quotations of the Antiphonary of Bangor.[4] The Cathach has in
addition to its remarkable text another curious feature, as the rubrics
which precede each psalm will reappear again in Northumbria in the
eighth century, in the Codex Amiatinus; they were most probably
transmitted from Iona to Lindisfarne in the seventh century and passed
on from there to Jarrow and Wearmouth.

The decoration of the book is not very impressive. The beginning is
missing and this deprives us no doubt of a decorated first page which

[1] *Vit. Col.*, II, 8.   [2] *Vit. Col.*, II, 9.
[3] As Lawlor remarks (op. cit., pp. 312 sqq.) the saint in question was not
Finnian of Clonard, Columba's first teacher, who was dead at the time, but Finnian
of Moville, who is supposed to have gone to Rome and to have brought back
'the complete Gospels' to Ireland; see Kenney, *Sources*, p. 391.
[4] Warren, *Antiphonary of Bangor*, II, p. 39.

would have been invaluable for our knowledge of Irish illumination. There remain only the large capitals (Pls. 9, 12) which, in the way of all moderately decorated psalters, mark the beginning of each psalm. They are very simple, traced in firm strokes of ink. Most of them were surrounded by red dots. In addition, some of the patterns, inside the letters, were painted, probably in yellow. So the decoration was sparse but already well organized as far as colour went, playing on the opposition between a flat tint and dots, and the sharp definition of a thick black line on the vellum. These lines in fact turn the letter into a series of ornamental curves combined with counter-curves and including sometimes the little leaf-pattern which occurs already on quite a number of metal objects from pagan times. Here and there one finds also some animal heads and simplified representations of fishes, which may derive from ornaments in sixth-century Italian manuscripts. Sometimes a little cross with expanded ends similar to those on the engraved pillar-stones is included in the capital or drawn beside it.

The extreme importance of the Cathach, whether it belongs to the actual time of Saint Columba or to the years immediately following his death, comes from the fact that it allows us to grasp what the decoration of manuscripts was before the contacts with the Continent had become closer, and much before the development of the Northumbrian scriptoria. This makes it an essential landmark in the history of Insular illumination. To what we learn from it can be added the Irish elements in the decoration of some of the oldest of the Bobbio manuscripts.

These Bobbio manuscripts belong to the years which followed closely upon the death of Saint Columbanus (A.D. 615).[1] They are written in Irish characters very similar to those of the Cathach and their script has the same archaic features, combined in some cases with Continental elements. Their scribes use a whole series of abbreviations which are characteristic of Irish manuscripts. So they give us an idea of the methods of writing which the first companions of Columbanus and their later successors had learned in the Irish scriptoria before coming to the Continent. The same thing applies obviously to their decoration where essentially Italian features are to be found side by side with others which occur later

[1] Lowe, *C.L.A.*, IV, pp. xx sqq.; Henry, *Débuts min. irl.*

in Irish manuscripts and in all the regions influenced by the Irish style.

One of them, the Codex Usserianus Primus (T.C.D. Library, Ms. 55),[1] is an incomplete Gospel-book in very bad condition. Its text is pre-hieronymian, and it has the Gospels in the customary order of such versions : Matthew, John, Luke, Mark. Nothing is known of its history before it came to Trinity College in the seventeenth century, but Lowe attributes it to the beginning of the seventh century on account of its archaic features, especially the shape of the letter G (which has close parallels in the Cathach), reminiscent of forms dating from the fifth and sixth centuries. He connects it with the scriptorium of Bobbio because of the close relation of its script with that of some Bobbio manuscripts (such as D.23.sup. and D.26.sup. of the Ambrosian Library). The manuscript is extremely decrepit, so that most of its decoration has disappeared. It seems to have consisted of a decorative panel marking the transition from one Gospel to the other. The only one which has survived bears a large cross, or better a Chi-Rho, in red and black with the Alpha and Omega on both sides of it, framed by lines of dots and curves (Pl. 58). It would be easy to find parallels to that page in Italian manuscripts of the time, for example in the Gospel-book of Valerianus (Munich, CLM.6224), written in northern Italy towards the end of the seventh century. The only unexpected feature is supplied by the dots framing the Chi-Rho.

It may be that Usserianus Primus was sent to Ireland from Bobbio. Though it would be dangerous to insist on what may be a fortuitous coincidence, the strange analogy of the cross-shape with that engraved on the slab at Loher (Kerry) (Pl. 16) must be pointed out.

Ms. D.23.sup. of the Ambrosian Library in Milan is an incomplete copy of the Chronicle of Orosius which bears the ex-libris of Bobbio.[2] It is written in a type of Irish majuscule very similar to that of the Usserianus Primus, but its decoration is altogether different. The book

[1] Lowe, C.L.A., 271; Henry, op. cit., p. 9.

[2] Lowe, C.L.A., III, 328; Henry, op. cit., p. 10; there is in E.Q.C. Lindisfarnersis, II, Pl. 20a an attempt at a restitution of the colours of the two first pages of this manuscript. It may well be done, as is claimed, with the correct pigments, but the saturation must be wrong, and this crude colour composition is unlikely to give any true idea of the original aspect of the manuscript, which is now very faded.

starts with two ornamental pages facing each other (Pl. 58) : on the left a page covered with various patterns, on the right the beginning of the text, with a large capital, of which the stem comes right down to the bottom of the page and which is followed by a line of ornamental writing. This is exactly the treatment of the beginning of a section of a book which was to be common in Ireland from the eighth to the twelfth century. Here again there are dots, either all around the letters, or in groups of three. The letters themselves do not have the complexity of curvilinear motifs found in the Cathach, but they have the same distinct tendency to ornamental tracery and the same slightly dancing rhythm. The terminal hooks which are not rare in the Continental manuscripts of the time are here remarkably developed, their curve continuing that of the letter itself.

To these manuscripts must be added another, the Ms. S.45.sup. of the Ambrosian,[1] a commentary of Saint Jerome on Isaiah, which bears the ex-libris of Bobbio. It is the work of several scribes, some writing in Irish script, others in a Continental script with some Merovingian features, a fact which lead Lowe to wonder if it was not partly written by scribes from Luxeuil. It seems to have belonged to Atalanus, the immediate successor of Columbanus in the abbacy of Bobbio who had previously been in Luxeuil, a fact which would perhaps account for these composite features. It is a palimpsest like many other Bobbio manuscripts, and it has suffered greatly from the efforts made to revive the original text. In spite of this it remains possible to trace the small capitals, some of them surrounded or overloaded with dots. They show the same tendency to enlarge the terminal hooks of the letters as we have found in the preceding manuscript, and the first page bears a large initial, blossoming into hooks, curves and spirals which is in many ways close to the capitals of the Cathach (Pl. VI); even the fishes reappear, drawn in the same simplified way. This is very much how one would imagine the capital which must have existed in the beginning of the Cathach.

---

[1] Lowe, *C.L.A.*, III, 365; Henry, op. cit., p. 8; F. Masai has queried the early date of this manuscript (*Regula Magistri* (Brussels–Paris, 1953), p. 49), chiefly because he thought that the name on the first page was not Atalanus, but Ataganus. In this he was unfortunately misled by a worm having nibbled at some parts of the letter (the corresponding hole can be seen on the opposite page). In any case the very archaïc type of script would remain a sufficient dating element.

After eliminating the elements which, in this decoration, conform to what is found in Italian manuscripts of the time – the Chi-Rho cross in the Usserianus Primus, the twists on the stems of some initials – several irreducible features remain : the tendency to insist on the curves of the letters and ornaments, attaining its maximum in the capital of Ms. S.45.sup., the use of dots, usually red, either over or around letters or patterns, and finally the composition of the two first pages of Ms. D.23.sup.

The use of dots has been often studied.[1] It is of Coptic origin and is found in paintings of the monasteries in the Egyptian desert. It passed into Byzantine art and though it is still not as common then as it will become later, it does occur in Byzantine manuscripts of the sixth century, such as the Dioscorides in Vienna Library or the Gospel-book in the cathedral of Rossano in Calabria. It is difficult to establish how the Irish scribes came to know it. In this context the Irish litanies enumerating Oriental monks who came to Ireland have been quoted. Amongst them are Egyptians, Armenians, and 'Romani' (which at that time means Byzantines).[2] Other elements of the decoration, and specially the decorated page of Ms. D.23.sup. which has close parallels in Coptic bindings of the sixth century, and in some carved panels from Coptic slabs, seem to indicate that we must look in the direction of Egypt to find the ultimate inspiration of these manuscripts. A quatrain in the poem on the rule of Bangor which was copied towards the middle of the seventh century into the Antiphonary of Bangor, points in the same direction :

'. . . Domus deliciis plena
Super petram constructa
Necnon vinea vera
Ex Aegypto transducta. . . .'[3]

---

[1] Åberg, *Occident-Orient*, I, p. 30; Masai, *Origines*, pp. 85–7, Pl. LVII.
[2] Ch. Plummer, *Irish Litanies* (London, 1925), pp. 57 sqq. and 61 sqq.
[3] '. . . House full of delight
Built on the rock
And indeed true vine
Transplanted from Egypt. . . .' Warren, *Antiphonary of Bangor*, II, p. 28.
This, of course, is a reminiscence of verse 9 of Psalm 79 : 'vineam de Aegypto transtulisti'; still the meaning seems to be taken very literally.

Indeed all the sixth-century monasteries would have been able to claim their origin from the first impulse given by the Thebaid monasteries. Still, here, there may be something more. If Coptic influences certainly play very strongly on Merovingian art, they produce there quite different results and do not introduce this characteristic element, the use of dots.

How these contacts between the very isolated Ireland of the sixth century and the Egyptian monasteries from which she claims to derive a monastic rule came about, we may never know. But it is essential not to lose sight of the intensive trade with Mediterranean lands of which the importation of pottery manifest in Garranes is the result. In the present state of our knowledge it seems that these importations took place directly by way of Gibraltar and that the objects came from the Near East, perhaps from Egypt and Byzantium. They continued until the end of the sixth century and may have declined very quickly at the time of the Arab invasion. Thus the door is open for all sorts of suppositions on the comings and goings which this commercial current may have facilitated, and the possibility for anybody who wanted to go to Egypt and the Near East to find occasionally a boat going there directly, on the possibility also of the arrival in Ireland of Oriental monks fleeing before the Arabs.

It is a profitable approach to deduce from carvings and manuscripts a fairly precise notion of the general appearance of Irish decoration in that period before studying the metalwork, as we will be faced now with the problem of deciding what, amongst a group of metal objects found in England, is of Irish or British origin.

In Ireland itself, in fact, the question of metalwork appears as very complex. Whilst there is no room for doubt where manuscript decoration is concerned, with metalwork it is difficult to decide how far the work was done in the monasteries or for them. Some of the brooches bear crosses and a few categories of objects clearly have a religious purpose, the portable shrines for example, and possibly the hanging-bowls. Some incidents in the *Vita Columbae* allow us to postulate the existence of a forge and probably metal workshops in Iona. But we have

F

seen that such workshops were to be found in Garranes and Bally-catteen, two sites which seem to have a secular character. Altogether it looks as if any settlement at that time had its specialized craftsmen. They enjoyed a position of importance. The smith's work retained something of the mysterious aura which had surrounded the beginnings of the working of iron. In the Irish texts, the smith is a seer, a man endowed with a prophetic gift. He and the goldsmith belonged to that social class intermediary between the warring aristocracy and the common people, which included beside the highest category of crafts-men, the lawyers, the poets, the historians and the clerics.

We have seen that on some objects which can be attributed to the sixth century or the beginning of the seventh, the art of the pagan period was going on without any very serious changes.[1] These are repoussé or bronze objects decorated with curvilinear motifs standing up, in very deliberate relief for the repoussé objects and in thinner and sharper lines for the others. The repoussé work is represented by a few large bronze discs of uncertain purpose, which are about a foot in diameter, some of which were found in County Kildare (Dublin Museum and British Museum) (Pl. 10), and by a brooch found in the Ardakillin crannog (Dublin Museum) (Pl. 10). The high relief curves on these objects have equivalents, as already mentioned, in repoussé silver objects found in the Scottish seventh-century hoard of Norries Law (Edinburgh Museum).

At first glance one might believe that the brooch is cast by the cire perdue process, all in one piece. Only by examining it closely is it possible to detect the joints of the three thin sheets of repoussé bronze, probably filled with mastic, which cover the framework of the object. The curves have the same bold firmness as is found in the initials of the Cathach. Still, the interlacing which covers the bow of the brooch is a new pattern which will have some parallels in enamelled objects and soon also in the decoration of stone and vellum. It may have the same Egyptian origin as the dots in the manuscripts.

Three groups of objects, a disc found in the Bann (Belfast Museum)

---

[1] See pp. 9–10.

(Pl. I, Fig. 30),[1] bronze horns discovered together in the bank of a river in Cork (Cork Museum)[2] and the fragments of unknown origin known as the 'Petrie crown' (Pl. 11), from the archaeologist George Petrie who owned them (Dublin Museum), indubitably have points in common as well as being connected with the repoussé objects. The Cork and Dublin objects may have been parts of horse-trappings, though in the case of the 'crown', there has been a remodelling, made regardless of the original arrangement, which transforms the reorganized fragments into one of those votive crowns so often hung above saints' tombs in the Early Middle Ages.

M. J. O'Kelly has recently studied the technique of these objects and reached the conclusion that they were not cast, as had been hitherto held, but that the reliefs, which are very low, had been obtained by the excision of the surrounding surface of bronze combined in a few places with repoussé work. We would have here, as in the case of the Ardakillin brooch, one of these substitutions of technique, so common in Celtic art, which are often prompted by subtle practical reasons – here most probably by the desire to keep the object very light, and maybe also to give the ornament that crisp and engraved look which contrasts with some mellower reliefs obtained by casting. The tracery of the design is of an extreme elegance and contrasts sharply with the large areas of smooth, slightly curved surface. In several places the spirals end in a few small hooks suggesting the appearance of animal heads. In the Petrie crown, however, some of these heads are given eyes of red enamel. The meeting points of the great scrolls are decorated by a few little leaves in relief, sometimes by leaves on a stem, an arrangement obviously meant to break up the strict geometric appearance of the design. This device had already been used by the bronze-smiths of pagan times and appears also on the bone slips of Lough Crew (Pl. 8), as well as on some of the initials of the Cathach (Pls. 9, 12).

To this can be added a whole series of trinkets and of objects derived

[1] J. Raftery, 'A Decorated Bronze Disc from the River Bann', *U.J.A.*, 1940, pp. 27 sqq.; E. M. Jope and B. C. Wilson, 'The Decorated Cast-Bronze Disc from the River Bann near Coleraine', *U.J.A.*, 1957, pp. 95 sqq.

[2] M. J. O'Kelly, 'The Cork Horns, the Petrie Crown and the Bann Disc', *J.C.H.A.S.*, 1961, pp. 1 sqq.

from Roman prototypes which are usually enlivened with enamel. We have seen that the penannular brooches and hand-pins, whose evolution in Roman times can be followed in England and on the Scottish border, were introduced into Ireland towards the end of the Empire and that they developed there on very original lines (Pl. 13).[1] To these one may add objects ending in a disc which are probably fasteners ('latchets') (Pl. 13, Fig. 5) and a whole lot of buttons, strap-tags, etc. All have a nearly identical decoration which is found also on larger objects such as bowls of beaten bronze whose hanging hooks are decorated, and small shrines meant to be suspended from the two ends of a strap. Nearly all the pins and the brooches have been found in Ireland, some of them in excavations: the unfinished ring of a penannular brooch and the pin of a brooch at Garranes, a hand-pin in Carraig Aille, another at Ballycatteen, a brooch in the crannog No. 2 of Ballinderry (Pl. 24), etc.

The case of the bowls is more complex and has led to violent controversies.[2] A large number of those with an enamelled decoration – at least sixty – have been found, usually partly broken up, in Saxon graves where they probably represent loot. As it is usually accepted that the bowls, which are likely to have been lamps, were used in churches, it is assumed that Saxon raiders found them in churches in England. This hypothesis, though it raises some difficulties, remains the most satisfactory of those which have been suggested. Everybody agrees that the

---

[1] See p. 14; Kilbride-Jones, *Brooches*.

[2] The bibliography of the hanging-bowls is by now very vast. The chief references will be found in: T. D. Kendrick, 'British Hanging-bowls', *Antiquity*, 1932, pp. 161 sqq.; F. Henry, 'Hanging-Bowls', *J.R.S.A.I.*, 1936, pp. 210 sqq.; Id., *Ir. enam.* (1956); G. Haseloff, 'Fragments of a Hanging-Bowl from Bekesbourne, Kent, and some Ornamental Problems', *Med. Arch.*, 1958, pp. 72 sqq. Various explanations of their use have been suggested. A. Leistöl ('The Hanging-Bowl, a Liturgical and Domestic Vessel', *Acta Archaeologica*, 1953, pp. 163 sqq.) proposed to see in them liturgical hand-basins, but, as Haseloff has pointed out (op. cit.), the vase on which he bases his explanation is not a hanging-bowl, and anyway the inscription in runes refers to its use after it was taken to Scandinavia, not necessarily to its use in Ireland. See also a series of interesting texts on decorative hanging vases in C. Peers – C. A. Ralegh Radford, 'The Saxon Monastery of Whitby', *Archaeologia*, 1943, pp. 27 sqq.; this is a tempting explanation, though the lamp remains the most likely one.

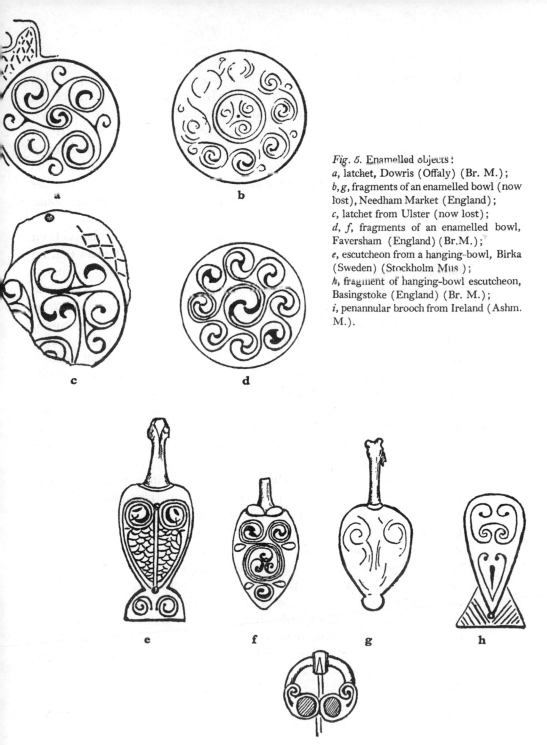

Fig. 5. Enamelled objects:
a, latchet, Dowris (Offaly) (Br. M.);
b, g, fragments of an enamelled bowl (now lost), Needham Market (England);
c, latchet from Ulster (now lost);
d, f, fragments of an enamelled bowl, Faversham (England) (Br.M.);
e, escutcheon from a hanging-bowl, Birka (Sweden) (Stockholm Mus);
h, fragment of hanging-bowl escutcheon, Basingstoke (England) (Br. M.);
i, penannular brooch from Ireland (Ashm. M.).

bowls are not Saxon work but come from 'Celtic' workshops. This means, at that time, Welsh, Scottish or Irish. The near identity of the ornaments with those on the pins, brooches and latchets on the one hand, and on the slabs and pillars on the other hand, seems to point clearly to the centre of production being in Ireland whence the bowls would have been exported to the surviving churches of Britain. It still remains possible that some bowls were made in Scotland or in Wales, given the Irish expansion towards the east. But the impulse came without doubt from Ireland.

For a long time, those archaeologists who held that the bowls had been made somewhere in Britain saw their best argument in the fact that no bowls had been found in Ireland. The argument had already lost most of its force when one remembered that in a Christian country, where the dead were not buried in the pagan fashion with all their most precious goods, the chances of finding an object of such large size as these bowls, which often reach a foot in diameter, were small: what usually turns up in excavations of Early Christian sites in Ireland is small enough to be easily lost in the earthen floor of a hut. In fact, in spite of this initial handicap, a certain number of bowls and of enamelled escutcheons or hooks have been found in Ireland in the course of the last twenty years, so that the objection has ceased to have any weight. We shall in consequence consider the hanging-bowls as one of the characteristic products of the Irish workshops.

The categories of objects which we have listed may in fact appear as rather odd. One may wonder, if churches were plundered, why the Saxon graves did not contain chalices, patens or crosses, but always these hanging-lamps. In actual fact, the sacred vessels were probably immediately carried to safety in case of attack, the chalices being anyway quite possibly made of glass. The lamps on the contrary, would have been abandoned, and the first thing to have met the eyes of the Saxon, lover of shiny things, on entering a church may well have been this glowing half-sphere, gilt, tinned and enamelled. The Vikings, centuries later, will show themselves quite as eager to grasp the large lamps with panels of millefiori which they will find in similar circumstances in Irish churches.

70

The decorative repertoire of all these objects is rather limited. Spirals are the staple motif. In the earlier examples, those which are nearer to Roman prototypes, the pelta often supplies the framework of the composition. This is so in the case of the Carraig Aille pin, the vessels from Baginton and Lackford and the escutcheon found in the River Bann. At this stage enamelling is generally reduced to thin lines of red. But the enamellers soon became bolder and after a while it is the pattern which is made of thin reserved lines of bronze standing out on a wider field of enamel. The ornament is now of a more assured design and on a smaller scale recalls the spirals of the Petrie crown or the disc in Belfast Museum. As in these last objects, there are often animal heads in the centre of the scrolls. Sometimes a marigold similar to those on some of the latchets covers the disc, or a Greek cross (Kingston, Faversham, Camerton). The same motifs are treated in various ways, a fact which seems to point to small local workshops each having its own methods, and not to large factories, as the centres of production of the bowls.

On a certain number of objects, little square or round sections of millefiori glass are combined with the enamelled decoration. This seems to occur from the beginning. Fragments of sticks of coloured glass and of rods of millefiori glass partly cut have been found in Garranes and in

Fig. 6. a, enamelled disc found at Garranes
(Cork) (Cork Mus.);
b, gold bird with filigree found at Garryduff (Cork) (Cork Mus.);
c, openwork bronze disc with lump of enamel found at Somerset (Galway) (N.M.D.).

a   b   c

Lagore. So there can be no doubt that this type of ornament was made in Ireland. How it was introduced remains so far an unanswered problem. The combination of champlevé enamel and panels of mille-fiori glass is in Roman times the near monopoly of a well-defined centre of manufacture, the workshops of the Roman villa excavated at Anthée, near Namur.[1] The villa was destroyed in a raid by the Franks in the middle of the third century A.D. Are we to accept that this technique was introduced into Ireland in the second century or the beginning of the third? Or were there other workshops in Gaul which survived until the end of the Empire, and did some craftsmen come from there to Ireland?

The little glass segments are in fact treated at first as intrusions: they are fitted here and there in between the champlevé patterns (Fig. 7), and this is not always a happy combination. It may be the reason why they were gradually confined to unpatterned panels where they were usually floating in a field of red enamel. This is for example what happens in the case of the terminals of the large penannular brooch found in the crannog No. 2 of Ballinderry (Pl. 24) and of several other brooches. This is also what the enameller who decorated the strap-mounts of a little shrine found in a Viking tomb at Melhus, in Norway (Trondheim Museum),[2] chose to do.

[1] Henry, *Em. Occ.*, pp. 123 sqq.   [2] *V. Ant.*, V, pp. 73–4.

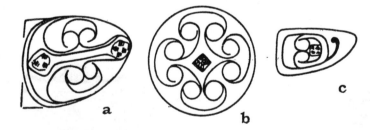

Fig. 7. Red enamel with millefiori:
a, terminal of penannular brooch from Antrim (Br. M.);
b, disc on the smaller bowl from the Sutton Hoo grave (Br. M.);
c, terminal of penannular brooch found in Ireland (Br. M.).

Beside these traditional ornaments, a few elements of zoomorphic decoration appear here and there. The Roman prototype of the hanging-bowl had suspension hooks in the shape of heads of birds or lions, or sometimes a bird with folded wings. This idea never disappeared completely and most of the suspension hooks end by a little bird head, often of fine modelling. Sometimes the general shape of the bird is only indicated on a flat sheet of metal (Fig. 5) or, as on a bowl found in York, the bird is modelled in relief, its wings tinned and the rest of the body gilt. An enamelled button found in Ballycatteen has two animal heads in relief of the same type as those used on the bowls.

In a few cases, other animal motifs appear: a vase from Faversham (British Museum) has escutcheons made of three dolphins (Fig. 20, c) — two on each side of a cross, drawn by thin lines of enamel, and the third in relief, forming the hook; these dolphins have exact parallels on a small ring-pin found in the North of Ireland (British Museum) (Fig. 20, b)[1]; a vase found at Benty Grange (Derbyshire) of which only fragments remain, had escutcheons enamelled in red and yellow whose design was made of three fish-like monsters (Sheffield Museum and Ashmolean Museum, Oxford) (Fig. 20, a). A bowl found near Cambridge has the double monster-head pattern which is so frequent in Saxon art. We shall meet other similar borrowings.

A quite exceptional bowl, that found at Lullingstone (British Museum) (Pls. 26, 29), has a series of zoomorphic applied plaques soldered on the surface of the bronze: affronted birds, birds holding a fish in their claws, all of very simplified design, accompanied by a procession of beautifully drawn deers.

Interlacing is not very common on the enamelled objects but a few examples can be found. A little tag enamelled in red and yellow which was found in Lagore previous to the 1934–6 excavations, has two knots of wide ribbon.[2] A similar knot, also enamelled in red and yellow, was found near Oxford.[3] A plaque discovered in the excavations of the monastery of Whitby has a Latin cross surrounded by three-lobed

---

[1] They may well be derived from Continental or English belt-buckles. See: S. Chadwick-Hawkes, 'Soldiers and Settlers in Britain', *Med. Arch.*, 1961, pp. 1 sqq.

[2] Wood-Martin, *Lake-Dwellings*, p. 138. [3] Henry, 'Hanging-Bowls', loc. cit., p. 232.

knots.[1] All these interlacings are made of large ribbons, like those on the Ardakillin brooch. Another small enamel from Whitby and the large openwork plaque of the Bekesbourne bowl have, however, interlacings made of fine threads. To this one may add the two repoussé discs of the York vase, where a ring is formed by the meanders of a fine thread (York Museum).[2]

Some of the techniques of gold filigree work current in the Roman world were known in Ireland from the end of the Empire, as witness the tiny gold bird (Fig. 6, b) decorated with fine spirals from the oldest level of Garryduff and a gold plaque with interlacings from the foundations of the crannog of Lagore.[3]

Of these objects some, for example those from Whitby, were in England as a consequence of the work of the Irish missionaries and may well have been made in England by Irish craftsmen or their English pupils. The problem of these mixed workshops and of their influence has not been studied very much as far as metalwork is concerned. It is quite possible that some objects found in tumuli of the north of England which bear interlacings may be imitations of Irish models, as the patterns of animal-interlacings which occur sometimes in the same tombs were imitated by Irish artists.[4]

This question becomes acute where the finds from Sutton Hoo are concerned.[5] The mound was the cenotaph of a king of East Anglia, and we have seen that these kings protected the monastery of Saint Fursa which had been founded by one of them around 630–35. The importance of this monastery and the strength of its links with Ireland are clearly shown by the fact that the monastery of Péronne, which was its continuation, remained completely Irish for at least a century and a half.

[1] Peers–Radford, 'The Saxon Monastery of Whitby', loc. cit.; the crescent-shaped terminals on this object have exact parallels on the Moylough belt (Pl. XX) and on a bronze plaque with animal decoration from Lagore (Hencken, *Lagore*, Fig. 11, No. 201, p. 65).

[2] The Lullingstone bowl has interlacings of two-strand ribbon.

[3] Hencken, *Lagore*, Fig. 23, p. 87.   [4] Åberg saw this problem, though he did not attempt to deal with it. (N. Åberg, *The Anglo-Saxons in England during the Early Centuries after the Invasion*, Cambridge–Uppsala, etc., 1926, p. 176.)

[5] R. L. S. Bruce-Mitford, *The Sutton Hoo Ship-Burial, A Provisional Guide* (London, 1947).

Opposite: Pl.A. Detail of large hanging-bowl found in Sutton Hoo

The three enamelled hanging-bowls found at Sutton Hoo are obviously of Irish workmanship. One of them has escutcheons with a pattern of very thin spirals in which some squares of millefiori glass are inserted. Pattern and insertions are found nearly identical on two Irish penannular brooches (Fig. 7). The large bowl is one of the most imposing of the whole series. Its escutcheons and discs have delightful garlands of spirals and panels of millefiori of a magnificent colour (Col. pl. A and Pl. 25). The spirals are nearly identical in their tracery to those on the latchet in Dublin Museum (Pl. 13) and the relief frame of the escutcheons is decorated with a guilloche identical to that on the ring of the Ballinderry brooch (Pls. 24–5). It seems likely in consequence that the lamps were either made in the monastery of Fursa or brought from Ireland. The first hypothesis may be the most likely given the obvious influence which Irish work has had on the workshop where the Saxon objects of Sutton Hoo were manufactured: these objects have pieces of millefiori glass which have not been fused as in the Irish enamels, but set as in Germanic jewellery.[1] The third bowl shows the same contamination with Saxon patterns as the bowl found not so very far away, near Cambridge. This is a phenomenon which could easily take place in these workshops where Irishmen worked on English soil.

The unity of ornamentation between the different techniques at the end of this formative period gives the impression of an art which is beginning to feel conscious of its methods and style and which will be capable of enlarging its repertoire without deeply upsetting its inner structure.

[1] Henry, *Ir. enam.*, pp. 82–3.

Opposite: Pl.B. Applied enamel plaque in the form of a human being from the Irish bowl found in a Viking tomb in Miklebostad, Norway

4. Sites and Architecture

I F W E now turn to the later period, from about 650 to the first Viking raids, we will find that a few sites which have been excavated since 1920 and some ruins give an idea of the appearance of the secular and religious establishments of that time. For the secular habitations,[1] the documentation comes chiefly from the excavations made in 1934–6 at Lagore (Meath) and at Cahercommaun (Clare) by the Harvard Archaeological Expedition to Ireland. For the monasteries, the data which can be gathered from the excavations made in 1921–4 at Nendrum (Down) by the Natural History and Philosophical Society of Belfast, may be complemented by the examination of several groups of monastic ruins.

The crannog of Lagore (Loch Gabair)[2] was an artificial island built near the shore of a lake now dried up. There was, a short distance away, at Dunshaughlin, on the shore of the lake, a monastery founded by Secundinus (Sechnall), one of Saint Patrick's companions. The crannog is only 6 miles from Tara and seems to have become a royal residence after Tara was abandoned. There are mentions of it from the middle of the seventh century on. The artificial island was probably built about that time, during a summer when the water level was low, by piling up successive layers of beams and earth mixed with rubbish of all kinds coming probably from older settlements: animal bones, broken objects, an old boat, demolition beams, etc. A post palisade of about 120 to 135 feet in diameter, deeply embedded in that substratum, obviously surrounded wooden buildings. But the centre of the crannog having been destroyed long before the excavations by the cutting of a drain, it is now quite impossible to know what they were like. In spite of this interference it was possible to distinguish three levels of occupation each

---

[1] For the raths, see Proudfoot, op. cit. p. 46.   [2] Hencken, *Lagore*.

corresponding to a rebuilding of the palisade on a slightly different plan.

The lower level yielded pottery of seventh-century type, probably imported from the Rhine valley, whilst a fragment of Gallo-Roman 'terra sigillata' was found embedded in the foundations. The lower level contained obvious traces of the working of metal and glass. There were crucibles and moulds for glass studs, one of which still contained a glass disc, as well as a plaque of slate covered with engraved sketches. Unstratified rods of coloured glass and fragments of millefiori help to complete the picture. A fragment of a bronze object decorated with an animal similar to the Benty Grange beasts also comes from that level and is a confirmation of its seventh-century date. We shall have to examine in more detail later some of the objects found in the crannog. It seems to have been occupied until the tenth century. But it was destroyed a first time 'so that it was level with the ground' in 848 or 849.[1] In the second half of the eighth century its kings are mentioned several times in the Annals. So that the two outstanding periods of occupation seem to be the middle of the seventh century to which the lower level corresponds, and the second half of the eighth century to which can be attributed a whole series of objects approximately dated by comparisons with the finds in the Viking graves.[2]

The fort of Cahercommaun[3] takes us to the other end of Ireland, to the limestone crags of County Clare (Fig. 8). It is built at the top of a cliff overlooking a narrow valley. The fort itself consists of an enormous circular dry-stone wall about 30 feet wide, still standing 12 to 15 feet high and enclosing a space about 100 feet wide. Two other concentric ramparts, much more lightly built, supply additional defences on all sides where the wall is not protected by the cliff. Inside the inner enclosure a layer of debris covered the inextricably confused ruins of several houses and their hearths, under which there were two souterrains. This was probably the dwelling of a local chieftain, built towards the

[1] *A.F.M.*, 848.
[2] A crannog about 3 miles S-W of Downpatrick has yielded some objects similar to those found at Lagore; A. E. Collins, 'Excavations in Lough Faughan Crannog, Co. Down, 1951–52', *U.J.A.*, 1955, pp. 45 sqq.
[3] Hencken, *Cahercommaun*; for the correct dating, see: *Lagore*, pp. 17–18.

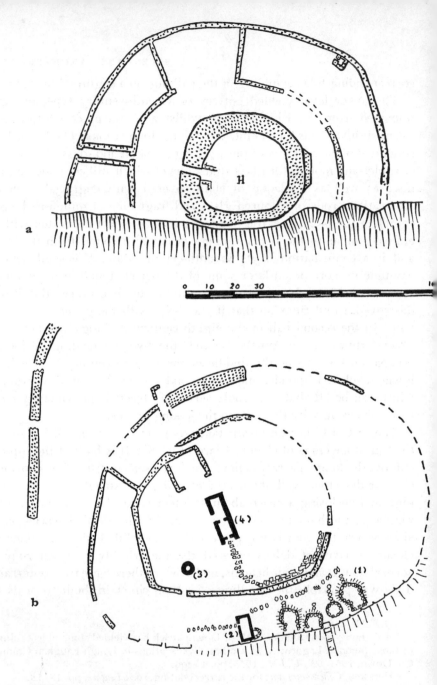

0   10   20   30

b

Fig. 8. *a*, plan of Cahercommaun (Clare):
    H, complex of ruined huts;
    b, plan of the Monastery of Nendrum
    (Down): (1) ruins of craftsmen's huts,
    (2) 'School', (3) round tower, (4) church.

middle of the seventh century and occupied over a fairly long period. A beautiful silver brooch found in one of the souterrains belongs most probably to the eighth century.[1]

Though the excavations of Nendrum (Fig. 8) did not solve all the problems connected with that complex entanglement of buildings,[2] it still remains possible to learn from them many things about the appearance of a monastery, its transformations and the various activities which took place there. It was built on one of the islands near the western shore of Strangford Lough, to the north of Downpatrick. Its origin goes back to Mochaoi, a fifth-century saint, but there are no mentions of the monastery in the Annals during the sixth century and it seems likely that it was permanently established only towards the middle of the seventh century, having been abandoned for a while. It was plundered by the Vikings in the early ninth century. However, names of abbots occur again in the Annals towards the end of the ninth century and in the beginning of the tenth, the last mention being in 974 that of 'Sedna O'Deman, abbot of Nendrum, burnt in his own house'.[3]

It appears obvious, both from archaeological data and the inferences deduced from some legends, that the monastery had been originally built inside a fort very similar to Cahercommaun. There is the same series of concentric enclosures, but at first sight they seem very much wider. The proportions are only seen to be similar when one realizes that the inner wall, which in Cahercommaun is the stoutest and surrounds the houses, has disappeared at Nendrum. It may have been destroyed to give more space to the monastic buildings. The various phases of occupation can probably be summed up thus : first, there was a fort with a thick inner wall and two flimsier outer ramparts; whatever of Mochaoi, who may simply have lived as a hermit somewhere on the island, the fort was inhabited until the seventh century. Then it was turned into a monastery. After a while, probably in the early eighth

---

[1] See p. 112.

[2] H. C. Lawlor, *The Monastery of Saint Mochaoi of Nendrum* (Belfast, 1925).

[3] *A.F.M., A.U.*; the hypothesis that in the later period of occupation converted Scandinavians had much to do with the monastery, which is based chiefly on the presence of an inscription in runes, would need re-examining.

century, the times being then peaceful and the monastery needing space to expand, the second enclosure, which is about 180 to 200 feet in diameter, became the limit of the monastery and the fort itself was razed, its stones and the accumulated rubbish of centuries being used to turn part of the third enclosure into a terrace on which several huts were built for the craftsmen employed by the monks. It seems rather difficult, in their present state, to take into consideration other fragments of walls which the excavators described as an outer rampart. Later, after the first Viking attacks, the round tower was built, and the church was modified.

The stonework of the terrace was interspersed with sherds, some from imported vases, others of a local pottery of which examples are often found in souterrains of the North of Ireland. Fragments of funerary slabs were found in the church. They bear Latin crosses with hollowed angles of a type frequent in the eighth century. A stone decorated with a complicated marigold pattern has equivalents in Clonmacnois and in Gallen. Of the monastery itself, little can be known, as its buildings were deliberately destroyed, probably in the last Viking attack.

The remains of the huts on the terrace constitute the most interesting part of the ruins. Only foundations and the base of the walls were left; the rest had probably been made of wood or wattle and daub. One of these huts was obviously the bronze-smith's workshop. It yielded a great number of crucibles, some with traces of bronze, and a stone mould for casting pins.

A rectangular structure built of stone and clay mortar which was near these huts may have dated only from the time when the monastery was rebuilt in the ninth century. The fragments of charred beams which it contained show that it was destroyed by a violent fire, perhaps that of 974. The excavators called it 'the school', because it produced many sketches of patterns, and studies of letter-shapes, inscribed on about thirty slate tablets; there was also a compass arm and several iron styli, one of them of the type used to write on wax tablets, so that the fire has no doubt deprived us of other interesting documents, melted in its heat.

This was not a very large monastery, though the mentions of its abbots in the Annals show it to have been comparatively important. Other islands had similar establishments. Some are in lakes, such as Inish Cleraun ('Quaker Island'), an island in Lough Ree, to the north of Clonmacnois, where the monastery was surrounded by an enormous circular rampart. Others are off the coasts. The most outstanding is Inismurray (Sligo).[1] There also the monastery was enclosed by a dry stone wall about 14 feet thick, surrounding a space about 130 to 170 feet wide where stone huts and churches conglomerated. On various parts of the island were found engraved slabs of a great variety of design, some of them with exuberant spiral patterns (Fig. 13). Caher Island, off the coast of Mayo,[2] had probably a similar wall, now nearly completely disappeared. Amongst rather shapeless ruins, there are still a number of stone slabs and a cross cut in a large slab and carved on both sides (Pl. IV).

A schematic plan of a monastery drawn on one of the pages of the book of Mulling[3] can be compared with these monasteries surrounded by a more or less circular rampart (Fig. 17): two compass-drawn circles indicate the enclosure whilst inside and outside are scattered a number of crosses whose names are indicated.

Much more important monasteries were also established in pre-existing fortifications, which often turned out, after a short time, to be too small for the needs of the community. This was probably the case at Armagh and Kells. The outline of the walls of Armagh can still be traced in seventeenth- and eighteenth-century maps[4] and indeed the present network of streets partly follows their general lay-out. On the top of a steep hill, the cathedral and a few other religious buildings, as well as the library, were enclosed by a wall; below, on the slope of the hill grew slowly a town where lived the students and possibly, as in Nendrum, the craftsmen attached to the monastery. Recent excavations

---

[1] Wakeman, *Inismurray*.

[2] F. Henry, 'The Antiquities of Caher Island, Co. Mayo', *J.R.S.A.I.*, 1947, pp. 23 sqq.

[3] Lawlor, *Mulling*, pp. 167 sqq.

[4] W. Reeves, *The Ancient Churches of Armagh* (Lusk, 1860).

made in Downpatrick[1] have abundantly demonstrated the pre-Christian character of the fortifications surrounding the monastery.

Glendalough,[2] established in a narrow valley of the Wicklow mountains which encloses two lakes, owed its origin to Saint Kevin who retired there at the end of the sixth century. The first establishment consisted of hermit huts of which some traces still remain near the upper lake. Later, towards the end of the seventh or in the eighth century, a monastery was established on an expanse of flat land farther down the valley. The Latin *Life of Saint Kevin*, written at Glendalough in the eleventh or twelfth century,[3] speaks of this new foundation, which it attributes symbolically to the time of the saint, in a way that suggests that here again, a 'fort' belonging to a local chieftain was the original setting of the new constructions. But this first enclosure soon became too small and the 'monastic city' extended obviously over all the plateau, from the cathedral to Saint Mary's church, as far as the lower lake. The outline of the enclosure can be traced to the east of the present graveyard wall; to the south, part of it is still standing in the graveyard itself and is continued farther by one of the walls surrounding Saint Mary's. There were, in fact, natural defences as the city stood at the meeting of two lively mountain streams and above the lower lake. Later, other churches were built elsewhere in the valley and even now ruins are scattered over a length of nearly two miles.

Of many other monasteries, Kildare, Durrow, Lismore, for example, the plan has been obliterated in the course of time. The appearance of Clonmacnois[4] in the eighth century is difficult to conjure up. The monastery had been founded in the sixth century on the side of an esker

[1] V. B. Proudfoot, 'Excavations at the Cathedral Hill, Downpatrick, Co. Down, 1953', *U.J.A.*, 1954, pp. 97 sqq.; B. Proudfoot, 'Excavations at the Cathedral Hill, Downpatrick, Co. Down', *U.J.A.*, 1956, pp. 57 sqq. An enormous rampart surrounds the remains of the monastery of Seir Kieran (Offaly), but so far it is impossible to date it.

[2] H. G. Leask, *Glendalough, Co. Wicklow* (Dublin, 1951).

[3] Plummer, *VV. SS. Hib.*, I, pp. 234 sqq.

[4] T. J. Westropp, 'A description of the Ancient Buildings and Crosses at Clonmacnois, King's County', *J.R.S.A.I.*, 1907, pp. 277 sqq.; R. A. S. Macalister, *The Memorial Slabs at Clonmacnois, King's County* (Dublin, 1909).

overlooking an immense stretch of marshland through which the Shannon wends its way. All that remains now is a group of late churches near a round tower. An overcrowded churchyard has invaded the space where stood part of the wooden constructions of the monastery. There is no satisfactory trace of a rampart and it is difficult to estimate the amount of ground originally built up.

Little remains of the monastery where Adamnan lived on Iona at the end of the seventh century and where he wrote the *Vita Columbae*.[1] In Lindisfrane, a priory dependent on Durham, built in the twelfth century, practically obliterated the old foundation. The site was a slight depression on the west coast of the island, opposite the mainland to which the island is connected by sandbanks at low tide. A few bases of crosses still standing here and there, and some funerary slabs found in the course of repairs, are all that remains of the pre-Romanesque monastery.[2] Vanished also is the monastery of Melrose (Old Melrose), which was established on a promontory surrounded on three sides by the Tweed, not very far from the site of the Celtic and Roman city of Newstead. A rampart can still be traced across the neck of the promontory, but there is nothing left of the buildings themselves, except a shapeless ruin beside a modern house. The very appearance of the place is changed, as the magnificent trees which now cover the hill hardly fit in with the 'bare headland' (Máel ross) described by the Celtic name.

Excavations carried out at Whitby some time before the last war[3] have brought to light part of the foundations of the monastery which owes its origin to Hartlepool, itself founded by Lindisfarne. It was occupied from 657 until its destruction by the Vikings in 867. There was a certain number of rectangular constructions separated by flagged areas; the bases of two crosses were found in situ, as well as many

[1] What remains has been excavated recently by Charles Thomas; the results of the excavation are not yet fully published. But see: S. Cruden, 'Excavations at Whithorn and Iona', *The Scotsman*, 4 – 5 – 1963.

[2] C. R. Peers, 'The inscribed and sculptured stones of Lindisfarne', *Archaeologia*, 1923–4, pp. 255 sqq.

[3] C. Peers–C. A. Ralegh Radford, 'The Saxon Monastery of Whitby', *Archaeologia*, 1943, pp. 27 sqq.

fragments belonging to stone crosses whose arms were not connected by a circle; there were inscriptions, partly written in Irish majuscules, and amongst the finds were several fragments of enamelled hanging-bowls. So that there were witnesses to both the Saxon and the Irish elements which formed the background of the monastery at the time of its foundation.

What can we know of the buildings inside these enclosures? A good number of them were made of wood. This was obviously the case for the craftsmen's huts in Nendrum, of which only the foundations were of stone. It was also the case for the church erected by Finan around 650 at Lindisfarne.[1] Still, there is no doubt that there existed at that time churches built of stone and mortar. The texts have two words for a church: daimliag, 'stone church', and durthech or dairthech, 'wooden church' (lit.: oak church). In 789 there is mention of a daimliag in Armagh,[2] and when the Vikings stormed the town in 839, it is stated that they destroyed there not only wooden oratories, but also a stone church.[3]

A few ruins may give some idea of the general appearance of these churches.[4] Their plan seems to have always remained very simple. There were no columns, no pillars, no arches. Most of them consisted of a rectangle of fairly small size (18, 30, 35 feet long), with no separate choir. The walls are usually about 3 feet thick and are often lined with large, comparatively thin slabs set on edge, Roman fashion, on a core of rubble. The side walls often protrude at each end, forming 'antae' which look like buttresses but whose structural function was really to support the overhanging roof. This feature is not absolutely constant and as it survived until the twelfth century when it is found for example at the west end of the church of Roscrea, it can not be used as an indication of date. The windows seem to have been narrow slits widening

[1] Bede, H.E., III, 25.   [2] A.F.M., A.U.   [3] A.F.M.
[4] On these churches, see: Petrie, Round Towers (1845); R. R. Brash, The Ecclesiastical Architecture of Ireland to the close of the Twelfth Century (Dublin, 1875); Dunraven, Notes; Stokes, Early Christian Arch.; A. Champneys, Irish Ecclesiastical Architecture (London, 1910); Leask, Irish Churches, I (1955).

towards the inside, their small size coming perhaps from the inability to glaze them. The door is always in the middle of the west wall, a mere rectangular opening, sometimes framed by a slightly raised band and surmounted by a cross on the lintel; occasionally it has also a cross or some other symbol engraved under the lintel or on one of the jambs.

There are substantial remains of churches of this type in all parts of Ireland. One of them is at Fore (Westmeath), on the side of a steep hill. It was originally 27½ by 37 feet inside. A choir of later date has altered its appearance to the east, but otherwise its walls are in their original state. They are built of large blocks of stone, only roughly dressed. Massive antae frame the west front; the door, which has slightly inclined jambs, is covered by a huge monolithic lintel bearing a cross in a circle, and is surrounded by a frame in very light relief (Pl. 23).

At Clonamery (Kilkenny), all that remains of the original building is the lower part of the west gable and some of the foundations of the other walls. The church seems to have been about 30 by 19 feet. It also has antae, a door with sloping jambs and a slightly raised frame. The cross, this time, is a Maltese cross whose stem comes down to join the frame (Pl. 22).

The church at Ratass, in Kerry, has the same arrangement of the west front, with antae and framed door, but no cross. Some of the Aran churches (Galway), may belong to the same type, but they are so featureless that their dating is difficult.[1]

Nothing is known of the early history of Ratass or of Clonamery, but the monastery of Fore was founded by Saint Fechin who died in 664. The similarity of the cross on the lintel with those engraved on pillars and slabs makes it likely that this may be the remains of a church built fairly soon after his death. This type of lintel bearing a cross is common in pre-Romanesque churches. It is found at the oratory of Mellebaude in Poitiers, usually dated seventh century,[2] and on doors of churches of

---

[1] The lintel found in the excavations at Gallen Priory (Offaly), which was originally decorated with three crosses of arcs, may have belonged to a small building of that period. But it is a very flimsy piece of stone. T. D. Kendrick, 'Gallen Priory Excavations', *J.R.S.A.I.*, 1939, pp. 1 sqq.

[2] C. de la Croix, *Hypogée-Martyrium*, Pl. VI.

North Africa and the Near East prior to the Arab invasion.[1] Champneys quite rightly remarked that the sloping jambs of the Irish churches which have sometimes been looked upon as an archaic feature inspired by local dry-stone constructions, are in fact typical of Roman architecture.[2] The facings of slabs on the walls may have the same origin. It would be dangerous to insist too much when dealing with such elementary methods of building, but it is possible all the same that these churches may retain something of a belated Roman tradition such as survived in some parts of the Empire up to two or three centuries after the invasions. How and when it was introduced into Ireland, whether about the time of Saint Patrick or much later, could hardly be decided.

The cathedral of Glendalough has been remodelled a great number of times: the addition of a large Romanesque choir, the re-building of the upper part of the walls, everything has contributed to alter its appearance. It is one of the larger churches of the type which have come down to us, being about 30 by 48 feet inside. The lower part of the north wall and the west front obviously belong to the original construction. This part of the wall is built of large slabs of micaschist put on edge on both faces of a rubble core. The cutting of the edges is very beautiful; they vary in size but are dressed so as to fit perfectly. Inside and outside, the door was surrounded by a raised frame in strong relief whose upper part has unfortunately been marred by an awkward repair. The arch above certainly does not belong to the original scheme and is also due to a reconstruction. The antae are very massive and widen about 8 yards or so above ground level no doubt in order to support a strong structure of beams on which rested the end of the roof (Pl. 32). This building, much larger than any we have seen so far,[3] is likely to go back to the time when the monastery was first established in this part of the valley. From the middle of the eighth century Glendalough figures prominently in the Annals, so that there does not seem to be much reason to hesitate

---

[1] See for example in North Africa: J. B. Ward-Perkins–R. Goodchild, 'The Christian Antiquities of Tripolitania', *Archaeologia*, 1953, pp. 1 sqq., Pls. Xc, XIVa, Fig. 20, and for the Near East, M. de Vogüé, *Syrie centrale* (Paris, 1865–76), *passim*; M. Gough, *The Early Christians* (London, 1961), Fig. 26.

[2] Champneys, op. cit., p. 36; Vitruvius, IV, 6.

[3] See plan in Leask, *Ir. Churches*, I, p. 64.

in dating it to that time. The numerous fires and Viking raids mentioned in the Annals during the following centuries account for the reconstructions to which the higher parts of the north and west walls and all the south wall bear witness. In the course of one of these restorations, fragments which had had a structural or ornamental role were used as building material: the top of a window and several drums of enormous half-columns. These have no equivalents in other pre-Romanesque Irish churches. The other churches of Glendalough may all be of later date than the cathedral. It is possible, however, that the lower part of the west front of Saint Mary's, with its framed door, may belong to the eighth century.

It is essential to remember that this is only one aspect of seventh-, eighth- and ninth-century architecture. All the wooden structures escape us, and some of them may have been very elaborate. Of the stone churches themselves, we have only bare shells. We know nothing of their roof which may have had carved beams and ornamented tiles. The illumination in the Book of Kells which shows Christ on the roof of the Temple can only be used with caution, but may, all the same, start us speculating (Fig. 9). As is the case for most representations of buildings up to the thirteenth century, the structure is described neither full face nor in profile: it is a sort of sum total of characteristic features. There is a rectangular door with a frame around it and there seem to be antae at both ends of the wall. The roof has a strange perspective, but the ornament formed at the top by the crossed ends of the beams terminating in animal heads provides an interesting clue, especially as several stone finials of similar shapes have been found in various parts of Ireland.[1] The regular ornament on the walls and roof of the Temple may be only a decorative conceit, but as it has no parallels in the usual patterns of the Book, we may be justified in considering it as a rendering of a mode of covering which the painter was used to seeing on the walls and roofs of churches – shingles or sheets of lead (there are mentions of both in texts). Up to a point, this representation of the Temple can help us to imagine the appearance of these primitive churches, with their wide overhanging roofs, their carved beams, and possibly brilliantly coloured

[1] Ibid., p. 46.

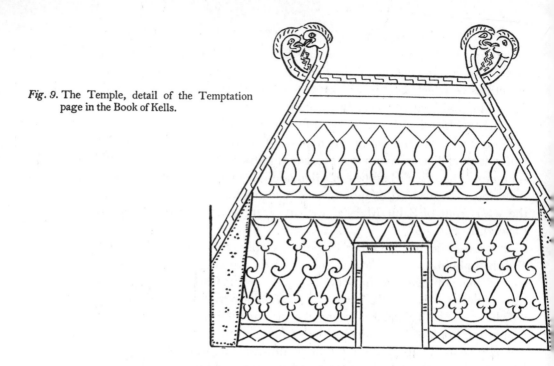

Fig. 9. The Temple, detail of the Temptation
page in the Book of Kells.

imbrications clothing all the surface. However in some cases, even for
important churches, the roof seems to have been made simply of thatch.

It sometimes also happened that the roof was made of stone. The
larger of the boat-shaped oratories date most probably from the seventh
or eighth centuries. But the use of mortar enabled builders to erect lighter
stone coverings over uncorbelled walls. The oratory on Friar's Island
(now moved to Killaloe), and the small church of Illaun-mac-Dara, a
tiny island off the Connacht coast, in the absence of larger buildings
which may have existed, give an indication of the method used (Fig. 10).
The Illaun-mac-Dara church is only 15 feet long inside. Its straight walls
are thinner than those of corbelled oratories (less than 3 feet instead of
5 feet) and its roof is triangular in section. It may have been held up by
wooden cross-beams. This miniature church has antae which have no
structural function and simply frame the whole gable.

Only at a later date will we find a more complex assortment of stone
coverings of various types. As for the round towers which are such a

Fig. 10. Oratory on Illaun
Mac Dara (Galway).

H. G. Leask, del.

characteristic feature of Irish monastic sites, they probably did not
appear until the ninth or even the tenth century and in consequence are
outside the scope of this study.

We may gain some idea of the inside appearance of the churches of
wood or stone from the description Cogitosus[1] gives of the church of
Kildare as he knew it in the seventh century. We have seen that he
wrote his *Life of Saint Brigid* towards the middle of the century. He
speaks of the church where 'the glorious relics of Bishop Conlaeth and
the Virgin Saint Brigid rest on both sides of the decorated altar in
monuments adorned with various embellishments of gold and silver
and gems and precious stones, with crowns of gold hanging from above'.
The church was enlarged because the number of the faithful had
increased. Cogitosus tells us that it was decorated with pictures
('decorata pictis tabulis'), had ornamented windows, and that one of its

---

[1] Mario Esposito, 'On the Earliest Latin Life of Saint Brigid of Kildare', *P.R.I.A.*,
1912 (C), pp. 307 sqq.; Kenney, *Sources*, pp. 359–60; the relevant passage is
quoted in Petrie, *Round Towers*, pp. 197–8, Henry, *Sc. irl.*, p. 174 and Bieler,
Ireland, p. 28.

doors was carved. Its internal layout was conditioned by the fact that Kildare, as happened frequently at the time, was a double monastery.[1] So there was a plank partition dividing the space allotted to the nuns from that given to the monks. Cogitosus speaks of another wooden partition extending from one to the other of the church walls and pierced by two doors, one providing access into the sanctuary for the 'summus pontifex' and the priests who accompanied him, the other allowing the nuns to enter the sanctuary for communion. This partition was 'decorated and painted with pictures and covered with linen hangings' (paries decoratus et imaginibus depictus, ac linteaminibus tectus). This description is remarkable from more than one point of view. The crowns hanging above the tombs recall those which accompanied the tomb of Saint Martin at Tours, as well as the hanging crowns in the Spanish 'treasury of Receswinth'; the iconostasis decorated with paintings has an exact parallel in the churches erected by Benedict Biscop only a few years later: in 680, he brought back pictures from Rome ('picturae imaginum sanctarum'), which he used for the decoration of Saint Peter's church in the newly founded monastery of Wearmouth; whilst some of these 'images' were hung on the north and south walls of the church,[2] others, representing the Virgin and the twelve apostles were on a transverse wall which seems the exact equivalent of that at Kildare. These pictures on wood were in fact no complete novelty in England, as it is likely that a church at Canterbury had kept the 'picture of the Saviour painted on a plank' which Saint Augustine carried with him when he went to meet the King of Kent for the first time in 597.[3]

We can more or less have an idea of the appearance of these icons, either definitely brought from Rome, or in some cases from the East, from paintings on wood which belong – whatever their exact date – to a period very close to that with which we are dealing at present, the Madonnas of Santa Maria nuova and Santa Maria in Trastevere in

[1] Mary Bateson, 'The origin and Early History of Double Monasteries', *Trans. Roy. Hist. Soc.*, 1899, pp. 137 sqq.; S. Helpisch, *Die Doppel-Klöster, Entstehung und Organisation* (Münster, 1928).

[2] Bede, *H. abb.*, 6.   [3] Bede, *H.E.*, I, 25.

Rome and some of the paintings from the monastery of Saint Catherine of Mount Sinai.[1]

So the grey walls which are all that remain now of these churches were really almost completely covered by various coloured revetments, and their effect rested chiefly on the glitter of paintings, embroidery and metalwork.

Within the enclosure of the monastery, all sorts of buildings were scattered, probably without much order, one or two stone churches being surrounded by wooden buildings of various shapes. Nothing allows us to assume the existence of cloisters, but paved pathways certainly connected the chief buildings and formed streets possibly of very irregular course some of which, those following the enclosing wall, for example, may have been sheltered by a lean-to roof (Fig. 8: Nendrum). Here and there stood carved crosses which may well have been painted and were one of the most original features of these monasteries. The plan in the Book of Mulling shows them standing outside as well as inside the circular enclosure (Fig. 17). It might seem a logical course to study them now, but so many things in their structure and their decoration proceed from the imitation of jewellery that it is better to examine the work done in metal before coming to the carvings.

[1] Kitzinger, *Icons of the Seventh Century*; P. Cellini, 'Una Madonna molto antiqua', *Proporzioni*, 1950; C. R. Morey, 'The Madonna of Santa Francesca Romana', *Studies in Art and Literature for Belle da Costa Greene* (Princeton, 1954), pp. 118 sqq.; Carlo Bertelli, *La Madonna di Santa Maria in Trastevere* (Rome, 1961); G. and M. Sotirou, *Icones du Mont Sinaï* (Athens, 1956).

5. Metalwork

OF IRISH metalwork of the eighth century, fragments only have come down to us. However scanty they enable us to guess at an art which was brilliant, colourful, at times fastidious, elsewhere strange and nearly frightening. The sumptuous appearance of metal objects must have contributed a great deal to brighten eighth-century churches. Chalices and book-covers on the altar glittered with silver and gold ornament; everywhere shone the crisp brilliance of gilding and studs on croziers, shrines and censers. The lamps were resplendent with multicoloured enamels. On the vestments of priests and probably on the cloaks of the laity, the hundred facets of penannular brooches sparkled in the light. Seldom has the art of the goldsmith and bronzer attained to such dazzling brilliance and to such technical virtuosity.

Perhaps, if one wished to be captious, that very sumptuousness may appear as a fault. As in the stone decoration and that of the manuscripts, the time had passed when a few well-chosen ornaments on a plain background were thought enough to satisfy the eye. Richness, profusion, luxuriance are now the rule. Closely packed ornament covers the whole surface; the artist seems to be impatient of any blank space and ashamed to leave an inch undecorated. It is an almost ostentatious art, as well adapted to the proud eighth-century schools, to the 'multitudinous' ecclesiastical cities with a world-wide reputation, as a more restrained decoration befitted the ascetic communities of earlier times.

A small number of objects have reached us nearly intact :[1] the Ardagh chalice (Col. pl. C, D), the Moylough belt-shrine (Pls. 34, 35), a whole set

[1] Photographs of most pieces of Irish metalwork, and studies of them with bibliographical references are to be found in *Christian Art in Ancient Ireland* (quoted as *C.A.A.I.*); for the objects found in Viking graves in Norway, the fifth volume of *Viking Antiquities* (*V. Ant.*) is the essential reference book. See also: Coffey, *Guide*, and Smith, *Guide Anglo-Saxon A.*

of penannular brooches (Pls. 38, 44, 45). Others, such as the objects in Saint-Germain Museum (Pl. 66), are important fragments of more complex pieces. Most of them are chance finds and nothing can be known of their associations or of the place where they were manufactured. However, a great number of broken gilt-bronze mounts and a few nearly complete objects, the Ekerö crozier-head (Pl. 69), the Birka pail (Fig. 25), the bowls from Hoprekstad, Miklebostad (Col. pl. B), Løland, have been found either in Viking tombs of Scandinavia, where they are associated with datable objects, generally of the ninth century, or in well-excavated sites like the Swedish emporia of Birka or Ekerö. From these objects some chronological data can be deduced. If we assume an average of twenty or thirty years to have elapsed between the day when they were taken from Ireland and the moment of burial, we may get some idea of when they were still housed in an Irish monastery. This gives in any case some sort of terminus ante quem.

The excavations of Lagore have supplied other indications.[1] Though the robber excavations of the nineteenth century had so far upset the site that many objects have no proper stratigraphical record, a certain number of others belong definitely to the first period of occupation (middle seventh century) and others again to the period which ends with the destruction of 848, the most brilliant time of the crannog. In addition, the remains of workshops give precious indications about the manufacture of some objects.

Glass studs of the same type as that discovered in its mould in the lower level of Lagore (Pl. 36) are to be found on the Ardagh chalice and on several penannular brooches which as a consequence are likely to belong to the early eighth century. From Lagore came also, besides crucibles and unfinished objects, little stone tablets covered with sketches. Similar drawings have been found in Garryduff and there were others in Nendrum, probably later in date. In addition, there were in Lagore some bones in which panels of chip-carving have been excised (Pl. 37); these were either more elaborate sketches or were cut in view of casting. Such carved bones have been found elsewhere, for example in Dooey (Pl. 9). Pages of sketches and preparations for casting constitute a

[1] See p. 76–7.

documentation capable of explaining the stages of fabrication of the chance finds.

If now we try to get a general impression of these objects and of their technique, the dominant features appear to be on the one hand their kinship in manufacture and general effect with Continental and English Germanic jewellery, and on the other, the very original way in which these borrowings are treated. Chip carving and the love of multiple facets are typical of the flashy Germanic jewellery of the seventh and eighth centuries. But the Irish version of it is mellower, with a tendency to modelling proper, and it mixes or alternates with areas treated differently. On the English belt buckles this chip carving is mostly obtained by casting, or sometimes by the cutting away of the metal skin. In Ireland, casting is the rule, and it is often 'cire perdue' casting. The same applies in fact to some objects which are practically in ronde bosse. The obverse of the plaques in Saint-Germain Museum (Pl. 66), of the little figures on the Miklebostad bowl (Col. pl. B) and of the Aghaboe figure in Dublin Museum (Pl. 47) show the characteristic depressions left in a sheet of wax when it is stamped into a mould, preparatory to casting.

Filigree is also of a curiously original quality. At first sight it seems very similar to that on Saxon work. Only when it becomes possible to put panels of Irish filigree work side by side with some of the most delicately wrought Saxon buckles, as happened when the Tara brooch was being cleaned in the British Museum Laboratory, does the difference of scale and the relative coarseness of English work become evident (Pl. II). The same elements are used on both sides: bronze or gold wires beaded or twisted – the starting point in fact of nearly all the filigree decoration of the Early Middle Ages. The first distinctive feature of the Irish work is its incredible delicacy. The wires are tiny and are soldered on to the background with such skill that very little of the solder ever shows. The most elementary method consists in soldering scrolls of gold threads onto a gold foil. But there are more complex cases, and in these the differences become obvious. In Saxon metalwork it often happens that a thick beaded wire is edged by two finer ones; from this arrangement the interlacing gains a sharper relief which makes it more legible. On the Ardagh chalice, a similar effect is obtained by a different method: a beaded thread is soldered on top of another, which has been previously hammered flat into a notched ribbon. The notches appear on both sides of the beaded wire, but, being lower, they give it a much more accentuated relief. In some cases different threads are soldered in superposition; in a panel of the chalice, for example, a beaded thread is soldered on top of another thread made of twisted wires (Col. pl. C). On the Tara brooch, tiny gold ribbons, mounted on edge, support beaded wires giving extraordinary depth to the design (Pl. 40). There are infinite variations proceeding from the same fastidious taste which in earlier times dictated the choice of unexpected techniques to produce effects of relief in bronze.[1]

Cloisonné work where glass or garnet is mounted in bands of metal, generally on a patterned metal foil, one of the staple ornaments of Germanic art, is rarely used by Irish jewellers. It only occurs in a few objects: the foot of the Ardagh chalice, the Kilmainham brooch, the Copenhagen shrine, and a few ring-pins. As a rule its appearance is imitated by processes involving the fusing of glass or enamel.

A series of objects, the Ardagh chalice, the Moylough belt, the Ekerö crozier, the Tara brooch, have red and blue studs of varying relief (nearly flat in the case of the Tara brooch) which are all made by a method already used centuries before by the enamellers who made the Somerset hoard boss (Fig. 6). When the Tara brooch was cleaned, what so far could only be a hypothesis was confirmed: these studs were made by placing a metal grille into a mould, enamelling some of the compartments in red and then dropping in a large pearl of blue glass in a viscous state; this filled the still empty compartments and formed the slightly translucent core of the stud. The result is a very rich coloured

---

[1] This ease in the handling of filigree may be the result of a long experience in the use of that technique. The Garryduff bird (Fig. 6) and the little gold mount from the substratum of the Lagore crannog (p. 74) may provide a link with Roman filigree work. Finger-rings with filigree of a slightly coarser type, found near the tumulus of New Grange with a Roman third-century coin, are Roman imported work (R. Smith, *British Museum Guide to the Antiquities of Roman Britain* (London, 1922), p. 61 (p. 28 of J. W. Brailsford's 1951 edition of the *Guide*); see Kendrick, *A.-S. Art*, Pl. XXXII, 4).

effect produced by the different natures of the two kinds of glass, the opaque red enamel and the blue glass full of variegated reflected light. These studs have kept all their brightness on the chalice (Col. pl. C) and the Tara brooch. On the Moylough belt which macerated for centuries in the acid juices of a turf bog, the red enamel has been dissolved and the blue has lost its intensity, but quite obviously the effect was originally the same. The blue and red harmony is too similar to the colours of Germanic jewellery not to be inspired by them. Other studs on some of the brooches are made by simply inserting a molten glass bead into a grille. This is again the same process, but the result is a monochrome effect. Other glass ornaments, on the Ardagh chalice and on some jewels, including the Tara brooch, are simply cast in a clay mould like the Lagore stud (Pl. 36). Sometimes their grooves are enamelled in red or yellow applied directly on the glass.

Beside these erratic techniques, real champlevé enamel is still used. But its appearance has changed. Curvilinear motifs have become very rare indeed. There are only a few examples of zoomorphic designs; one may quote a fragment of a brooch from Westmeath (British Museum), some compartments of an enamelled cross (private collection) and some of the details of the Moylough belt (Dublin Museum) (Pl. 34). The most usual arrangement is a combination of lines of bronze forming geometric patterns in the shape of T, L, S or a cross (Pls. 26, 29, 34, 35). Red enamel generally constitutes the background whilst the patterns are in yellow or green enamel or in blue-and-white or black-and-yellow millefiori. These enamels can attain gorgeous effects when spread over a fairly large surface as on the Miklebostad bowl. This new appearance of the cloisons may well be influenced by the angular designs of Germanic jewellery.

The omnipresent influence of Saxon objects so manifest in these works can easily be explained by the contacts which existed in the seventh century between England and Ireland. Some Saxon objects may have reached Ireland by trade or through travellers whilst England was still pagan. Later the Irish missions in England were an obvious means of transmission of patterns and objects. Those princes and their retinue and all those hundreds of students who came to Ireland must have worn belt buckles and brooches which drew the attention of native craftsmen. Several penannular brooches ending in little birds' heads of which examples have been found in the north of Ireland[1] may be local imitations of Saxon silver brooches of which examples have been found in Kent (Fig. 20, f) and Yorkshire, or simply adaptations to a native form of a motif frequent in Saxon jewellery. There is no doubt anyway that the type of animal head found on one of them which comes from Co. Antrim (British Museum) is of Saxon inspiration (Fig. 21, a). There is, amongst the few late objects discovered in the crannog of Lisnacroghera (Belfast Museum) a gold bead which is an exact parallel of the beads forming the necklace from Desborough (Northants) in the British Museum[2] and also of the beads of another necklace with gold medallions found in Scandinavia.[3] Whatever its ultimate origin, this bead is likely to have reached Ireland through England. These few finds are enough to show how the stream of influence sprang up. The knowledge of English and possibly Continental metalwork is so evident in Irish jewellery that it becomes clear that these objects are only a few survivals of much more numerous importations and direct imitations. It is, however, essential to mark firmly from the start the true character of these connections. There is obvious imitation, but never a copy. We are faced with constant adaptations, where different techniques are used to give a similar effect and a few motifs are chosen carefully and completely incorporated into the current of Irish repertory. The Irish artist is never overwhelmed by what confronts him. He assimilates what he borrows and submits it to the inner rhythm of his ornament. He is infinitely superior to the Saxon artist in craftsmanship and less easily satisfied with his achievements. He seldom limits his efforts to producing the same effects by the same means. To him, each object represents a new adventure and ever renewed experiments.

[1] One of them (from Co. Antrim) is in the British Museum (Smith, *Guide Anglo-Saxon A.*, Fig. 174), another, from the old finds of Lagore is in Dublin Museum (Hencken, *Lagore*, Fig. 10) and another is in Belfast Museum (see our Figs. 20, d; 21, a). [2] Smith, *Guide Anglo-Saxon A.*, Pl. IV.

[3] M. B. Mackeprang, *De Nordiske Guldbrakteater* (Aarhus, 1952), Pls. 23, 16. Amongst the medallions, there is one of Anastasius (491–518). Similar beads, also associated with a medallion of Anastasius, occur in the necklace of the princess buried in Cologne cathedral; see: *Germania*, 1960.

Enamelling is not the only technique which distinguishes him from his Saxon counterparts. There are many others which it would be tiresome to examine in detail. Suffice to quote metal engraving which is very popular in Ireland at this time. It takes the shape of a design deeply cut into a sheet of bronze or silver which still retains something of the freedom of a freehand sketch. The backgrounds are filled either by hatchings (Domnach Airgid (Pl. 55), Hoprekstad pail (Pl. 87), Birka pail (Fig. 25),[1] Copenhagen shrine,[2] etc.) or by dots (Ardagh chalice, Monymusk reliquary,[3] brooch in Stavanger Museum (Fig. 11),[4] etc.). Or they may be openwork, allowing a sheet of metal of a different colour to show through (back of the Saint-Germain objects, fragment in Vidalen Museum, Norway, Clonard pail). Are we to see in this a survival of engravings such as those of the Lisnacroghera scabbards, of the Somerset 'box', or of the Lough Crew bone slips? It would be hard to say. At the time we are dealing with, engraving on metal is essentially a southern technique which was never popular in England or in the north of Gaul. The only possible comparison would be with the Aquitanian belt buckles of the seventh century which have also an engraved decoration with dotted backgrounds.[5] But this is probably a futile analogy when in fact the most immediate affinities may have to be sought in another technique of drawing, that of manuscript decoration.

One would like to describe the general appearance and the structure of the chief types of Irish metalwork objects, but nothing is more difficult. Most things have come down to us broken and in disconnected pieces. The habit of inserting panels of decorated metal into compartments is partly responsible for this. No less the impatience of plunderers who, at the time of the Viking invasions, hacked at objects so as to take away fragments or share them. We know nothing of such ecclesiastical objects as patens and flabella. And still the paten was essential and

---

[1] T. J. Arne, 'Ett kärl i irisk stil', *Fornvännen*, 1924, pp. 142 sqq.; H. Arbman, *Birka I, Die Gräber* (Uppsala, 1940–3), I, Pls. 203–4, II, pp. 147–8; it was found with two tortoise brooches.

[2] *V. Ant.*, V, p. 79.   [3] Allen–Anderson, I, Fig. 18.

[4] *V. Ant.*, V, pp. 42–4 (the other side has chip-carving).

[5] Åberg, *Occident-Orient*, III, pp. 40 sqq.

some texts mention flabella.[1] It remains possible that chalices and patens may have been made of glass, in which case their breakable nature would explain their disappearance. Of metal chalices[2] we have one complete example in the Ardagh chalice, and the bronze boss which was found under the church at Steeple Bumpstead (British Museum) (Pl. 43) may be the foot of a less elaborate one.[3] An object from a Viking tomb in Bergen Museum may be a censer.[4]

The Annals mention several times the making of shrines for the relics of saints[5] and we have seen that there were two in the church of Kildare in the seventh century. The destruction and carrying away of shrines by the Vikings is mentioned in numerous texts and several small ones reached Scandinavia in a nearly perfect state. Others have been found in lakes or rivers where they had been thrown. They are small-size reliquaries made to be carried about like the Melhus shrine, held by a strap passing around the neck of their bearer.[6] Such box-like portable

[1] L. S. Gogan, *The Ardagh Chalice* (Dublin, 1932), pp. 75 sqq.

[2] See art. 'Calice' in Cabrol–Leclercq. The two-handled type of chalice seems to have been obligatory in the time of Gregory the Great (590–604). The Merovingian chalice from Gourdon (Paris, Cabinet des Médailles) is two-handled, and so was the lost chalice in the treasury of Monza. Still, the now destroyed chalice of Chelles (known from a drawing), attributed to Saint Eligius (7th century) had no handles. See: R. Lantier–J. Hubert, *Origines de l'art français* (Paris, 1947), Fig. 14, p. 115 and Fig. 46, p. 130.

[3] As Reginald Smith suggested it might be Viking loot; Smith, *Guide Anglo-Saxon A.*, pp. 137–40.

[4] Bøe, 'An Irish bronce object found in a Norwegian grave', *Bergens Museum Aarb.*, 1924–5.

[5] See Reeves, *St. Columba*, notes pp. 313 and 317 (eight mentions between A.D. 743 and 800).

[6] Apart from that found at Melhus, the best examples are the shrine in Copenhagen Museum, the Monymusk reliquary (Edinburgh Museum), the 'Emly shrine', for a long time on loan in the National Museum, Dublin, now in the Museum of Fine Arts, Boston (*Bulletin Mus. of Fine Arts, Boston*, 1957, p. 61), the Shannon and Lough Erne shrines, and the shrine discovered in 1961 at Setnes, in Norway (S. Marstrander, 'A New Norwegian Find from the Viking Period with Western European Imported Goods', *Lochlann*, 1963, pp. 1 sqq.). They are roughly of the same shape as the Anglo-Saxon reliquary in Mortain which is indicated by its inscription as being a chrismal (Salin, *C.M.*, IV, Pl. IX). In fact the word 'chrismal' may be interpreted in various ways (see Cabrol–Leclercq, art. 'Chrismal') and these boxes, including that from Mortain, may all be simply portable reliquaries.

reliquaries are not uncommon on the Continent at the time[1] and the type may have been introduced into Ireland at any time from the fifth century on. Larger examples are likely to have existed also.[2] If the objects in Saint-Germain Museum are really the gable finials of a shrine,[3] this must have been nearly of sarcophagus proportions. An enamelled cross in a private collection may have been applied on a somewhat smaller reliquary.[4] Its shape explains the purpose of several fragments hitherto unidentified. The heart-shaped enamelled object in Dublin Museum is likely to have been the finial of a shrine intermediate in size between these large chests and the small portable boxes. A few fragments and the Athlone openwork plaque (Pl. 46) come probably from book-bindings, but it is impossible to visualize the whole metal decoration of a book.

From carvings where it is represented we can form some idea of the crozier of an abbot or bishop in the eighth century (Carndonagh pillar, Drumhallagh slab (Fig. 15), cross of Old Kilcullen (Pl. 73), base of the north cross at Ahenny (Pl. 79), cross of Kilrea, Banagher slab (Pl. 94)).[5] It seems to have been comparatively short, with a crook like that of an ordinary walking-stick, not unlike the Continental type at the same time as represented by the Délémont crozier.[6] Two frag-

[1] For example the shrines in the treasuries of Sens and Tournai, the shrine of Saint-Bonnet-Avalouze, the shrine of Saint-Maurice d'Agaune, etc.; others may be in their turn influenced by Irish models. The Lough Erne shrine contained a smaller box of the same shape as the shrine itself which was the relic-box proper; similar boxes were found in some of the Sens shrines. On this type of reliquaries, see: W. M. Conway, 'Portable Reliquaries of the Early Medieval Period', *Proc. Soc. Ant. Lond.*, 1919, pp. 218 sqq.

[2] There were on the Continent at that time large metal-work 'tombs'; see Salin, *C.M.*, II, pp. 178 sqq.; none has survived.

[3] J. Hunt, 'On two "D" shaped objects in the Saint-Germain Museum', *P.R.I.A.*, 1956 (C), pp. 153 sqq.; on these objects, see F. Henry, 'Deux objets irlandais au Musée des Antiquités nationales', *Préhistoire*, 1958; there are two fragments of apparently identical objects among the group of Irish objects found at Gausel, in Norway (Bergen Museum), *V. Ant.*, V, pp. 31–2; for illustration, see *C.A.A.I.*, I, Pl. 34.

[4] *Frühe irische Kunst* (Mainz, 1959), No. 112.

[5] See also the bronze figure from Aghaboe (Pl. 47).

[6] G. Haseloff, 'Der Abstab des Heiligen Germanus zu Delsberg (Délémont)', *Germania*, 1955, pp. 210 sqq.; F. Henry, 'Les crosses pré-romanes', *Iris Hibernia*

ments, both found in Scandinavia, may have belonged to croziers, though the identification remains uncertain in both cases, as the Ekerö crook (Pl. 69) – were it not for its iconography – might be the top of the side-post of the back of a chair similar to those animal-headed thrones on which the Evangelists are accommodated in some miniatures, and the fragment of staff found in Norway which is in Copenhagen Museum[1] could just as well have belonged to a processional cross. A third fragment in Dublin Museum[2] comes certainly from a crozier, but it may be slightly later than the eighth century.

The bell, a small portable one derived from the dinner-bell of Roman times, seems to have been in Ireland an essential attribute of some ecclesiastics.[3] It is represented beside the crozier, and sometimes a book, on several carvings. A great number have come down to us, several found in ecclesiastical sites. But they seldom bear any ornament. Those which do and the elaborate metalwork boxes in which several of them

---

(Fribourg, Switzerland), 1956, pp. 35 sqq.; it is generally said that the distinctive feature of the Irish crozier is the fact that it is the reliquary of the walking-stick of a saint or at least that stick embellished with a metalwork casing (cf. M. Stokes, *Early Christian Art in Ireland* (chapter on croziers); art. 'Crosses (Chrétientés celtiques)', by Dom Gougaud, in Cabrol–Leclercq); this is probably true, but the same may well be true also of the Continental croziers of the same time; the only ones which can be dated of before the ninth century with some probability are the fragments of the sixth-century crozier of Saint Césaire in Arles, whose wood was originally covered with metal, and the Délémont crozier, which is similarly decorated. The crozier kept at Montreuil-sur-mer is probably slightly later.

[1] *C.A.A.I.*, I, Pl. 27, 2.   [2] Ibid., Pl. 27, 1.

[3] Three Roman bells similar to the Irish ones were found in a well with objects of the third century A.D. at Epernay (Epernay Museum). A passage in the *Tripartite Life* of Saint Patrick (p. 345 of W. Stokes' edition), seems to indicate that Irish bishops received a bell and a crozier when consecrated; there are several carvings where bell and crozier appear together: on the cross of Old Kilcullen, the Carn-donagh pillar, and (probably a little later) the Killadeas pillar. There are some bells of Irish type on the Continent: that known as the 'cloche de Sainte Godeberte' in the treasury of the cathedral of Noyon, and that in the cathedral of Saint Gall (which comes from a nearby hermitage), may well have a close connection with Irish bells. J. O. Westwood, 'On the Ancient portable Hand-Bells of the British and Irish Churches', *Archaeologia Cambrensis*, 1848; there is much information about Irish bells in: H. T. Ellacombe, *Church Bells of Devon* (Exeter, 1872).

have been enshrined, belong to a later period and can not be dealt with here.

The wooden pails, usually covered by a thin sheet of engraved metal (Pl. 87), are probably derived from those wooden pails covered with panels of stamped bronze, which come from Merovingian graves.[1] Like them, they were probably used to carry holy water. A few nearly complete hanging-bowls from this period have been found in Norwegian graves; from others only the escutcheons have survived. These are not vastly different from the examples of earlier times, except that spiral patterns are replaced by angular motifs and that millefiori panels become very common.

Penannular brooches are plentiful and profusely decorated, but the zoomorphic enamelled brooch disappears and is replaced by silver gilt or bronze gilt brooches with filigree and studs whilst the hand-pin makes room for a great variety of ring-pins. Some of the brooches are likely to have been used as chasuble-fasteners, but a good deal of this jewellery was probably made for the use of the lay population. Crannogs and forts yielded it in quantity; and the wearing of brooches as insignia of rank and social position is mentioned in the collection of laws, the Senchas mór.[2] Their decoration is in no way different from that of objects

---

[1] See an example in Beauvais Museum, another in the Röm. Germ. Museum in Mainz. (G. Behrens, *Merovingerzeit*, Mainz, 1947, Fig. 139), etc.; some may have been meant to carry holy water (G. Chenet, 'La tombe 319 et la buire chrétienne du cimetière mérovingien de Lavoye', *Préhistoire*, 1935, pp. 34 sqq.); however there was in the treasury of the Abbey of Saint Denis an 'escritoire' (wooden tablet with inkstands) to which a pail for carrying a provision of ink was attached; this wooden pail was covered with leather and contained another vessel of bronze which was the real container of the ink; it is not impossible that some of the Irish pails were meant for such use (see: M. Conway, 'The Abbey of Saint Denis and its Ancient Treasures', *Archaeologia*, 1914–15, pp. 103 sqq.; pail, p. 122 and Pl. VII).

[2] When they are in fosterage, there must be 'brooches of gold, having crystal inserted in them, with the sons of the king of Erin and of the king of a province, and brooches of silver with the sons of the king of a territory; or the sons of each king is to have a similar brooch as to material, but that the ornamentation of all these should appear in that brooch' (*Ancient Laws of Ir.*, II, pp. 146–7); the so-called 'Dalriada brooch' in Dublin Museum is the only penannular brooch of solid gold which has come down to us (*C.A.A.I.*, I, Pl. 21, 3), but brooches of gilt bronze or silver may have been meant also.

destined for church use. The same remark would apply to the few horse-trappings which have come down to us, chiefly strap-tags and chariot-rings.

It would be a vain task to try to make localized groupings of these objects. They probably issue from workshops which each had their own methods and traditions. But there may also have been travelling craftsmen offering their services wherever they were wanted. However intricate their work may appear, it is likely to have been produced in the same casual way still characteristic of metalworkers in Oriental bazaars, over some charcoal burning in a hole, and with fairly primitive tools. Skill and the knowledge of some technical processes were the essential things.

With the small number of excavations which have been done, one hesitates to give too much significance to the few known examples. As the Garranes excavations have produced millefiori glass whose pattern is identical with some of the millefiori of the large Suttton Hoo bowl, and still one would not feel entitled by that to say that the vase was made in Garranes, in the same way, one hardly dares to follow the leads given by the Lagore excavations; these can only give indications of what may have happened there as well as elsewhere, in lay or ecclesiastical workshops still awaiting the spade, or dispersed long ago. The existence, in the crannog, of fragments of millefiori glass, of glass rods which were prepared for their manufacture, of a bronze plaque whose enamel has floating sections of millefiori glass, and also of a belt-buckle very close in shape, general appearance, and type of enamelling, to the Roman buckles of the second and third centuries, might cause us to wonder if some of the experiments which led to the elaboration of the characteristic Irish millefiori decoration did not take place in that vicinity. But better not to insist. And it is probably equally futile to ask ourselves how far metalwork was in the hands of the monks. The monasteries, like all human communities in this time, had their work-shops. This is made clear by the excavations of Nendrum. Lay specialized craftsmen were probably employed when none was available amongst the community itself. The close similarities existing between some of the metalwork and certain pages of manuscripts which are without a doubt the product of a monastic scriptorium, entitles us to postulate a close link between scribes and metalworkers and in some cases a common training. In actual fact this is the impression given by the 'school-house' at Nendrum.

These various objects can be roughly classified in several groups, from the aspect of technique and style.

Millefiori and champlevé, or champlevé alone, combined with high-relief castings, are the only ornament of a few hanging-bowls devoid of chip-carving, which were buried in Norway towards the middle of the ninth century (at Miklebostad, Hoprekstad, Løland) and of the wooden bucket from the Oseberg tomb (Pl. 91). The rings or handle were held by squat little men or by birds. The base of the Miklebostad bowl had a gorgeous decoration consisting of a three-rayed star of enamel in a circular frame.[1] The enamelled birds from Hoprekstad have a nearly exact parallel in an escutcheon found in Clonmacnois (Pl. 29). Shrines also were decorated in this way; the finial in Dublin Museum has enamel of identical type; the little animal head from Ireland in the Ashmolean Museum (Pl. 29) which may be the end of a ridge-pole is connected with that group; and the applied enamelled cross, another shrine fragment, belongs to it also.

At first sight, one might think that one or several workshops were turning out objects of this type, ignoring or despising chip-carving and repoussé work. This would be, however, a rash hypothesis: what do we know of the background of the enamelled cross, or of the appearance of the reliquaries to which the Dublin and Oxford finials belonged? An enamelled bird-escutcheon found at Ferns,[2] whose enamels are surrounded by cast interlacing patterns might act as a warning, but two much more important objects now give full proof of complex juxta-positions: one of them is the belt-reliquary dug out of a turf bog in 1942 at Moylough (Sligo), the other is a crook, probably from a crozier, found in 1955 at Ekerö, near Stockholm.

[1] See F. Henry, *Early Christian Irish Art* (Dublin, 1954), Pl. 33.
[2] *C.A.A.I.*, I, Pls. 41–4.

The Moylough reliquary (Pls. 34, 35) is formed by two sheets of bronze encasing a leather belt which had probably belonged to a saint.[1] Several texts mention such relics preserved in various monasteries. The outside bronze sheet, which was probably covered by a thin foil of decorated metal, carries a series of relief mounts – buckle, hinges, crosses – which have enamelled frames. These frames are mainly of the most current type of pattern, with compartments in the shape of T and L, enamelled in yellow on a red background, and the insertion of panels of blue-and-white millefiori. But on the ends of the buckle-plates and the fastening ring itself, there are animal patterns : monster-heads threatening an enamelled boss and birds' heads with long curved beaks, both derived from well-known traditional Germanic patterns here transferred to enamelling. The frames surround panels of repoussé silver, some simply stamped, others in high relief. Their patterns are very varied : spirals, accompanied sometimes by little thread-like serpents, interlacings, animal heads, etc. Above the frames stand some bosses of glass and enamel, some with angular cloisons, others inlaid with three little metal coils. In all this, there is no real chip-carving. But in the other object, it plays an essential part.

The Ekerö crozier (Pl. 69)[2] consists of a volute mounted on a socket and thickly covered with ornaments. The curve ends in a monster-head with wide open jaws whose sharp teeth hold a human head. One side and the socket are covered with enamel and millefiori. On the other side the pattern is modelled in sharp relief and covered with violent hatchings. It would be difficult to imagine a more integral combination of enamel and chip-casting and we are drawn to the conclusion that there is no incompatibility whatsoever between these techniques. At the most we may say that some workshops preferred one of them at the expense of the others. It may be also that there were different currents of tradition : the little enamelled figures are not without some kinship with the symbol of Saint Matthew in the Book of Durrow (Pl. 57). The chip-

[1] M. Duignan, 'The Moylough (Co. Sligo) and other Irish Belt-Reliquaries', *J.G.A.H.S.*, 1951, pp. 83 sqq.

[2] W. Holmqvist, 'An Irish Crozier-Head found near Stockholm', *Ant. Journ.*, 1955, pp. 46 sqq. ; Id., *Excavations at Helgö*, I (*1954–6*), (Uppsala, 1961), Pls. 23–5.

carvings are more closely connected with the styles of the Book of Lichfield and the Book of Lindisfarne. This need not necessarily mean chronological differences, but possibly a certain archaism on one side, a more modern trend on the other, or even local styles.

Some of the gilt bronze objects borrow very little, however, from the Saxon themes of ornament, as witness the two objects preserved in Saint-Germain Museum.[1] These, like the Ekerö crozier, derive their inspiration from themes which belong to a far-away Celtic past, monsters devouring a human head, snakes, coiled spirals. The sort of frozen and immobile ferocity which they emanate is found also on some broken pieces of gilt bronze from Norway, especially the plaque from Romføejellen (Oslo Museum) (Pl. 90) where bosses of spirals uncoil into snakes in very high relief, snouts uplifted, glass eyes staring, more terrifying even because of the meticulous precision of their execution. The high relief brutes covered with finely carved ornament which keep watch heavily around the Steeple Bumpstead boss belong to the same universe of muffled anguish. They have an obvious kinship with the stylized boars which stand out on a background of interlace around the silver hanging-bowl from the Saint Ninian's Isle hoard (Shetland).[2] As for many others of the objects from the same hoard, this is likely to be an imitation of an Irish object made in some Scottish workshop.

These animals in relief are not all made by casting processes. In the case of the little ducks stylized into triangular masses which are applied on one of the brooches from the Ardagh find (Pl. 39), a break reveals a core of carved bone on which is applied a thin sheet of metal. A similar example of relief obtained by repoussé work has been supplied earlier by the Ardakillin brooch. In all processes this continuity of tradition asserts itself.

Up to a point the Ardagh chalice and some of the penannular brooches seem to form a fairly coherent group, distinguished by the use of chip-carving and of filigree work. But again it would be dangerous to establish too rigid categories and to lose sight of their close relation in other respects with some of the objects just examined.

[1] See p. 100.
[2] A. C. O'Dell, *St Ninian's Isle Treasure* (Aberdeen University Studies, 141), Pls. 28–30, 32; see: *Antiquity*, 1959, pp. 241 sqq.

Opposite: Pl.C. Handle of the Ardagh Chalice

The chalice was found in the autumn of 1868 by a boy who was digging potatoes in the rath of Ardagh (Limerick),[1] to the south of the Shannon estuary. With it were four brooches and a small bronze chalice. They were all concealed under a stone slab within the roots of a thorn bush. It may be that the objects were hidden at a late date, as tradition has it that mass was said in the rath during Penal times and it is not impossible that a priest might have hidden there some of the treasury from a disestablished monastery which had come into his keeping.

The chalice is made very simply of a large cup and a semi-spherical foot of beaten silver[2] united by a robust metal rod (Col. pl. D). The edge of the cup is strengthened by a thick brass roll on which rest the ends of the handles. Its general outline has a massive beauty, a fullness of line which attains to elegance by the economy and variety of the ornaments. There is something superfluously rich in the appearance of the ordinary eighth-century penannular brooches. Here, on the contrary, great soft surfaces of silver are left untouched, and on their quiet curve the ornaments emerge with extraordinary brilliance, glittering of colours and variegated surface. Between them a subtle link is established by the animal terminals and the inscription lightly engraved on the cup below the golden band. The whole balance of the composition has still the strength and restraint of the best seventh-century work and belongs to that moment of perfection which marks the turning point between a youthful, impetuous, though already experienced art, and a surfeited and over-elaborate decoration.

This regal feeling for balance is served by a technical virtuosity which is such as to cause stupefaction. We have seen by what various processes of near-enamelling the bosses and the glass plaques of the handles have been made, as well as some aspects of the filigree work.

---

[1] Dunraven, 'On an Ancient Chalice and Brooches lately found at Ardagh, in the County of Limerick', *Trans. R.I.A.*, 1858–71, pp. 433 sqq. (the plates are reversed); L. S. Gogan, *The Ardagh Chalice* (Dublin, 1932); *C.A.A.I.*, I, pl. 51–53; for an unlikely attribution of the chalice and the Tara brooch to a Northumbrian workshop, see: *E.Q.C. Lindisfarnensis*, pp. 250 sqq. (Bruce-Mitford).

[2] There is absolutely no foundation in the oft-repeated assertion that silver is rarely used in Ireland before the Viking period. Many silver objects have gone unnoticed through their being gilt.

Opposite: Pl.D. The Ardagh Chalice

These range from the delicate scrolls fixed immediately on the surface of a gold foil on the cruciform discs (executed nearly in the same way as the Garryduff bird), to the superpositions of the handle escutcheons and of the top border. The ornaments of the foot are made of cast bronze deeply gilt so as to match the gold filigree (Pl. 33).

Though the chalice is more sophisticated and shows greater technical skill than the belt-reliquary, the kinship between the two objects is very striking. Even if we take into account the thin metallic foil which originally covered all the surface of the reliquary and whose decoration was obviously either engraved or cut-out, the relation between this nearly smooth surface and the high-relief motifs remains the same. In both cases there is the slightly rustic tubular edge framing the object. The enamelled glass bosses are practically identical and so are glass beads with three metallic spirals inserted into their surface. Reliquary and chalice have been conceived by artists who had the same notions of the composition and structure of an object, who had at their disposal the same studs, but who, for reasons best known to themselves, have planned their decoration one from the angle of filigree work, the other from that of repoussé and champlevé. Here again it seems difficult to separate objects decorated by different technical methods.

Nearer even to the chalice is another object, the so-called Tara brooch (Pl. 38).[1] It is a fairly small brooch, some 3½ inches in diameter, whose ring is completely closed as is usually the case at that time. Its name, purely fanciful, is the product of the imagination of a dealer who owned it for a while. In actual fact, it was found in a wooden box, with some Scandinavian objects, near the mouth of the Boyne.[2] It had obviously been looted, it is impossible to know from where.

[1] For bibliography, see: *C.A.A.I.*, II, pp. 25–6. The brooch was cleaned in the Laboratory of the British Museum in 1962, where, with the kind permission of Dr Lucas, Director of the National Museum of Ireland, and the invaluable help of the Laboratory staff, I was able to study it in detail. Slight discrepancies between the French and English versions of this book have resulted from the fact that I visited the Laboratory before the cleaning was completed. The latest findings have been incorporated in the present text.

[2] At least this is one of the versions of the discovery. The facts are far from clear. See: H. A. Wheeler, 'The Tara Brooch: Where was it found?', *Co. Louth Arch. Journ.*, 1949–52, pp. 155 sqq. In the first detailed account of the brooch, that by

Its structure proceeds from the same simple and direct outlook as that of the chalice and the belt-shrine which once again comes as a contrast to the elaborateness of the details. It consists basically of a cast-silver ring prepared on one side with a series of raised frames made to hold the tiny panels of filigree.

The back of the brooch is decorated essentially by panels of gilt chip-carvings in the very style which we will find on many other brooches of that time. But when examined closely it reveals a more elaborate execution. It has two nearly flat discs of enamelled glass made exactly like the bosses of the chalice (Pl. 40). In three places there are sheets of metal with threadlike sunken spiral patterns (Pl. 27). This play of incredibly fine lines running on a shiny surface has practically no parallels and the lines are so thin that one may wonder if they were not cut into the surface by an acid. To the spirals and animal interlacings which form the main decoration are added borders of fat birds biting each other's legs which show a direct connection with illumination and are very rare in metalwork (Pl. 42). Still, the treatment of the bodies of the animals, with its heavy hatchings, is very close to that of the Ekerö monster, the animals in the panels of the Steeple Bumpstead boss and the snakes of the Saint-Germain objects, so that this ornament takes its place quite normally in that group of Irish jewellery.

However, this side was not usually seen. The other is the one which was exposed when the brooch was fastened in a garment (Pls. 40, 41), and the goldsmith in consequence has done his best with it. It must be remembered that the Tara brooch is a rather small object, one of the smallest of the ornamented brooches. The work in consequence is of an unusually delicate quality. But it remains strangely effective in its minuteness. Beasts designed by an amazingly fine and intricate network of gold wires glitter amidst raised bands of amber; gold wires twisted, knotted, coiled, frame them with their subtle, unfailing tracery.

George Petrie in the *P.R.I.A.*, 1851, p. 36, there is no mention of the circumstances of discovery. Whatever they were, the fact that the chain has been cut seems to point to looting. E. C. R. Armstrong, 'Catalogue of the Silver and ecclesiastical Antiquities in the Collection of the Royal Irish Academy, *P.R.I.A.*, 1914–16(C), pp. 287 sqq.; see p. 310.

Contrasting with this arachnidean embroidery, fierce-looking reptiles skirt the outlines of the jewel and add a wild punctuation of upturned heads. The blues and reds of the studs, the mellow transparencies of two little human heads of moulded dark glass, combine with the gilt surface and the mat yellow of amber bands in warm and glowing accord.

Here again, as on the chalice, the treatment of the filigree is of extreme versatility, going from threads which seem nearly embroidered on their gold foil to the strong effects of light and shade produced by the little gold ribbons soldered upright, and the more subtle modellings of the animal whose body is covered with hatchings and bosses made with different kinds of wires.

Many other brooches have filigree, but only two have an animal decoration in filigree which could be compared with that of the Tara brooch.[1] Both were found in Scotland, but may very well have only come there as loot taken by the Vikings. Of one of them there is only a fragment left (Edinburgh Museum); it was found right at the north tip of Scotland, at Dunbeath (Caithness).[2] Its filigree is nearly as fine as that of the Tara brooch. But the little animal in one of the compartments is covered in gold granulations while its outline is indicated by a wire. The same technique occurs on the other brooch, which was found at Hunterston, in Ayrshire, opposite to the north-east coast of Ireland (Edinburgh Museum).[3] It belonged in turn to two Vikings, as is indicated by the runic inscriptions scratched on the back.[4] It is appreciably larger than the Tara brooch and its filigree is coarser. Ought one to see in this technique of gold granulations a process peculiar to Scotland?[5] In fact it might be the special method of a workshop or of several, as gold

[1] A third one has been acquired by the National Museum of Scotland in 1964.

[2] Allen–Anderson, I, p. xciv.

[3] Allen–Anderson, I, p. xcvii; J. Anderson, *Scotland in Early Christian Times* (2nd series, Edinburgh, 1881), pp. 1 sqq.; *V. Ant.*, II, pp. 187 sqq.

[4] G. Stephens, 'Note on the Hunterston Brooch, Ayrshire', *P.S.A.Sc.*, 1886–7, pp. 462 sqq.; one of the names (Maelbrigte) is a Celtic name, but the fact that it is written in runes shows that we are dealing with somebody belonging to one of those families of mixed Scandinavian-Celtic blood common in the tenth century.

[5] At least at the time we are dealing with. It was originally a Greek technique, like most of the filigree work; see R. A. Higgins, *Greek and Roman Jewellery* (London, 1961), pp. 18 sqq.

granulations in a circle of wire occur on a number of the large penannular brooches found in Ireland.

The other brooches and the ring-pins deserve a more detailed study than they have received.[1] From a typological point of view, there would be the problem of the change from the enamelled brooches with zoo-morphic terminals, which are simple open rings, to the eighth-century type which has both ends linked by one or several metal tags or has an uninterrupted ring. The variations of the pin-head of these last brooches should also be considered : it is sometimes simply folded over the ring, or it carries a large shield, generally triangular in shape. The various arrangements of the compartments on the surface should be taken into account. The conclusion to be drawn from such an analysis might well be that all these elements existed side by side, inextricably mixed together. But in the absence of such a study, all that one can do is to dwell on a few general points.

Let us take for example the type of brooch which has trilobe motifs in high relief. The first to come under consideration might be the 'Breadal-bane brooch' (British Museum)[2] which has an open ring. It has some fairly coarse filigree in the centre of the trilobes and a little filigree snake pattern on the ring. The top of the pin is simply folded over the ring, with a panel of interlace on the curve. Next comes a brooch from the old finds of Lagore (Dublin Museum)[3] which is in cast bronze, without filigree. The ends of the ring are connected by a transverse plaque and the top of the pin has a large triangular shield. With the brooch from Co. Cavan in Dublin Museum (Pl. 44) we come to the most beautiful of all this series. It is made of silver, cast and gilded and has remarkably fine filigree work. The ends of the ring are linked by three bands of silver on which are little human heads in relief. The top of the pin has a third trilobe, similar to those on the ring. A brooch of this type, in gilt bronze lined at the back with a sheet of silver, was found at Snaasa, near

---

[1] Reginald Smith's article, 'Irish Brooches of Five Centuries', *Archaeologia*, 1914, pp. 223 sqq. is only a cursory survey and is now out of date because of new discoveries and publications.

[2] Smith, *Guide Anglo-Saxon A.*, Pl. XIII.

[3] Hencken, *Lagore*, Fig. 8, p. 62.

111

Trondheim (Oslo Museum)[1] with Scandinavian brooches of the middle ninth century. It seems in consequence that the whole series can be attributed to the eighth century or the beginning of the ninth.

Another group consists of brooches which have a lozenge-shaped panel at each end of the ring.[2] To this belong the Ballyspellan (Kilkenny) brooch,[3] that found at Killamery (Kilkenny) (Pl. 45), two of the brooches from the Ardagh find (Limerick),[4] the brooch found in the souterrain of the fort of Cahercommaun (Clare)[5] and one of the brooches which were preserved in the Library of Trinity College, Dublin and are now in Dublin Museum.[6] It is remarkable that all, except this last one which has no location, belong to the half of Ireland which is south of a line drawn from Dublin to Galway. Several have very fine filigree with sometimes little pyramidal coils of threads. The terminal plaques which remain smooth, apart from the lozenges, are edged by little elongated

[1] *V. Ant.*, V, pp. 66–7.

[2] The terminals of these brooches have generally a lead filling on which was fixed a panel of filigree inserted in the lozenge-shaped frame.

[3] *C.A.A.I.*, I, Pl. 38, 2.

[4] Ibid., Pl. 56.   [5] Hencken, *Cahercommaun*, Fig. 11, p. 28.

[6] *C.A.A.I.*, I, Pl. 48; E. C. R. Armstrong, 'Four Brooches preserved in the Library of Trinity College, Dublin', *P.R.I.A.*, 1914–16(C), pp. 243 sqq.

Fig. 11. Engraved design on terminals of penannular brooch found at Bergøy (Norway) (Stavanger Mus.; drawing Oslo Mus.).

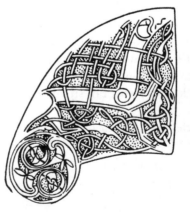

and short-legged animals in fairly high relief. The whole group belongs also no doubt to the eighth century, as a very worn fragment of a brooch of this type, which had been turned into a fibula, was found in a woman's grave in the neighbourhood of Bergen (Bergen Museum)[1] with Scandinavian brooches dating from about 850. Given its derelict condition, it had probably been in use for a long time before being buried and it is likely to have been carried out of Ireland early in the ninth century.

Beside these well-defined groups, there are isolated specimens like the beautiful 'Londesborough brooch' in the British Museum,[2] and a curious series is represented by a brooch from Co. Antrim in Dublin Museum,[3] several found in Scotland and one of the brooches in the Saint Ninian hoard; they all have an open ring and little birds' heads or busts emerging from the terminal. They may be a Scottish type, though it is indeed very hard to distinguish between what was made in Ireland or in Scotland at that time.

The representation of man does not occupy a very important place in these metal objects. When it occurs, it is often absorbed by a network of ornament; sometimes, however, the figure or the head only assumes a remarkable massivity, cylinders and half spheres standing out violently from the background. The handling of faces is often a curious mixture of simplified modelling and fine chiselling. They have an impassive and implacable expression, the mouth drooping at the corners is half open, the eyes are strictly almond-shaped, the eyebrows are strongly marked and the cheeks are sometimes engraved with the sharply marked outline of a short beard.

A little head found in England, at Furness (Pl. 69), is one of the best examples (British Museum). It is one of those broken fragments of Irish metalwork which were mounted on a little cushion of lead by the Vikings who used them as weights. It is impossible now to know to what type of figure it originally belonged. The arrangement of its hair, with

[1] *V. Ant.*, V, pp. 56-7 (No. 73); Hencken, *Cahercommaun*, Fig. 12, p. 28; see another example of this type in: Paor, *E.C. Ireland*, Fig. 42, found in the neighbourhood of Trondheim.

[2] Smith, *Guide Anglo-Saxon A.*, Pl. XI, 1.   [3] *C.A.A.I.*, I, Pl. 20, 2.

the interval in the curly locks on the forehead, is also found on some of the heads engaged in fights and whorls on the Saint-Germain objects (Pl. 66). Some of these last ones are caught between the teeth of monsters. This is the theme of the devouring beast which is found several times carved on the crosses, a theme which is capable, in spite of its mythological antecedents, of a Christian interpretation: on the Ekerö crozier it is most probably meant for Jonah emerging from the whale, a symbol of resurrection which occurs frequently on croziers of a later date.

What was the meaning of the little figures which have a square of enamelling in guise of a body? Puppets without arms of the Miklebostad bowl (Col. pl. B), two-headed plaques of the Løland vase, cross-legged figures of the Oseberg bucket (Pl. 91), they all seem to come from the hands of the same craftsmen, fond of beautiful smooth relief. The squatting figures on the bucket, akin to that carved on the North cross at Clonmacnois (Pl. 91), belong to the same hazy borderland where there lingers still something of the formal appearance of the Celtic gods.

But strongly modelled figures of this type may be made also to serve Christian iconography, as shows a little figure from Aghaboe (Leix; Dublin Museum) (Pl. 47). Its body is a slightly flattened cylinder, its face has a haunting massivity. Wear may, however, be partly responsible for this smooth appearance. Originally, the dress was nearly completely covered with ornament merging into that of the background. The same arrangement is also seen on the openwork plaque found in Athlone (Westmeath; Dublin Museum) (Pl. 46) which comes most probably from the binding of a book. In this Crucifixion, all that is significant is firmly stressed: the regal serenity of the large oval face, the widely outstretched arms. Apart from that, ornament is dominant and covers nearly all the surface in an uninterrupted network raised on the breast into a strongly modelled spiral pattern. A small angel found in Norway (Oslo Museum)[1] is similarly covered with ornament. It is probably also a fragment torn from a book-binding, as it clearly formed part of a wider composition to which it was connected by a plaque of interlace, now broken. On a shrine mount in Dublin Museum (Pl. 90),

[1] Ibid., Pl. 24, 2.

Fig. 12. Pattern on an Irish object found in a Viking grave in Norway (Trondheim Mus.) (see pl. II).

the little figure – probably Daniel between two lions – has a body reduced to a pattern of triangles with its head fitted into a lozenge-shaped frame.

Of these exuberant ornaments, it remains to draw up a repertory. First there are spirals, enlivened by vegetable patterns, spreading all over a surface, as floriated, as fanciful as they were on the enamelled plaques of the Sutton Hoo bowl or the latchet in Dublin Museum. Then there are interlacings, comparatively simple in tracery, of one or two strands; they only seem to appeal to the craftsman as an element of diversity and he does not seem to look upon them as a source of really interesting effects. His attitude to chequers and key-patterns is very much the same; they are rarely used and only occupy an important place on the foot of the Ardagh chalice, on the Athlone Crucifixion and on the Domnach Airgid. Besides the spiral, one of the favourite motifs is the animal-interlacing. In this, as we will see, the metalsmith shows an attitude widely different from that of the sculptor in stone, and may well have derived his inspiration from pages of manuscripts. But from what he found there he evolved fairly quickly a little creature all covered with

115

hatchings, with a long rectangular snout, better fitted to the sharp definition required by gilding. It is found already on the back of the Tara brooch, strongly connected as this is with illuminated ornament. Birds, so essential a part of the decoration of some of the manuscripts, here occur very seldom. They form a border on the Tara brooch, and there are a few examples of them on the brooch in Stavanger Museum, one of the Ardagh brooches and the Londesborough brooch. Little panels of snakes are, on the contrary, very frequent, and may be derived from Saxon metalwork. It is curious to note in this connection that they will only become a frequent element of illuminated decoration in the beginning of the ninth century, when they are very plentiful in the Book of Kells. Only once, on a little roundel found at Togherstown, near Uisneach,[1] is found the human interlacing which is such a feature of the Book of Kells and occurs already in the Book of Mac Regol and the Ms. 1395 of Saint Gall.

The chronology of these objects can only be established in a very wide manner. For technical reasons indicated above, it seems however that the belt-reliquary, the chalice, and a few objects closely connected with them such as the Tara brooch and the Ekerö crozier, belong to the first half of the eighth century, whilst some of the brooches may, given the dating indications of the Norwegian tombs, belong to the second half of the eighth century or the beginning of the ninth.

[1] *C.A.A.I.*, Pl. 19, 4; see also : R. A. S. Macalister–R. L. Praeger, 'The Excavation of an Ancient Structure in the Townland of Togherstown (Co. Westmeath), *P.R.A.I.*, 1931, pp. 54 sqq. This disc was not a 'saucer-brooch' as the authors of the report state, but an ornamental plaque, probably for a shrine : it has a tag at the back, but no hinge or clasp.

6. Carvings

In the primitive establishments, in the hermitages, no more was needed than a pillar marked with a cross or a slab bearing a few symbolical ornaments to mark the tomb of a few ascetics and sum up in cryptic fashion the hope which had governed their life. The monastic cities inhabited by hundreds of students will require a more sumptuous ornamentation. This will be supplied by crosses carved on all sides and most probably painted, whose surface is often a picture-parable in carved figures and scenes.

A study of seventh- and eighth-century carvings[1] centres of necessity on the moment when the one type of monument yields to the other. Cogitosus, when talking about the church at Kildare, has a passing reference to a decorated doorway. But we know little of stone portals and nothing at all of wooden ones. So it is from the isolated monument, slab or cross, that we gather all our notions about the art of carving stone at that time.

Towards the end of the seventh century, pillar and slab alike begin to assume a more monumental appearance. They cease to be just rough blocks of stone, they begin to be cut to a more regular design and grow larger, until they reach 6 feet or more in height. One may wonder how far Coptic slabs which are rectangular in outline or rounded at the top, or have a triangular pediment, have had an influence on this evolution, and, looking nearer, if some carvings from Visigothic Spain may not

---

[1] See : H. S. Crawford, *Handbook of Carved Ornament in the Early Christian Period* (Dublin, 1926); A. Kingsley Porter, *The Crosses and Culture of Ireland* (New Haven, 1931); Henry, *Sc. irl.* (1932); E. H. L. Sexton, *A Descriptive and Bibliographical List of Irish Figure Sculpture in the Early Christian Period* (Portland, Maine, 1946) and the books quoted for general reference in the chapter on Sites and Architecture.

have played their part in it.[1] The shape of the cross itself participates in this more organized design. A Greek cross in a circle occupies all the upper part of the flag, or is inscribed fully on its axis. Often it is a Maltese cross drawn usually by compass in sections of arcs; this has parallels in Gaul, specially in one of the slabs found in the oratory of Mellebaude, in Poitiers.[2] It often happens that the ends of the cross curl up into complicated spirals; the cross may also be made of interlace, either by a few knots of thin threads or by a thick plait of large ribbons. Sometimes the cross, framed in a circle, has a long handle. This is likely to be meant for a flabellum, a liturgical fan which had become, on account of the peacock feathers of which it was sometimes made, a symbol of watchfulness and sometimes a symbol of the faithful disciple. Gradually the cross with which it is engraved or carved seems to dictate the actual shape of the monument. There was a dramatic moment when it looked as if some driving force was struggling to shape the inanimate matter. The idea of the cross was still embedded in the stone, unable to free itself, yet pushing out at the sides and the top. Finally it fought its way out of the inert frame and the first free-standing crosses appeared.

Monuments of different purpose seem in fact to go each their own way at that time : the standing slab and pillar are replaced, as funerary monuments, by recumbent slabs covering the tombs.[3] Meanwhile, something of the role which the cross-bearing stone had come to assume in the monastery passes to the monument deriving from it, the sculptured high cross, which loses all funerary character and becomes probably, in its turn, a centre for the recitation of prayers and offices, and perhaps in some cases the mark of a place of asylum.

One of the large pillars is approximately dated by an inscription and may help up to a point to fix the chronological place of others, though it is important to remember here that dates used too dogmatically can only be dangerous, when most probably monuments of very different

---

[1] J. Baum, *La Sculpture figurale en Europe à l'époque mérovingienne* (Paris, 1937), Pl. LXII (No. 165); Masai, *Origines*, Pl. XLIX, 6.

[2] C. de la Croix, *Hypogée-Martyrium*, Pls. 15, 22.

[3] Lionard, *Grave-Slabs*, pp. 95 sqq.

shapes were being carved at the same time, some of them archaic and traditional, the others venturing boldly into new styles.

This pillar, cut out of a very thick piece of stone, is nearly 7 feet high and, surrounded by a few stones marked with crosses, stands in the middle of a field at Kilnasaggart in South County Armagh (Pl. 49). It was on one of the chief roadways of Ireland, that which connected Tara with Emain. The inscription, cut in rather irregular Irish majuscules, tells us that 'this place has been given by Ternoc, son of Ciaran-the-Little, under the protection of Peter the Apostle'.[1] This Ternoc is known from Annalistic entries: he died in 714 or 716. If the monument, as is likely, was erected in his lifetime, it may date from around A.D. 700. The south-east side, carefully smoothed and nearly regular in outline, has a beautiful boldness of composition. The back is more unexpected in arrangement and bears eleven discs each marked

[1] W. Reeves, 'Kilnasaggart', *U.J.A.*, 1853, p. 221; G. H. Reade, 'The pillar-stone of Kilnasaggart', *J.R.S.A.I.*, 1857, pp. 315 sqq.; Petrie, *Chr. Insc.*, II, p. 27; Macalister, *Corpus*, II, p. 114; there has been some hesitation as to the meaning of a word which might be translated either *gave* or *bequeathed*; on the whole, *gave* seems the most likely translation (see: *Contribution to a Dictionary of the Irish Language*, T (Dublin, 1943), art. 'Timne', and Id., D (Dublin, 1960), art. 'Do-im(m)na').

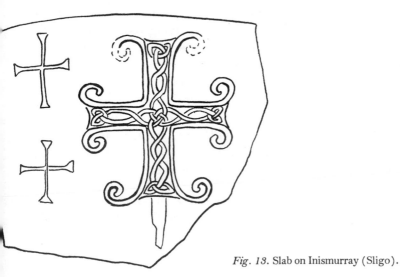

Fig. 13. Slab on Inismurray (Sligo).

with a cross, carved in very low relief and irregularly distributed on the surface. With the large disc on the other side (probably meant for Saint Peter), they are likely to represent the twelve apostles, whilst the Latin cross is probably an emblematic figuration of Christ. This inscription has been compared with that of a small pillar found near Whithorn (Candida Casa) which bears also, below a Maltese cross inscribed in a circle, a dedication to Saint Peter (Pl. III). They may be both examples of affirmations of fidelity to the Chair of Saint Peter as a consequence of the Synod of Whitby.[1]

The large slab which stands in the graveyard of Killaghtee, in Donegal (Pl. IV), was elaborated in the same symbolical atmosphere as the Kilnasaggart pillar, and is very close to it in its technique also. It proceeds from the same art as the Clonamery and Fore doorways, and draws, as they do, its chief effect from the juxtaposition of the rough stone, hammered into shape with a few masterly strokes, and the smooth surface where the design appears in low, infinitely delicate relief. But the sculptor who made the Killaghtee slab showed an even greater sensitiveness, inventing the slightly concave disc, giving a hardly perceptible curve to the arms of the cross and boldly putting a trifold knot on one side of the slab, which might have upset the whole composition, yet successfully avoids doing so. This knot stands most probably for a symbol of the Trinity and the whole cross seems to be an awkward version of a Chi-Rho, the Rho having its loop turned the wrong way round and being cut out of the top arm of the cross.

Three slabs on Inishkea North[2] repeat this composition of a monument shaped by a large cross-bearing disc (Fig. 14), with the addition of complicated motifs of thick spirals which cover the lower part of the slab, indicating clearly on one of them the handle of a flabellum. A slab in Glendalough has the same structure (Pl. 21), but here the flabellum comes very near to the cross in a circle which will soon become so common.

A series of smaller slabs on the island of Inismurray (Sligo),[3] some

[1] Macalister, *Corpus*, I, pp. 497–9 (No. 519, 1).

[2] Henry, *Inishkea*. A small stone figure also found in north-west Mayo may belong to the same time (J. Raftery, 'A stone figure from Co. Mayo', *J.R.S.A.I.*, 1944, pp. 87 sqq.).

[3] Wakeman, *Inismurray*.

Fig. 14. a, b, slabs, Inishkea North (Mayo),
   c, pattern on one of the Carndonagh pillars (Donegal);
   d, slab on Inishkea South, detail.

of them perhaps recumbent grave-slabs, show several variants of the same type, amongst them crosses covered with thread-like interlacings whose extremities curl up in a rich flowering of spirals (Fig. 13).

Up to now we have only met a more orderly and imposing version of a type we knew already. On other monuments appears this great novelty : the representation of the human figure, and they are most probably the equivalents in stone of paintings such as those in the church of Kildare described by Cogitosus.

In fact, one of them, the Killeen Cormac pillar (Pl. IV),[1] bears an engraving of a figure in bust, carrying a cross, which seems to be an extremely simplified version of some icon of the type of the Mount Sinai Saint Peter,[2] and may well derive directly from one of the pictures in the church at Kildare, only about 15 miles away. Icons again, but on a much larger scale, are the two closely related Crucifixions which stand on two islands near to each other off the coast of Mayo, Inishkea North and Duvillaun (Fig. 14 and Pl. 51). The designs are reduced to a few simple lines : a figure of Christ indicated broadly – with a very large head in the case of Inishkea – and on each side the sponge and lance bearers very small, and looking as if they were floating in the air. On the back of the Duvillaun Crucifixion, the slab – which is like a huge plank raised in front of an infinite perspective of sea and cliffs – carries an engraved Maltese cross in a circle (Pl. III).[3]

This same type of cross is engraved on both sides of the slab at Ballyvourney (Cork) (Pl. 50).[4] There, a little figure walking over the circle has been drawn in a few beautifully firm lines. A comical figure indeed, with a dress shaped like a bell, a round face, and the most surprising pointed nose. But for all its singular appearance, there is a strange vitality in the eager movement of its little feet, shod with

---

[1] R. A. S. Macalister–R. L. Praeger, 'Report on an Excavation recently conducted in Killeen Cormac, Co. Kildare', *P.R.I.A.*, 1928–9 (C), pp. 247 sqq. Though the lines of the engraving have been deepened in modern times, the design has not been altered (see op. cit., Pl. XX).

[2] Kitzinger, *Icons of the Seventh Century*, Pl. 7.

[3] Henry, *Slabs and Pillars*, p. 271.

[4] Ibid., p. 275; F. Henry, 'The Decorated Stones at Ballyvourney, Co. Cork, *J.C.H.A.S.*, 1956–8, p. 41.

pointed shoes, and in the decided way in which it clutches the crozier.

On all these monuments there is very little more than engraving, than the transcription on to a stone surface of the essential outlines of a painted image. It is indeed extremely likely that touches of paint came as a complement to these schematic designs which would then become the very exact equivalents on a more resistant support, of an icon painted on wood. Their stone-plank appearance comes only as a confirmation of this general impression.[1]

This, however, is only a transition stage. Other monuments are carved in relief and come nearer to carving proper, or, if they are still engraved, take on a new monumental appearance. Most of the slabs in this category have protuberances jutting out of their rigid frame at the sides or at the top. These appendices are to be found on the Glendalough slab. They occur also on the Fahan Mura slab (Donegal) (Pl. 52), on those of Drumhallagh (Donegal) (Fig. 15) and Gallen (Offaly) (Pl. 64) and on the slab which is in the graveyard at Carndonagh (Donegal) (Pl. 59).

The big slab at Gallen Priory, near Ferbane (Offaly) (Pl. 64)[2] is one of the most remarkable of this series where a feeling for relief is beginning to appear. It is divided into several panels a little like a manuscript page. That at the top has a large cross of interlacings whose arms are curved back at the ends into spirals. Underneath there are two affronted animals, perhaps stags, with curved and knotted antlers; the lowest part of the slab is occupied by a key-pattern framing the figure of a small stag in combat with a snake.

The Drumhallagh slab is much smaller (Fig. 15). It has a Latin cross on each side. One of them is covered with very irregular interlacing and in each of the quadrants there is a little figure: below, two ecclesiastics carrying one a crozier, the other a Tau-shaped staff,[3] above, two exactly

---

[1] For some icons, a carving of the wood in very low relief helps the effect of the paint. See for example an icon of the tenth or eleventh century in Sofia Museum (*Antiquity*, Sept. 1938, pl. IV).

[2] T. D. Kendrick, 'Gallen Priory Excavations, 1934–5', *J.R.S.A.I.*, 1939, pp. 1 sqq.

[3] These Tau-shaped croziers existed in Ireland and in Scotland in the pre-Romanesque period. There are several representations of them on Scottish slabs;

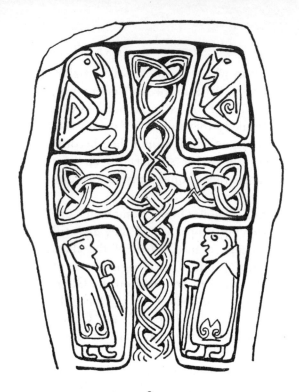

Fig. 15. a, slab at Drumhallagh (Donegal);
b, c, slabs on Iniskeel (Donegal).

symmetrical figures, sitting hand in front of face. Similar compositions are found on slabs in the islet of Inishkeel, on the west coast of Donegal (Fig. 15), where the compartments are occupied by human figures and swans.[1]

Other monuments which are all in the Inishowen peninsula (Donegal), north of Derry, form a group coherent in its diversity. The unity of style is firmly established by the treatment of figures some in full face, others in profile, but all of a similar type, and by the use of large ribbons sometimes double edged. A strong outside impulse can be felt there, manifest not only by the complexity of the iconographical programme and the preponderance of motifs such as marigolds and interlacing, but also by the text of an inscription itself. The links with the monuments we have just studied are, nonetheless, just as evident and are made manifest by the identity of the spiral pattern on one of the Carndonagh pillars with those on the Inishkea slabs (Fig. 14), by the similar figuration of a full-face body with feet in profile on the cross of Carndonagh (Pl. 56) and the Duvillaun slab (Pl. 51) and by the analogy in shape of one of the interlace crosses on the Fahan Mura slab (Pl. 54) with the cross on the Gallen slab (Pl. 64).

The Fahan slab is an imposing monument, in size as well as in decoration (Pls. 52, 54). It would stand nearly 9 feet high if its base were completely cleared, and the ornament, devised on a large scale, stands out vigorously. The frame is clearly marked and ends in a triangular canopy. The plaits and elaborate knots of a large double-edged ribbon compose, on each side, a Greek cross with a stem. Though the surface is nowhere very deeply cut, the cross stands out boldly, and on one side its striking design is enhanced by two little figures, very square, absolutely unconcerned with proportion and as determined as those on the Ballyvourney slab. The cross on the other side has a perfectly

---

it is not impossible that the staff carried by the figure on the Ballyvourney slab would be an awkward rendering of a Tau crozier. The only example which has survived in Ireland is a late one in Dublin Museum (eleventh or twelfth century). There are eleventh- and twelfth-century examples on the Continent.

[1] *J.R.S.A.I.*, 1934, p. 262 (H. Wheeler); another slab has been discovered on Inishkeel in 1963 by P. McGill who kindly sent me a photograph of it; it bears a Crucifixion with a cross of the same outline as the Carndonagh Cross.

plain background below the triangular compartment occupied by two affronted birds, which recall birds placed in similar fashion on Coptic slabs[1] or on the marble slab from the church of La Major in Narbonne.[2] The patterns on the dresses of the two little figures give the illusion, which is probably deceptive, of an inscription.[3] But on the north edge of the slab a perfectly clear and well-defined inscription has been cut (Pl. VII). It was R. A. S. Macalister who first read it and stressed its historical import.[4] It is written in Greek uncials and is the Greek version of a form of the *Gloria Patri*: 'glory *and honor* to the Father and to the Son and to the Holy Ghost', whose use is attested in the seventh, eighth and ninth centuries. That it was known in Ireland in the seventh century is proved by the fact that it is given as an antiphon to the *Gloria in Excelsis* in the Antiphonary of Bangor (middle seventh century).[5] As Macalister pointed out, it is quoted in canons 13 and 15 of the Fourth Council of Toledo which was presided over by Isidore of Seville in 633. But the second of these canons give the impression that the formula had been in use for some time and was then in process of

---

[1] Henry, *Sc. irl.*, Pl. 15.

[2] M. Durliat, 'Un groupe de sculptures visigothiques à Narbonne', *Etudes mérov.*, pp.93 sqq., see Pls. 2 and 3.

[3] For Macalister's reading, see: *Corpus*, II, p. 118.

[4] R. A. S. Macalister, 'The inscription on the slab at Fahan Mura', *J.R.S.A.I.*, 1929, pp. 89 sqq. (also: *Corpus*, loc. cit.). In his article 'Sur quelques exégètes irlandais' (*Sacris Erudiri*, 1955), Father Grosjean wonders if the inscription and its possible connection with a seventh-century council has not influenced the dating of the slab. Actually, I did not know about Macalister's reading of the Greek inscription when I wrote my article, 'Les origines de l'iconographie irlandaise' (*R.A.*, 1930), where I suggested a seventh-century date on stylistic grounds. I had tried to read the inscription, but had been defeated by bad weather. I have examined the slab very carefully since, with an excellent light, and am absolutely satisfied that Macalister's reading of the Greek inscription is correct, though I cannot follow him in his reading of the inscriptions on the figures. As for its genuineness, on internal evidence alone, one could hardly doubt it.

[5] Macalister was unaware of this. See: Warren, *Antiphonary of Bangor*, I (facsimile), fol. 33v., II, p. 31. The complete formula is here: 'gloria et honor Patri, et Filio, et Spiritui Sancto, et nunc et semper et in saecula saeculorum.' The second part of the doxology (omitting 'sicut erat in principio') is quoted in the ninth century by Walifrid Strabo as being the Greek form (*De Rebus Ecclesiasticis*, cap. XXV).

being superseded by the modern formula: 'glory to the Father. . . .'[1] However, perhaps thanks to the efforts of the council, the formula survived in the mozarabic liturgy where it is constantly found.[2] There has been a tendency, in consequence, to see in the Fahan inscription the proof of contacts between Ireland and the Spain of Saint Isidore.[3]

In actual fact, the spread of the formula is much wider than has been said generally. Warren, in his study of the Antiphonary of Bangor remarks that it is to be found in the Ambrosian liturgy. It is also widely attested in Greek liturgies at least from the ninth century onwards,[4] and no doubt goes back in this context to an earlier date. It is then likely to have been introduced into Ireland in the seventh century in its Greek version, and to have been copied on the Fahan slab (with slight errors) from the page of a Greek manuscript – perhaps the same manuscript from which originated the inclusion of the 'glory and honor . . .' formula in the liturgy of Bangor. A direct influence from Greek manuscripts has caused the appearance in Ireland of a form of Greek uncials which is not only found in this inscription (Pl. VII), but occurs also in the copy of the *Vita Columbae* of Adamnan written in Iona at the end of the seventh century (Schaffhausen, Ms. 1) where, as well as the Greek text of the *Pater* (Pl. VII) there is a Latin colophon written in Greek letters.[5] On a manuscript which belonged to the library of Lindisfarne (Durham, Ms. A.II.10)[6] and which may have been brought there from Iona or from Ireland, there is also the *Pater* in Greek, but this time written in Latin characters (Pl. 53).

The monastery of Fahan Mura was of considerable importance in the seventh century.[7] Saint Mura was the patron saint of the chief branch of

---

[1] Warren, op. cit., note, p. 75; Masai, *Origines*, note, pp. 86–7.

[2] Cabrol-Leclercq, art. 'Doxologies'.

[3] J. N. Hillgarth, 'The East, Visigothic Spain and the Irish', *Studia Patristica*, 1961; Id., 'Visigothic Spain and Early Christian Ireland', *P.R.I.A.*, 1962, pp. 167 sqq.

[4] F. E. Brightman, Liturgies, *Eastern and Western* (ed. E. Hammond), Vol. I, *Eastern Liturgies* (Oxford, 1896), p. 310. The Greek connection is already indicated by Warren, though he seems to have been unaware of how far back it can be traced.

[5] Reeves, *St. Columba*, facsimile p. xiv.   [6] See pp. 163–6.

[7] See: J. H. Todd, *P.R.I.A.*, 1851 (C), pp. 100 sqq.; Reeves, *U.J.A.*, 1863; W. J. O'Doherty, 'The Abbey of Fahan', *P.R.I.A.*, 1881, pp. 100 sqq.; A. Spence, 'The Antiquities of Fahan and Inis-Eoghan', *U.J.A.*, 1911, pp. 17 sqq.

the Northern Uí Néill whose seat was the fortress of Aileach, on a nearby hill. They no doubt contributed to the wealth of the monastery. There was also in the immediate vicinity, the Columban monastery of Derry. Colgan, the Franciscan seventeenth-century historian, who may well have been brought up in Fahan, gives a list of a few of the books which the monastery still owned in his childhood,[1] and he attributes its foundation to Saint Columba himself. This need not be taken as being literally the historical truth, but it shows that there was a tradition of strong links with the Columban monastery of Derry and probably with Iona, the metropolis of the order. So this inscription helps to place the slab within the sphere of influence of the Columban monasteries at the end of the seventh century, and may help us to visualize the now completely vanished stone carvings which no doubt existed on Iona at that time. Connections with Bangor are also in no way surprising, given the short distance between the two monasteries.

The Carndonagh cross, which stands a few miles farther north from Fahan, and is obviously a product of the same workshop, marks the final victory in the attempt to free the cross from the slab. It is cut from a thin slab of sandstone, its contours sinuous and slightly irregular, drawn by a man who shrank from the use of straight lines, and stands a little more than 10 feet high (Fig. 16, Pl. 56). One side is completely covered by a close weaving of broad ribbons. On the other, patterns and figures, sharply engraved, form a continuous ornament, ever on the same level of the stone. The whole composition is organized around the oval of a head, emphatically stressed, that of Christ in glory, surrounded by four simplified figures which, like the figures on the Fahan slab, are shown without arms.[2] Above is a large cross of ribbons; below, three figures in profile.

The cross was accompanied by two little pillars carved in the same style and obviously by the same hand. One has a panel of spirals which are a thicker and broader version of the spirals on the Reask and Inishkea monuments (Fig. 14, c). On two other sides there are men; one with

---

[1] Colgan, *Trias Thaum.*, pp. 495, 510; Id., *AA. SS. Hib.*, p. 588.

[2] The latest photographs, taken in specially good conditions, show clearly that the right hand of Christ is raised in blessing (Pl. 56).

128

Fig. 16. Carndonagh cross (Donegal).

an enormous round eye and broad feet, clutching a diminutive round shield and a sword (Pl. 59); the other holding between his bare feet and his chest a barrel-shaped harp, which he touches with a ghostly hand. They may stand for two representations of David, as a harper and as a warrior. On the other pillar, a big head in profile, emerging from the mouth of an erect fish, is evidently intended for Jonah. There are two less intelligible figures; one with crossed arms holds a bell and a book over a crozier placed horizontally; the other has horns protruding out of a wide forehead, small ears like the handles of a pot, and holds two discs and a hammer. The first, although certainly representing an ecclesiastic, has crossed arms which are strangely reminiscent of the Boa Island double idol, whilst the horned figure is not without a suggestion of the cross-legged horned figures of Gaulish carvings. Whatever new meaning may have been ascribed to them, their formal appearance seems to be due to earlier, pre-Christian representations.

The slab which stands in the graveyard at Carndonagh, a short distance from the cross and pillars (Pl. 59), though it belongs to the same group, is a monument much cruder in execution which shows even more clearly the strong foreign influences at work on all of them. The marigold-flabellum and the large quadrilobe interlace which it bears both belong to the repertory of the decoration of Merovingian sarcophagi.[1]

This cross cut in a stone plank is far from being unique. There is in Inishkeel the broken stem of another cross covered with interlacings.[2] Still another, slightly different in outline, has survived in Caher Island (Pl. IV): above a thick knot of ribbon, a Crucifixion is just suggested, the head only being carved at the top of a cruciform frame, but it is not impossible that the body may have been painted. On Tory Island, on the other hand, there are the remains of a cross with a figure in

---

[1] See for the marigold: Salin, *C.M.*, II, Fig. 73, p. 141; Fig. 95, p. 159 and *passim*; for the fourfold knot: Ward-Perkins, *Sculpt. of Visigothic France*, Pls. XXXV, 1 and XXXVI, 3 and 6; C. Enlart, *Manuel d'archéologie française*, I, 1 (3rd ed. Paris, 1927), Fig. 69 bis, p. 204.

[2] H. Wheeler, in *J.R.S.A.I.*, 1934, p. 262.

fairly strong relief. All this points to a series of parallel experiments leading to various solutions.

It is more than likely that the high cross carved in relief was up to a point the result of these researches. Slabs, pillars and crosses probably went on existing side by side for a long time. To group them in two series excluding each other chronologically and devoid of interpenetrations, would be a completely wrong approach to the whole problem. The characteristic features of this period are, on the contrary, hesitations, gropings, lingerings of traditional formulae, and it is probably only towards the middle of the century that the high cross becomes the standard decoration of the yards and greens which divided the buildings of a monastery.

It is necessary to pause here awhile to place the Irish high crosses in a broader picture. During the Early Middle Ages, the only countries of western Europe where high stone crosses, covered with ornaments and figures, are to be found are Britain and Ireland. They occur in all parts of England,[1] in Wales,[2] the Isle of Man[3] and Ireland. In Scotland,[4] the most usual monument is a large carved slab having a low relief cross on one side. Still, there are a few stone crosses in the east of Scotland and an important group in the west is connected with the Irish ones.

These crosses cover a long period and were carved from the eighth to the twelfth century. The question of interrelations between the various groups – English, Scottish, Irish – has sometimes been raised. It is too complex to be dealt with here in detail and it is sufficient to point out that its solution is not necessarily to be found in the influence of one group on the others, but rather in a parallel evolution proceeding from

[1] There is no general publication of the English crosses; see: Collingwood, *Northumbrian Crosses* (1927); A. W. Clapham, *English Romanesque Architecture before the Conquest* (Oxford, 1930); Kendrick, *A.-S. Art* (1938), and the *Victoria County Histories*.

[2] Nash-Williams, *Wales*.

[3] P. M. C. Kermode, *Manx Crosses* (London, 1907).

[4] Allen–Anderson (1903); C. L. Curle, 'The Chronology of the Early Christian Monuments of Scotland', *P.S.A.Sc.*, 1939–40, pp. 60 sqq.; R. B. K. Stevenson, 'Pictish Art', in *The Problem of the Picts* (Edinburgh, etc., 1955), pp. 97 sqq.

similar impulses. The problem appears clearly in this light if one accepts the chronology proposed in 1927 by Collingwood for the English crosses, which places their first development shortly before the middle of the eighth century. This chronology has received confirmation from the analysis made in 1960 by R. I. Page[1] of the runic inscription on the Bewcastle cross. He has shown that some hitherto often accepted readings were untenable and he concludes that the cross at Bewcastle and consequently that at Ruthwell which is to a great extent its model, are likely to date between 750 and 850 and not from the late seventh century as Baldwin Brown had suggested.[2]

If this be accepted, the development of Irish and English crosses would appear as roughly contemporaneous. There can be no question, however, of merging them into a unified series. Each group has its own structure of monument, its repertoire of decorative patterns, a particular treatment of figures. But a similar cause may have contributed to the transformation of the stone-plank – slab or cut-out cross – into an articulated monument, edged with mouldings and modelled in relief. This may perhaps be due to a stimulus from outside and to the teaching of a few wandering craftsmen.[3]

The Early Christian civilization of the Near East certainly knew carved monumental crosses. The Copts seem to have had a predilection for flat slabs carved in low relief, but the Armenians probably wrought crosses covered with ornaments and figures. Strzygowski[4] and Baltrusaitis[5] have published fragments of pillars from Thalin and Haridscha, carved on all four sides and mounted on cubic or pyramidal bases, which are nearly certainly fragments of crosses. They are usually attributed to the sixth or seventh century, or even to the fifth. There can be little

[1] R. I. Page, 'The Bewcastle Cross', *Nottingham Medieval Studies*, 1960, pp. 36 sqq.

[2] Baldwin Brown, *Arts in E. England*, V (1921), pp. 127 sqq.

[3] For a discussion of this, see: L. Stone, *Sculpture in Britain: the Middle Ages* (Harmondsworth, 1955), pp. 11 sqq.

[4] J. Strzygowski, *Die Baukunst der Armenier und Europa* (Vienna, 1918), Figs. 678–85.

[5] J. Baltrusaitis, *Études sur l'art médiéval en Géorgie et en Arménie* (Paris, 1929), Pls. LXX and LXXXI.

doubt in any case that they belong to the period prior to the Arab conquest.[1] There may have been monuments of the same type within the Byzantine Empire. In this regard one may perhaps take into consideration stone crosses of later date which are to be found in the Balkans (in Bulgaria and Yugoslavia) and which may embody an early tradition.

There would be nothing surprising in the arrival in Ireland at that time of Oriental sculptors, not only when the pressure of Arab occupation began to make itself felt too heavily in the Near East, but also at the time when the iconoclastic quarrel was turning the work of painter or sculptor in the Byzantine Empire into an uncertain, if not dangerous occupation. The possible intervention of sculptors originating from Mediterranean lands has been mentioned in connection with some phases of the development of English crosses, especially with the introduction of the vine patterns and with figure carvings such as those on the Ruthwell cross.[2] It sounds perfectly natural in England where a Greek from Tarsus had just been on the chair of Canterbury, where Benedict Biscop had brought masons from Gaul to build his churches and had called the archcantor of Saint Peter's of Rome to train the choirs of Jarrow and Wearmouth and where Coelfrid had had manuscripts imported from Italy copied as exactly as possible. In fact it would be in no way more surprising in Ireland which we have seen in close contact with Oriental monasteries and where imitation of imported icons was in full swing at the time we are dealing with. Here, all the same, it appears less blatantly because Irish artists already had their own repertoire of ornaments which they were not prepared to give up and to which they simply added new elements, and because a perfectly natural evolution had brought them already to the point of cutting

[1] Strangely enough, Strzygowski does not mention them in *Origin of Christian Church Art*, whose English edition (Oxford, 1923) has an additional chapter on 'Hiberno-Saxon Art in the Time of Bede' (pp. 231 sqq.); instead, he gives a small and unconvincing drawing of the pillars at Odzun which he says are covered with figured scenes (on the side not represented).

[2] A. Gardner, *A Handbook of English Medieval Sculpture* (Cambridge, 1935). Saxl only suggested the imitation of Mediterranean models (F. Saxl, 'The Ruthwell Cross', *Journ. Warburg and Courtauld Institutes*, 1943, pp. 1 sqq.; see p. 7).

standing crosses out of stone slabs. Another element also played its part in the shaping of the Irish high cross : the influence of metalwork, which leaves its mark both in the structure of the cross and the technique of its decoration.

So the origins of the Irish high cross are probably complex and multiple, and this is why an outside influence is less evident on them than in the case of the English crosses and has been less often suggested. This is also the reason which explains the great variety in appearance of the Irish crosses of the eighth and the beginning of the ninth century. They are distinguished from the English crosses by several features. First of all by the choice of ornament where spirals, interlacings and angular patterns are the chief motifs whilst the vegetable scroll with or without animals is one of the favourite elements of decoration in England. Then, there is the general shape of the monument. The English crosses never have a circle connecting the arms of the cross. In Ireland, the circle is the rule, though in a less absolute way than is generally assumed. In the early stages, it is rarely found. It does not occur on the Carndonagh cross, nor on that of Caher Island or on that of the Skellig; that of Inishkeel is hardly likely to have had it, and it is absent from a more sophisticated cross, all covered with ornament, which is in the graveyard at Kilbroney (Down); the cross at Old Kilcullen may not have had it. It is not certain that it was present on all the crosses of Clonmacnois. In Iona some of the crosses have a circle, others not. The sculptured slabs which remain the most usual monuments in the East of Scotland and which have often the same lateral protuberances as the Irish slabs, generally have on one side a cross carved in low relief. This cross may or may not have a circle.[1]

The monastery plan drawn on one page of the Book of Mulling gives some idea of the way in which the crosses were scattered inside as well as outside the sanctuary enclosure (Fig. 17). In many places several, sometimes of different dates, have survived, scattered here and there in the graveyard which now covers part of the grounds of the monastery.

[1] For an attempt at making the Scottish slabs the origin of the Irish crosses, see : R. B. K. Stevenson, 'The Chronology and Relationship of some Irish and Scottish Crosses', *J.R.S.A.I.*, 1956, pp. 84 sqq.

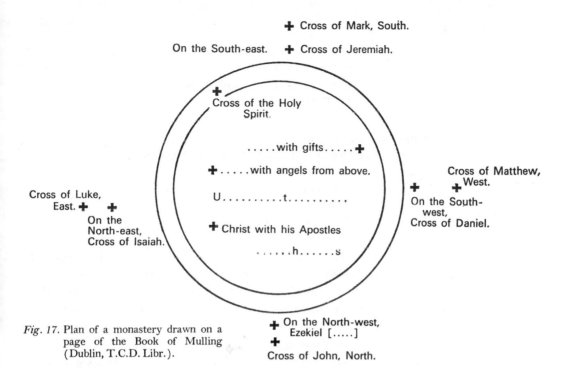

+ Cross of Mark, South.

On the South-east. + Cross of Jeremiah.

+
Cross of the Holy
Spirit.

.....with gifts.....+

+.....with angels from above.

Cross of Matthew,
+West.

On the South-
west,
Cross of Daniel.

Cross of Luke,
East. + +

On the
North-east,
Cross of Isaiah.

U.........t.........

+ Christ with his Apostles

......h......s

+ On the North-west,
Ezekiel [.....]

+
Cross of John, North.

Fig. 17. Plan of a monastery drawn on a page of the Book of Mulling (Dublin, T.C.D. Libr.).

They are always strictly oriented, facing east and west. As a rule, Irish crosses do not seem to have a funerary character, perhaps unlike those of England and Scotland. The inscriptions which have survived in Ireland are of the type: 'Pray for X who has caused this cross to be made.' They may have been places of gatherings for prayers or offices. When they had figured scenes, a didactic element was added, similar to that of carved doorways in gothic churches. They seem also to have had a protective role, that of watchmen warding off the evil forces of the four corners of the world. A poem on Oengus–Céli-Dé gives that impression:

'Disert Bethech, where dwelt the man
Whom hosts of angels were wont to visit;
A pious cloister behind a circle of crosses, . . .

.   .   .   .

135

> 'Tis in Clonenagh he was reared,
> In Clonenagh he was buried;
> In Clonenagh of many crosses
> He first read his psalms.'[1]

Another poem, relating to an abbot of Durrow, seems to conjure up a picture of a monastery as a place bristling with crosses :

> 'O Cormac, beautiful thy church,
> With its books and learning;
> A devout city with a hundred crosses.'[2]

Each had its name, not necessarily connected with its decoration. In the Book of Mulling plan, those around the rampart are dedicated to the four great prophets and the four Evangelists. The cross of the Holy Ghost is indicated on the wall itself, and was probably near the entrance gate. Three other crosses marked inside the circle were obviously near the churches. With these indications one may connect a reference, in the Tract on the Monastery of Tallaght, to a 'slab at a cross in front of the enclosure',[3] and that, by the Four Masters at the date of 848, of a cross which was 'on the green' of the monastery of Slane.[4] Two of the crosses of Iona are known to have been called after the Evangelists Matthew and John. There were obviously also crosses dedicated to other saints. One of the crosses of Iona is called Saint Martin's cross, and a cross at Kells bears the inscription : 'Patricii et Columbe crux.'

They do not vary widely in size. Most of them are between 10 and 15 feet in height, including a base of 2 to 3 feet and a finial which in some cases is more than 1 foot high. They are usually made of a fine-grained sandstone, either white as marble, or slightly cream coloured with reddish patches of iron deposit. But at the foot of the

---

[1] Meyer, *A. Irish Poetry*, p. 88.   [2] Reeves, *St Columba*, p. 269.

[3] 'For aulaid oc cros ind dorus lis', *P.R.I.A.*, 1911 (C), p. 151.

[4] The fact that this cross behaved in the most extraordinary way, exploding, as it were, so that its fragments were found in three fairly distant places (possibly a weird description of Viking plunder) does not minimize the value of the information. It remains that the 'green' of the monastery was a normal place for a cross.

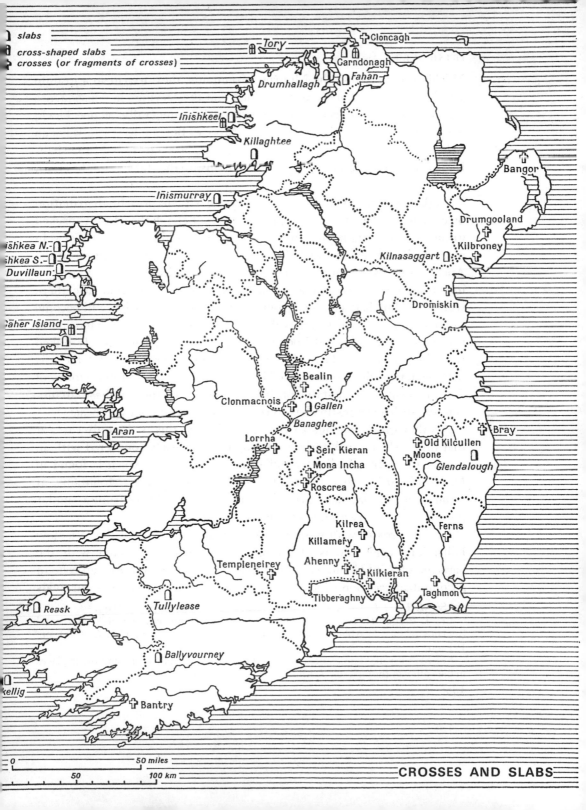

slabs
cross-shaped slabs
crosses (or fragments of crosses)

Tory
Cloncagh
Carndonagh
Fahan
Drumhallagh
Inishkeel
Killaghtee
Bangor
Inismurray
Drumgooland
Kilbroney
shkea N.
shkea S.
Duvillaun
Kilnasaggart
Caher Island
Dromiskin
Bealin
Clonmacnois
Gallen
Banagher
Aran
Bray
Lorrha
Old Kilcullen
Seir Kieran
Moone
Mona Incha
Glendalough
Roscrea
Kilrea
Ferns
Killamery
Ahenny
Templeneirey
Kilkieran
Taghmon
Tibberaghny
Reask
Tullylease
ikellig
Ballyvourney
Bantry

0   50 miles
0
50
100 km

CROSSES AND SLABS

Wicklow Hills and in the Mourne Mountains, they are cut in a granite which is often hard and coarse grained and the carvings in consequence take a heavier appearance. The cross itself is generally of one block, except when it is of a large size as in Moone. But the base is always an independent stone in which a deep cavity has been cut to hold the shaft. It is made in a pyramidal shape in order to insure the stability of the cross.

A glance at the map (p. 137) shows that their present distribution owes a good deal to chance preservation. Behind the closely packed group which exists in the south-west of the old kingdom of Ossory, in monasteries so obscure that they hardly ever deserve a mention in the Annals, one is tempted to postulate an impulse from Lismore, so important during the whole of the eighth century. In this case there would be a link between this group of high crosses and what will become the reform movement towards the end of the century. The extension of this group to Lorrha and Loch-Cré (Mona Incha), both closely linked with the reform, would tend to reinforce this impression. But there is nothing left of the monastery of Lismore, except a few tomb-stones of the ninth century and a statue probably of the same time.[1] In these circumstances, such a suggestion has to remain in the realm of hypothesis.

Another group belongs to Clonmacnois, and this is the only case, at that time, when a sculptor's workshop can be clearly connected with an important centre. A slightly different type of cross, which is found in Dromiskin and is repeated to the north of the Mourne Mountains, at Drumgooland, may have originated in Bangor, judging from a similar fragment found on the site of the monastery.[2]

Granite crosses with figured scenes occur at the foot of the Wicklow Hills. The chief one is at Moone, a monastery affiliated with the paruchia of Saint Columba,[3] and it may have preserved for us an echo of a Columban tradition which can only be traced in Iona by some survivals

[1] See *J.R.S.A.I.*, 1937, p. 306, and Macalister, *Corpus*, II, pp. 107 sqq.

[2] F. J. Bigger–H. Hughes, 'Some notes on the Architectural and Monumental Remains of the old Abbey of Bangor, in the County of Down', *U.J.A.*, 1900, pp. 191 sqq.

[3] F. M. Carroll, ' Some notes on the Abbey and Cross of Moone and other places in the valley of the Griese', *J. Kildare Soc.*, 1891–5, pp. 286 sqq.

occurring on crosses dating from the period immediately preceding the attack of the Vikings. Other non-decorated crosses of which examples have survived in Fore, Finglas, Killeen Cormac, Old Kilcullen, Tullow, Kilkieran, Ferns, etc., help to complete the picture and add a new element to its extremely varied appearance.

The chronology of these crosses, with one exception, can only be established by comparisons with metalwork and up to a point with manuscripts. It remains in consequence rather vague. The close analogy with metal objects belonging most probably to the beginning of the century leads to the conclusion that the Ossory crosses (Pls. 75–80), chiefly those of Ahenny, and some others of the same group, such as those of Lorrha (Pl. 86), belong at the latest to a period around 750. The Clonmacnois group is dated by the inscription on the Bealin cross and belongs to the last decade of the century.[1] These are the only more or less fixed points. The other crosses can be grouped around these, but it would be hard to say to which part of the eighth century they belong or whether they have in some cases been carved in the early years of the ninth century. We have tried to gather here everything which belongs to the eighth-century *style*, even though some examples may not belong to the century as defined in terms of absolute chronology.

Some of the best preserved crosses, those of Kilclispeen (Ahenny) (Pls. 76–80), Kilkieran (Pl. 78), Killamery (Pl. 67), Kilrea (Pl. 75), and the pillar of Tibberaghny (Pl. 83), are scattered about in the rolling fertile countryside of South-West Ossory[2] over which stands the low dome of Slievenamon, the mountain haunted by the mythical hunts of Finn-mac-Cool. With these are connected in style the two ruined crosses of Lorrha, much farther to the north-west, near the Shannon, a re-used base at Mona Incha (the Céli-Dé hermitage of Loch-Cré; Pl. 80),[3] the South cross of Clonmacnois (Pl. 84), the base at Seir

---

[1] F. Henry, 'L'inscription de Bealin', *R.A.*, 1930, pp. 111 sqq.

[2] See: Henry, *Sc. irl.*, pp. 164–5, and H. M. Roe, *The High Crosses of Western Ossory* (Kilkenny, 1958); also, for the various sites, W. Carrigan, *The History and Antiquities of the Diocese of Ossory* (Dublin, 1905).

[3] Henry, *Sc. irl.*, p. 106; an eleventh- or twelfth-century cross has been stuck in that base which is fairly certainly older.

Kieran,[1] a small cross on the shore of Waterford Harbour,[2] and fragments at Ferns and Taghmon (Wexford).[3]

They nearly all have the same elaborate structure. From whatever angle you consider them, they offer to the eye a complex perspective of mouldings and well-organized planes. In all of them the sides are marked by a play of deep vertical grooves cutting into the relief. All this owes much to metalwork: they are really processional crosses or reliquary crosses turned into stone monuments. The big rope mouldings seem to be there to cover the joints of sheets of bronze; the bosses play the part of glass or enamel studs covering the riveting of the two sides. And as happens with most metal objects at that time, not a square inch of the surface remains unadorned; ornaments run on the stone, covering it like embroidery. Either they are each confined to a separate panel or, more often, various patterns merge into each other, the spiral becoming an interlacing, the interlacing blossoming suddenly into animal heads. There are very simple weavings of threads, spirals with foliage patterns nearly identical to those on the Tara brooch and the Lagore belt-buckle, and, on some crosses, a great profusion of step-patterns and key-patterns. Though there are monster heads, animal-interlacing proper, which occupies such a prominent place in some of the manuscripts and on some of the metal objects, is found only once, on the Kilkieran cross (Fig. 26), under the guise of a cruciform arrangement of four animals. This links these crosses with some objects like the Moylough belt, where animal-interlacing is absent and which belong probably to an early part of the eighth century and possibly even with the Echternach Gospels, devoid of zoomorphic ornament. On the South cross at Clonmacnois there is a panel of foliage inhabited by birds and climbing animals. We shall see another vegetable motif on the Old Kilcullen cross (Pl. 74). This derives from Mediterranean models, possibly through some ivory carving.

On some of these crosses, at Ahenny, at Kilkieran, and probably at

---

[1] *J.R.S.A.I.*, 1937, p. 294.

[2] On Great Island, on the Wexford side of the estuary. This cross is still unpublished. I am indebted to Liam de Paor for showing me photographs of it.

[3] Henry, *Sc. irl.*, Pl. 97.

Lorrha, the cross itself is covered with decorative patterns, spirals or interlacings, and it is only on the bases that figured scenes are carved. They take a special importance on the base of the North cross at Ahenny which is covered with cavalcades and processions. Still on the Kilrea and Killamery crosses, where step-patterns occupy an important place, there are figured scenes, very confused and worn, on the cross itself and at the ends of the arms. The South cross at Clonmacnois has a Crucifixion on one side of the shaft. All these scenes are carved in very low relief on two planes, practically without modelling.

To this group of crosses are strongly connected a few fragments from the Scottish monastery of 'Nova Ferna', at Tarbat (Ross-shire),[1] which was probably a cell of the abbey of Ferna (Ferns), in Wexford. They are the broken pieces of a cross which, in the type of the patterns and their execution, comes curiously near to the Ahenny crosses. The chiselled treatment of the spirals is so identical that one may wonder if we are not faced with the work of the same sculptor who may have been called from Ireland to the new foundation in Scotland. In this case the cross had definitely a funerary character indicated by the wording of a beautiful Latin inscription carved in relief[2] where Romilly Allen read the name of that Reothaide or Reodaide, 'Ab[bat] Ferna', whose death is mentioned in the Annals of Ulster at the year 762 and in the Annals of Tigernach at 763. If this reading is not, as Macalister says,[3] 'wishful thinking', this inscription would give an interesting confirmation of the hypothesis placing this series of Irish crosses in the middle of the century.

A similar treatment of figured scenes carved in flat, though slightly higher, relief is found on the cross at Moone and that at Old Kilcullen. The cross at Moone (Pls. 68, 70–72) is one of the strangest and most

[1] Allen–Anderson, III, pp. 94–5, Fig. 96, 96A; the fragment with the inscription appears to be too thick to have belonged to a slab (12 by 6½ in). Other fragments, probably from slabs, were also found from time to time in the graveyard at Tarbat (Ibid., pp. 88 sqq.). One of them has also a pattern of spirals of a type very unusual in Scotland.

[2] It is to be noted that the inscription on the Bealin cross (see p. 143), completely different as to the lettering itself, has also raised letters.

[3] Macalister, *Corpus*, I, p. 489.

impressive of the whole series.[1] Its base is a very elongated pyramid continued by a long, square-sectioned shaft. Ornaments here are given little space. They are replaced by panels of figured scenes or animals, treated in a violent style where square bodies, sometimes devoid of arms, carry enormous heads, where uncompromisingly geometrical shapes are involved in expressive gesticulation. Some of these figures, the apostles especially (Pl. 71), recall the human-shaped enamelled handles of hanging bowls and can hardly be very different in date. The animals carved on the shaft of the cross (Pl. 81) have parallels on the pillar of Tibberaghny (Pl. 83) which also bears a disc of spirals exactly similar to those on the Ahenny crosses. The whirl of monsters which occupies the centre of the cross on one side has very near analogies on the Dromiskin (Pl. 82) and Killamery crosses (Pl. 67). So the cross at Moone is closely connected with eighth-century work.[2] Its strangeness comes mostly from the very genius of the sculptor and to a certain extent from the unyielding granite in which it is cut as this has dictated the economy of detail of all the panels.

The Old Kilcullen cross (Pls. 73–74) is now reduced to a block of nearly square section which shows at the top the beginnings of an attenuation corresponding probably with the crossing itself. There does not seem to have been a circle connecting the arms. The panels are again carved in a flat, low relief but without quite the wild undertone of the Moone cross. The base of a cross near Bray (Wicklow) has the same general shape as the base of the Moone cross. Its carvings are now hopelessly defaced, but there seems to have been a Crucifixion, the Sacrifice of Abraham and Daniel in the lions' den.[3]

A whole series of crosses carved in the same granite, at Castledermot, Saint Mullins (Tech Moling), Ullard, etc., will carry on in the same

---

[1] It was first studied in detail by Margaret Stokes ('Notes on the High Crosses of Moone, Drumcliff, Termonfechin and Killamery', *Trans. R.I.A.*, 1896–1901, pp. 542 sqq.); see also: W. Hawkes, 'The High Cross of Moone', *Repertorium Novum*, 1955, pp. 228 sqq.

[2] In the first edition of this book I suggested a date in the ninth century for the Moone cross, but since then, I have been struck by its many connections with eighth-century art. For a later dating, see: Paor, *E.C. Ireland*, pp. 149–50.

[3] Henry, *Sc. irl.*, Pl. 97, 1, 6; *J.R.S.A.I.*, 1959, p. 97 and Pl. VII (L. Price).

neighbourhood right into the ninth century this same style of flat relief carvings, but with an infinitely more complex iconography.

A slightly later group, dated by the inscription on the Bealin cross, seems to be the product of a Clonmacnois workshop (Pls. 88, 91–95). It consists of five pillars and fragments of crosses and a complete cross with circle. Most of them are not in their original position. In the eighteenth century, the deserted ruins of the monastery of Clonmacnois seem to have supplied the whole neighbourhood with garden ornaments. This explains why a cross, which is marked on a seventeenth-century plan of Clonmacnois[1] in the south-east part of the graveyard, is now about 15 miles away, on a hillock above the entrance gate of Bealin House. A carved pillar which is probably the stem of a cross was taken in the same fashion to Banagher (it is now in Dublin Museum). One may wonder whether the pillar (turned into a fountain) which used to be in a garden near Roscrea, and is now opposite the doorway of Roscrea's Catholic church, has not a similar origin, though it may have originated in Roscrea itself or the neighbouring monastery of Mona Incha (Loch-Cré).[2] Two other pillars are still in Clonmacnois (one of them usually referred to as 'the north cross') and a fragment of a cross probably devoid of circle was discovered during the repair works of the monastery in 1957.

The Bealin cross has an Irish inscription carved in raised characters on one of the panels of the cross: OROIT AR TUATHGALL LAS DERNATH IN CHROSSA (Pray for Tuathgall who caused this cross to be made). The Annals give the year 810 or 811 for the death of Tuathgall, Abbot of Clonmacnois.[3] The name Tuathgall, differing linguisti-

[1] J. Ware, *De Hibernia et Antiquitatibus ejus Disquitiones* (London, 1658), p. 304; the cross is indicated in the south-east part of the graveyard, south-east of Temple Rí; the Cross of the Scriptures is marked in its normal place. There is no indication either of the North or South cross; there is an adaptation of this plan in Brash, *Eccles. Arch.*, Pl. 25, where the cross is No. 14. The demesnes of Tynan and Caledon (Armagh and Tyrone) were decorated in the same way with crosses taken from neighbouring graveyards.

[2] It was bought at Rockforest, about one mile from Mona Incha, and preserved for a long time nearby, at Timoney Park, before being moved to Roscrea around 1935–40.

[3] See note, p. 139.

cally from the more common Tuathal, is found only once in the Annals. It seems obvious, as a result, that the cross was erected by Abbot Tuathgall who seems to have governed the monastery of Clonmacnois from 798 to 810 or 811. The wording of the inscription implies that it was erected in his lifetime. The beginning of his rule seems a likely time for such an addition to the decoration of the monastery. Given the close similarities between this monument and the others, the whole group is likely to belong to the late eighth century.

Except the Bealin cross, whose shape is perfectly normal,[1] they are all odd fragments of monuments whose complete appearance it is now hard to conjure up. Three of them have one undecorated side (the North cross of Clonmacnois, one of the small Clonmacnois pillars and that of Roscrea). They are all about 15 inches wide, but their thicknesses vary, and anyway it would be hard to imagine the two small ones arranged on top of each other to balance the height of the highest one (the North cross), otherwise it would be tempting to see in them the two sides of the frame of a rectangular door. In the present state of our knowledge all one can do is to point out their kinship. New discoveries may one day enable us to understand their original purpose. As for the fragment now in Dublin Museum, it seems to be the shaft of a rather flat cross.

The whole appearance of these monuments is different from that of the crosses of the Ahenny group: the mouldings have hardly any relief and the whole surface is kept as flat as possible, an outlook which comes closer to that of the Moone carvings than to the Ahenny type of cross. The lavish use of ornaments and their lace-like appearance is, however, more in keeping with the second group. They are very fine interlacings, spirals of complicated designs, and also animal-interlacings; to these are added figured scenes showing hunting riders and dragons.

These hunting scenes (Pls. 94, 95, Fig. 18) are carved with an extraordinarily sensitive feeling for flattened but modulated relief, and an almost fierce elegance of design which brings them very close to many

[1] H. S. Crawford, 'Bealin Cross, Twyford, County Westmeath', *J.R.S.A.I.*, 1907, pp. 320 sqq.; Id., 'The Early crosses of East and West Meath', *J.R.S.A.I.*, 1926, pp. 1 sqq.

of the little figures included in the text of the Book of Kells. Although they have a more sculptural quality than the corresponding scenes of the Scottish slabs and are also more static in presentation, they have in common with Scottish art a method of composition of which we have hardly seen any example so far and which is practically unique in Western art at this time: animals and figures are placed one above the other without any indication of ground or perspective, each fitting exactly in the space left by the others. It is an art of infinite skill where only an extreme precision in the drawing of the outlines allows the building of perfectly balanced compositions. This type of arrangement is found in Late Antique mosaics where the figures are often scattered about the surface in the same way.[1] A similar system is also found on large silver Byzantine dishes. It is a curious coincidence that in both cases the subject is often a lion or boar hunt, but this is not necessarily evidence that the Insular artist borrowed his motifs from mosaics, or even from silver plate which he was more likely to know. This is really a very old Oriental method of composition, found already on Assyrian reliefs. Celtic artists had imitated it before. The silver cauldron from Gundestrup, which was made by Gaulish artists about the first century B.C., shows some examples of a similar scattering of figures on a surface.[2] Thus it would be difficult to decide whether the Irish and Scottish compositions really go back to traditional themes, transmitted over centuries, or whether they are imitated from silver dishes brought to the West from the eastern Mediterranean, as were the large dishes in the Sutton Hoo grave. The combined effect of the two orders of model, one reinforcing the other, can not be completely ruled out.

The close connection between the Irish and Scottish monuments is made more obvious by the occasional use of nearly identical motifs in both. One of them is the arrangement of interlacings ending in two busts of human figures shaking hands: these are found on a slab at Saint Andrews[3] and on the Banagher pillar, as well as in some of the initials of the Book of Kells. The Irish monuments have in fact other

[1] See for example a mosaic from Antioch, Morey, *E.C. Art*, Fig. 31.
[2] O. Klindt-Jensen, 'The Gundestrup Bowl', *Antiquity*, 1959, pp. 161 sqq.
[3] Henry, *Sc. irl.*, Fig. 132, p. 165.

L

parallels of which there is no equivalent in Scotland: some of the Clonmacnois dragons recall in their general outline the animals carved on English monuments in the Museums of Durham and Derby.[1] The connections between Ireland and the north of England in the time of Alcuin may explain these similarities.

These rhythmic compositions are very close to animal-interlacings. This is shown clearly by one of the sides of the North cross where a series of monsters are placed on the surface according to the general lines of a plait, though the arrangement has not the rigid composition of a real interlacing. Some of these beasts have strangely flattened snouts, which are also seen in the dragons with foliated tails. The two lions of the recently discovered cross-fragment are of the same type and they are also not far from forming an interlacing. Again, they have close parallels in some of the small initials of the Book of Kells. The shaft of the Bealin cross is covered by a pattern which brings us to the inter-lacing proper, of the type which simulates a vegetable scroll (Fig. 25). This, and another animal-interlacing on the side of the Banagher pillar, is very close to what is found in illumination.

The similarities between Irish crosses and slabs from the east of Scotland can be explained by the constant inter-communication which existed at the end of the eighth century between the Churches of the two countries. But at the same time in the part of Scotland which was in fact Irish territory, in Iona and its neighbourhood, one finds crosses which, although very close to the Irish ones, differ from them up to a point. (Pls. 85, 96). The general layout is the same in both cases: there are crosses with a circle, though some have none, crosses made of several pieces, central discs as on the Bealin cross, bosses in relief. But the spirals generally swell up into half-spheres and figured scenes are inserted in the ornament. The Virgin and Child between angels, a subject never treated by Irish sculptors, appears twice (in Iona and Islay). Altogether it is a baroque art with deep hollows, violent relief, rather different in spirit from the flattened treatment of most of the Irish carvings, and it is closely connected from this point of view with some exceptional

[1] Kendrick, *A.-S. Art*, Pl. XLVII.

East Scottish monuments such as the Saint Andrews' sarcophagus and the slab at Nigg.[1]

If we try to sum up the elements of the figured decoration of all the monuments we have examined, they fall clearly into two groups: on the one hand, familiar and easily identified scenes of Christian iconography, on the other, war and hunting scenes, with horsemen, hounds pursuing their prey, processions of horses, and sometimes the passing of a dragon, a griffin, some fantastic creature.

Most of the scenes of traditional iconography belong to the series of the Help of God, prefaced by the Fall, as the cause which made the Redemption necessary, and the killing of Abel, prefigure of the Crucifixion, scenes which are found already on the sarcophagi of the fourth and fifth centuries in Gaul and Italy. One finds thus: Daniel in the lions' den on the base of the South cross at Ahenny, Adam and Eve and perhaps the murder of Abel, the sacrifice of Abraham, the three young Hebrews in the fiery furnace and Jonah and the whale on the base at Seir Kieran, Adam and Eve again and perhaps the murder of Abel on the base of the South cross at Clonmacnois. Both at Killamery and Kilrea, on the ends of the arms of the cross, there are scenes distributed in four small compartments where one can identify Jacob wrestling with the angel and the sacrifice of Abraham. The Templeneirey cross has a few very worn scenes, one of which is nearly certainly the murder of Abel. On the base of one of the Lorrha crosses, Noah calls the animals into the Ark.[2]

As all these subjects will reappear on the ninth- and tenth-century crosses, treated in greater detail and accompanied by others which complete them, it will be easier to deal with them in detail in the second part of this study of Irish art. It is enough to point out here that the types of the Help of God from the Old Testament are enumerated in the conclusion of the Martyrology of Oengus,[3] which means that they were known in Irish literature in the eighth century; one may assume that the

---

[1] C. Mowbray, 'Eastern Influence on Carvings at St Andrews and Nigg', *Antiquity*, 1936, pp. 428 sqq.
[2] See: Henry, *Sc. irl., passim*.　　　　　[3] Stokes, *Martyr. Oengus*, pp. 283 sqq.

corresponding pictures had reached Ireland in the form of paintings or ivories, and that these inspired the sculptors.

The Crucifixion to which this series of scenes leads up is represented twice on slabs and three times on high crosses (Killamery cross, South cross at Clonmacnois, base of the Moone cross). While Christ is represented unclothed on the Duvillaun and Inishkea slabs, on the crosses he wears a long garment as on the Athlone metal plaque. This most probably shows the influence of models of different origin, and not necessarily a great difference in date, as the two types seem to exist nearly side by side and certainly at the same dates in Italy and the Near East during the Early Middle Ages.[1] On the Inishkea slab two little crosses are engraved in the upper compartments produced by the meeting of the cross and the frame (Fig. 14). Sometimes angels occupy this part of the picture. One may wonder if the two figures carved above the arms of the interlace cross at Drumhallagh (Fig. 15) are not weeping angels, extremely deformed, but, as we shall see, they may at the same time belong to an entirely different type of iconography. The one feature common to all these representations of the Crucifixion is the presence of the sponge and the lance-bearers, either standing or kneeling; there are never any other attendant figures, not even the Virgin or Saint John. On the slabs the whole composition is engraved; on the crosses it is carved in low relief and on a fairly small scale. Instead of being in the centre of the stone cross as in the later crosses, it is brought down to eye level either on the shaft or on the base and limited by a rectangular frame like a picture. As for the large figure which is carved in the centre of the arms of the Moone cross, it is probably meant for a Christ in glory. At Carndonagh also the large figure surrounded by four small ones does not seem to be meant for a Crucifixion, but probably also represents Christ in glory,[2] blessing with his right hand.

Scenes from the life of Saint Anthony, the first hermit of the Egyptian

---

[1] P. Thoby, *Histoire du Crucifix des Origines au Concile de Trente* (Nantes, 1959), ch. II; J. D. Martin, 'The dead Christ on the Cross in Byzantine art', *Late Classical and Medieval Studies in Honor of A. M. Friend, Jr.* (Princeton, 1955), pp. 189 sqq.; K. Wessel, 'Die Entstehung des Crucifixus', *Byzant. Zeit.*, 1960, pp. 95 sqq.

[2] See note, p. 128.

desert, patron and model of monastic life, are sometimes put alongside the biblical ones. The meeting of Saint Paul and Saint Anthony is probably represented on the end of one of the arms of the Killamery cross, but it is at Moone, where the figures are on a larger scale and in better condition, that it can be studied properly (Pls. 71, 72). There, the two saints are seated face to face, on two chairs with high backs ending in animal heads; they hold between them the round loaf which they will have to divide; the bird which brought it still hovers above, enormous. The temptation of Saint Anthony is represented by a little abbreviated figure of the saint standing between two nondescript creatures with animal heads. Lower down, a panel of monsters may be an allusion to the lions which buried Saint Paul the Hermit, but may be simply an effort to create a suitable atmosphere: the desert in the Middle Ages is the abode of monsters, dragons, all sorts of terrifying creatures. In the *Life of Saint Paul of Thebes* (Saint Paul the Hermit) by Saint Jerome, a centaur hovers in its precincts, and the sentence: 'those deserts so fertile in monsters', gives the keynote to these phantasies.[1] These incredible beasts may well be a means of indicating, as by a sign-post: 'desert'. After this hint of local colour, the artist, who has only a dim notion of the reality of what he is describing, feels quite justified in showing his two anachoretes sitting on incongruously sophisticated chairs.

The sequence of the panels at Moone is of great interest. They have to be read starting from the east side and, at first, going from top to bottom: Adam and Eve, the sacrifice of Abraham, Daniel in the lions' den; then, on the south side: the three young Hebrews in the fiery furnace (Pl. 70), followed by the Flight into Egypt (Pl. 72), and the five loaves and two fishes which are an abbreviated version of the Multiplication. So there is first the Fall, followed by three of the most commonly represented Old Testament examples of the help given by God to the faithful and by two examples of his protection in the New Testament. On the west side comes the Crucifixion accompanied by a

---

[1] Compare the inscription on the Ruthwell cross: 'Salvatorem Mundi bestiae et dracones cognoverunt in deserto' (beasts and dragons recognized the Saviour of the World in the desert), Allen–Anderson, III, p. 444.

representation of the twelve apostles (Pl. 68) – the outcome of this elliptic summary of the Redemption which gets its final touch from the representation of Christ in glory in the upper part of the monument. Then come the panels of the life of Saint Anthony, symbolizing the contemplative life. This clear and well-thought-out series has to be read by turning around the cross clockwise, or more exactly by 'showing it one's right', an expression which occurs over and over again in the epic tales where 'showing one's left side' is a sign of hostility and malediction.

This programme has some points in common with that governing the arrangement of the scenes on the cross at Ruthwell (Dumfries-shire):[1] there also the Crucifixion is placed very low on the cross; there is a representation of the Flight into Egypt, a scene very rarely found on Insular crosses, and a panel accompanied by an identifying inscription[2] shows Saint Paul and Saint Anthony face to face, holding the bread between them, but this time they are standing up. Apart from these few points and its slender shape, the Ruthwell cross is very different from the monument at Moone, as to the general iconographical programme and even more the style of the figures. It seems to be a striking example of the parallelism which we mentioned at the beginning of this study of the crosses.

The cross of Old Kilcullen, the only other cross which has well preserved biblical representations does not seem to follow such a strictly defined programme. The twelve apostles are distributed in three panels one above the other. The rest, except for two panels representing Samson and the lion and David and the lion respectively, is more difficult to interpret. The most interesting composition shows an ecclesiastic holding an axe in one hand and in the other a crozier whose end rests on a small recumbent figure; a book and a bell fill the remaining space, as on one of the Carndonagh pillars, and combine to emphasize the ecclesiastical quality of the person represented. This panel has been interpreted as depicting a scene in the life of Mac Tail, the local

[1] Allen–Anderson, III, pp. 442 sqq.

[2] 'Scs Paulus et Antonius eremitae fregerunt panem in deserto' (Saint Paul and Saint Anthony hermits broke bread in the desert), Allen–Anderson, III, loc. cit.

saint and founder of the monastery; it might just as well show an episode in the breaking down of idols.

In fact this figure holding a crozier supplies a good introduction to so many similar figures in even more enigmatic scenes which we shall now have to consider. It is a good scheme to approach them by the study of the base of the North cross at Ahenny, where the carvings are comparatively well preserved. The four sides bear one scene each. That on the west side appears at first glance as the most important (Pl. 79), and its symmetrical composition is striking. It might very well represent, as Helen Roe has suggested,[1] the Mission of the Apostles, Christ holding a book occupying the centre, between two groups of three apostles, each holding a crozier, or better a shepherd's crook, and wearing cloaks with hoods, the costume of the traveller. The panel on the north side (Pl. 79) shows two figures in a chariot drawn by prancing horses and preceded by two horsemen. We shall meet these chariots again and these horsemen sometimes hunting a deer or surrounded by dragons. These hunting pictures have pagan antecedents, but in the hands of the Christian artist they have of course taken on a completely different significance, or perhaps several interchangeable meanings. Saint Columbanus probably gives us the key to these allegories and their imprecisions when, adapting the Paulinian simile of the Christian-athlete, he writes to Bonifacius IV: 'From that moment when the Son of God deigned to become Man, and riding over the sea of nations on those two most fiery steeds of the Spirit of God – I mean the apostles Peter and Paul –, . . . , disturbed many waters and increased with countless thousands of people the fleet of his chariots, himself the highest Charioteer of his own carriage, who is Christ, the true Father, the Herd of Israel, over the channels' surge, over the dolphins' backs, over the swelling flood, reached even unto us.'[2] So this panel at Ahenny is probably yet another allegorical image of the spread of Christianity

[1] *Western Ossory*, p. 19.
[2] *Epistulae* V; Walker, *S. Columbani Op.*, p. 48; in the ninth century, Sedulius Scottus will write of his four Irish companions in Liége as 'quadrigae Domini, Scottensis gloria gentis' (the four chariot-horses of God, the glory of the Irish race), *Carm.*, II, 33.

151

and shows Christ and the apostles riding through the world in search of souls, perhaps even riding the seas towards Ireland.[1]

The south panel (Pl. 80) has a scene tragically described which may yet form part of the same programme: a horse carries a naked and decapitated body, the legs falling on each side of the neck, the arms hanging inert. Ravens are attacking it. A man who follows the horse is holding a round object, the head of the dead man. Leading the procession walks an ecclesiastic carrying a cross and followed by a man with a crozier. We have here a realistic representation of a sight which was not alien to the world where the sculptor lived. In the epics as in Irish history, any vanquished man is decapitated. But his head is usually brought back as a trophy by the victor who carries it hanging from his waist or hidden in a bag. That head and body should here be brought together may give some hint of the real significance of the scene: it probably depicts the transfer of a holy body and of relics brought in solemn procession.[2] Are we to assume that it is necessarily those of a decapitated saint?[3] Or is decapitation to be taken here as simply a symbol of death and martyrdom?

The east side (Pl. 83) is rather strange: it shows a man under a palm tree of which he is holding the trunk while in front of him there are a number of wild animals, passing and fighting, which do not seem to be aware of his presence. Are they a personification of his passions or merely, as we have suggested à propos of the Moone cross,

[1] The only subject, in the carvings of the sarcophagi, which includes a chariot is the meeting of Saint Philip and the queen's eunuch. But it differs in several ways from the Ahenny panel. See: G. Wilpert, *I sarcofagi cristiani antichi*, I (Rome, 1929), pp. 25 sqq.; Pls. XXI–XXIV.

[2] For processions transporting relics, see a Byzantine ivory (D. Talbot Rice, *The Art of Bzyantium* (London, 1959), Pl. 70), or, at a later date the fresco depicting the transfer of the relics of Saint Clement in the church of San Clemente in Rome (Wilpert, *R. Mosaiken*, IV, Pl. 239).

[3] The original name of Ahenny was Kilclispeen or Kilcrispeen – the church of Crispin. It may be pure coincidence that Saint Crispin and his brother Crispinian are supposed to have been beheaded (*AA. SS. Boll.*, Oct., Vol. XI). Still, it is in the seventh century that their relics were enshrined at Soissons in a shrine made by Saint Eligius, and their fame was great in all the region of Northern France where Irish monks used to travel (for the enshrinement, see *Vita Eligii* (*M.G.H., Sc. R. Mérov.*, II, p. 373).

the emblem of the 'desert' as imagined by those who have never seen it, in other words is this a temptation scene or does the little figure under the palm tree represent a hermit in his retreat? This is far from unlikely and would complement in a fairly satisfactory way the three other images; the whole series would then illustrate the spreading of the Faith, ascetic life in the desert and the part played in the Church by martyrs and their relics. Going still further, one may wonder, as loading an image with several related meanings is a normal process of thought at the time, if at the same time these are not illustrations of the three types of martyrdom enumerated in the 'Cambrai Homily', a text in Irish of the beginning of the eighth century preserved in a manuscript of the Municipal Library of Cambrai (Ms. 619) : 'There are three kinds of martyrdom which are counted as a cross to man, that is to say, white martyrdom, and green martyrdom, and red martyrdom. This is the white martyrdom to man, when he separates for the sake of God from everything he loves, although he suffers fasting or labour thereat. This is the green martyrdom to him, when by means of them (fasting and labour) he separates from his desires, or suffers toil in penance and repentance. This is the red martyrdom to him, endurance of a cross or destruction for Christ's sake, as has happened to the apostles in the persecution of the wicked and in teaching the law of God.'[1]

These scenes have a very abbreviated equivalent on the cross at Dromiskin (Louth) (Pl. 81) where on one side a horseman is hunting a stag while on the other a horse carries a decapitated body in the same way as at Ahenny; a man walks in front holding the head and is received with open arms by another figure. So it looks as if the cavalcade of horsemen and chariots could be equated in some way with the stag hunt which probably means Christ pursuing a soul.[2] The two arms of the

---

[1] A. Tardif, 'Fragment d'homélie en langue celtique', *Bibl. École des Chartes*, 1852, pp. 193 sqq.; H. Zimmer, *Glossae Hibernicae* (Berlin, 1881), pp. 213 sqq.; Dom Louis Gougaud, O.S.B., 'Les conceptions du martyre chez les Irlandais', *Rev. bénédictine*, 1907. This point of view is not entirely new. The notion that a pious life and mortification are equivalent to martyrdom is found inter alia in Saint Jerome (*Vita Paulae*, ch. XXXI) and Sulpicius Severus (*Epist.*, II, IX and XII).

[2] The stag 'thirsting for running waters' is a constant emblem of the faithful in Early Christian art, but in medieval symbolism it can also represent the sinner, as

Killamery cross[1] have very worn carvings from which one can still guess at the presence of a more elaborate version of the same themes: stag hunt on one side, on the other, figures in a chariot, preceded by a man carrying a cross: so there seems to be a perpetual shifting from one scene to the other and it is essential to refrain from too much precision in their definition and interpretation. With these representations one should probably connect the friezes of horses or horsemen on the bases of the crosses at Kilkieran and Lorrha and the South cross of Clonmacnois and the figure seated between two horses or horsemen on the Kilrea cross.

In the Clonmacnois–Bealin group, traditional iconography disappears completely and we are faced again with strange hunting-scenes where there appear sometimes dragons with foliated tails and all sorts of monsters; in one case there is also a deer caught in a trap (Pl. 92). The Christian significance of all this is clearly indicated by the fact that one of the horsemen carries a crozier (Pl. 94) while another is accompanied by a three-lobed knot, emblem of the Trinity (Fig. 18). So this too applies the same complicated symbolism of the hunt, essentially Christian in inspiration, a symbolism which was not unknown in other parts of Christendom, as witness a few monuments: a sarcophagus in the Museum of Cordoba,[2] a slab in Narbonne Museum[3] and some Merovingian sarcophagi.[4] But in Ireland it seems to have been elaborated more fully and to have been appreciated very specially.

---

it does in this text of the *Hortus Deliciarum*: 'The chase of the Christian is the conversion of sinners. These are represented by hares, by goats, by wild boars, or by stags. These beasts . . . we pursue . . . with dogs when we arouse their fears by preaching of the word.'

[1] Henry, *Sc. irl.*, Fig. 89, p. 117.

[2] Sarcophagus in Cordoba Museum: A. Kingsley Porter, *Spanish Romanesque Sculpture* (Florence and Paris, 1928), I, Pl. 5; see also a sarcophagus in the cathedral of Civita Castellana: A. Haseloff, *Die Vorromanische Plastik in Italien* (1930), p. 56.

[3] For the Narbonne slab, see: M. Durliat, op. cit., *Études mérov.*, Pl. IV (right).

[4] E.g. the 'Castor and Pollux sarcophagus' from the cemetery of Saint Sernin, Toulouse (Le Blant, *Les sarcophages chrétiens de la Gaule* (Paris, 1886), No. 151; for a slightly different type of 'hunting' sarcophagus, see: Ward-Perkins, *Sculpt. of Visigothic France*, p. 98.

One of the reasons for this popularity may be that the purely formal aspects of these representations is likely to be of pagan origin. The engraved bone of Lough Crew which bears a fragment of deer hunt is a clear indication of it (Pl. 7). It is probably a case of transfer of familiar images similar to the adaptation of Hermes into the Good Shepherd in the catacomb paintings. The predominance of the stag and the horse, the two Celtic animal-shaped divinities which appear most frequently in Gallo-Roman carvings suggests it strongly. A confirmation is given by a panel from the North cross of Clonmacnois which shows a figure with crossed legs similar in its attitude to the two enamelled figures which act as handle fasteners to the Irish bucket found in the Norwegian grave of Oseberg (Pl. 91). It has on each side of the head a bunch of interlacing or antlers which brings it very close to the representations on Gaulish monuments of Cernunnos, the god of plenty, who is shown with crossed legs and stag's horns.[1] One may also wonder if the two figures in the upper compartment of the Drumhallagh slab which seem to bite their thumbs (Fig. 15), are not the result of a strange combination of weeping angels with some traditional figure of Finn-mac-Cool, the seer, biting his 'thumb of wisdom' which allowed him to foresee the future and to know hidden things. The birds on the two Inishkeel slabs, which are obviously swans (Fig. 15), owe something perhaps to the legend of the Children of Lir, turned into swans for many years and finally brought back to human shape by Saint Brendan who baptized them before their death.

Fig. 18.
Hunting scene, Bealin cross (Westmeath).

The animals which are represented on some crosses have connections with these scenes and their general meaning. They are especially remarkable on the pillar at Tibberaghny and on the Moone cross (Pl. 83). The Tibberaghny pillar has a nearly square section and is obviously a broken fragment of a larger monument. It has on one side a disc of spirals very similar to those on the Ahenny crosses. Still the flat mouldings at the corners, like the square section, are more reminiscent of the Moone–Kilcullen type of carvings. The three other sides

[1] R. Lantier, 'Le dieu celtique de Bouray', *Mon. Piot*, 1934, pp. 1 sqq.

bear animals in very light relief, a stag, a quadruped with a human head
and a centaur holding an axe in each hand. The style is animated, with
a great sensitiveness in the tracing of the outlines and the slight
modulations of the relief; there is a curiously humorous feeling for
the comical aspect of some of the beasts, with more than a hint of cari-
cature. They are simply juxtaposed, not combined into patterns as
the animals and figures of the Clonmacnois–Bealin group. Some of the
animals may have been imitated from pictures in Bestiaries. But the
centaur wielding axes is found again on Scottish slabs.[1] There he
sometimes also holds a long, trailing branch, a motif which occurs
already, centuries earlier, on certain Anatolian carvings.[2]

The animals on the high cross and on a smaller, broken cross at
Moone are of the same type and present parallel series: a sort of
sphinx, a dog with long, drooping ears, etc. There also a slightly
ironical touch can be felt in the definition of shapes.

Another remarkable feature of these crosses where animal-interlacing
proper is not common, is the interlacing ending in monster heads
or the pattern of monsters with snake-like bodies. It is found in a mild
form at Ahenny. It occurs in much more vehement versions at Killamery (Pl. 67), on the two crosses at Moone (Pl. 68), at Dromiskin
(Pl. 81) and on a slab at Gallen (Pl. 65). We saw it on metal objects,
specially on the objects from Saint-Germain and on the Ekerö crozier.
There are monsters fighting, swallowing snakes, threatening either
ornamental bosses, or a small figure, or a human head, making up a
swarming, barking and growling zoo. They may still keep something of
old Celtic renderings of devouring monsters of which the Noves beast is
one of the most revolting examples.[3] It happens in fact that this motif
becomes occasionally a representation of Jonah emerging from the
whale and consequently a symbol of the Resurrection. We have seen

[1] Allen–Anderson, Pl. XXXVI (Aberlemno), Pl. XLI and Fig. 234 (Glamis
No. 2), Pl. LXI and Fig. 311 (Meigle No. 2).

[2] In the Phrygian castle of Pazarli, Anatolia (c. 500 B.C.) Hamit Zübeyr Kosay,
Les fouilles de Pazarli (Istambul, 1938).

[3] Varagnac–Fabre, *Art gaulois*, 'Sculpture', Pls. 24–5; H. Hubert, 'Le carnassier
androphage et la représentation de l'océan chez les Celtes', *Congr. inter. arch.*,
Geneva, 1912 (C), pp. 220 sqq.

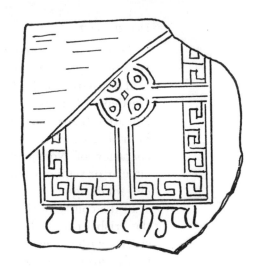

Fig. 19. Grave-slab of Tuathgall,
Clonmacnois (Offaly).

that this is obviously what is to be found on the Ekerö crozier (Pl. 69);
other examples of it are found on Scottish slabs.[1] What the meaning of
the motif was supposed to be when it involved only monsters and snakes,
it would probably be impossible to guess.

A series of monuments of much humbler appearance still remains
to be dealt with. We have seen that, as the high cross was losing its
funerary character, the use of grave-slabs became common.[2] In fact they
are already to be found in the seventh century. A quantity of small slabs
found in Clonmacnois probably go back to that time. They are irregular
in shape and bear a design which is sometimes enclosed in a small
frame. The most usual device is a cross with circular, square or triangular ends. Others have Maltese crosses made of arcs of a circle.
Sometimes a name is engraved quite irregularly on the edge of the
pattern. They are so small that they may well have been placed inside
the grave, under the head of the corpse, as is often the case in Merovingian tombs. Some of the Aran slabs, amongst them that found in
Saint Brecan's grave may have been used in that way, though larger.

[1] Allen–Anderson, III, p. 7 (Bressay) and *passim.*
[2] Lionard, *Grave-Slabs*, p. 156.

This early version of the Irish grave-stones is probably the origin of a type of very small funerary slabs which have been found in the graves of Lindisfarne and of a few Northumbrian monasteries, especially Hartlepool.[1] They are more regular in outline than the Irish stones and are either rectangular or rounded at the top; they bear inscriptions in Irish characters or in runes – a striking illustration of the hybrid character of Northumbrian monasteries. Their crosses have usually circular or semi-circular ends. They are lightly engraved and are of very elegant design.

In the course of the eighth century, crosses of other types appear on the Irish grave-slabs: crosses with hollowed angles, crosses potent, crosses with circles. The slabs become larger and are probably meant to partly cover the tomb. A number have very simply worded inscriptions asking for a prayer for the deceased (OROIT (or $\overline{\text{OR}}$) DO X, or OROIT AR X: pray for x, or: a prayer for x). The inscription is often of very beautiful epigraphy, but accompanies the cross with a certain carelessness, being often thrown across the slab or confined to one corner. Some of the names can be identified in the Annals and as a consequence several monuments can be dated. Amongst these is the funerary slab of Tuathgall (Fig. 19) who caused the Bealin cross to be erected. Its extreme simplicity and its absence of ornaments shows that we are dealing with a much humbler production than the carvings executed at the same date.

[1] C. R. Peers, 'The inscribed and Sculptural Stones of Lindisfarne', *Archaeologia*, 1923–4, pp. 255 sqq.

7. The Decoration of Manuscripts

A.D 650 800

NOTHING IS more difficult than to attempt a summary of the history of Irish manuscript decoration at the end of the seventh and during the eighth century. First of all, only about fifteen manuscripts which show that kind of decoration remain, scattered over a hundred and twenty years or so. This probably represents only a small portion of the production of Irish scriptoria at that time, and whole chapters of their history escape us.[1]

Then there is the difficulty that an Irish origin is really well attested for only a very small number of manuscripts. Even these few do not give us such secure information as would seem at first sight. Books travel only too easily, with or without the consent of their owners. They are borrowed, often for an indefinite term; some of them are small enough to be slipped easily in the pocket or the satchel of a traveller. Copies are made of them and are presented to friends, sometimes far away. It often happens that the copyist transcribes so faithfully the colophon where the first scribe has mentioned his name or the place where he was working, that it becomes difficult to date and localize the new manuscript. Worse still, these indications of origin may be falsified. Altered colophons, erasures, deformed names, are common occurrences. The total indifference of medieval people to historical truth is always to us a disconcerting phenomenon, but where manuscripts are concerned, it assumes overwhelming proportions. They make a virtue of forgery and we are left to fight our way as best we can in a maze of false allegations.

The problem is made more complicated in that to judge a manuscript one has to take into consideration as well as its decoration, its text,

---

[1] Most of the illuminations referred to in this chapter are reproduced in Zimmermann, *Vorkarolingische Miniaturen*.

the characteristics of its script and the way in which its vellum sheets have been prepared and assembled, all highly specialized subjects. For the manuscripts we are going to examine the study of most of the texts has hardly been tackled at all,[1] and that of the script in many cases has not gone beyond the general data given by Lowe in his monumental corpus.[2] This means that we can hardly hope to come to very definite conclusions. The most we can do in the circumstances is to attempt to outline the most plausible hypothesis and to link, up to a point, the decoration of the manuscripts with that of the crosses and the metal objects within the general framework of those of the historical events which are known to us.

The problem has been made even more awkward to handle in recent years by a growing tendency to ascribe to Northumbria manuscripts which had been usually considered as Irish.[3] There can be little doubt that one at least and perhaps several of the manuscripts we are going to study were written at Lindisfarne. To call them 'Northumbrian' or 'Saxon' betrays a warped approach to the history of northern England at that time. Like the Bobbio manuscripts they are too intimate a part of Irish decoration to be cut off from it. Our purpose is to study the development of that type of illumination which has the same characteristics as the other relics of the Irish style which we have been studying, whether the manuscripts where it is found were illuminated in Ireland, in Iona, at Lindisfarne or on the Continent. In so doing we may use the convenient term 'Insular manuscripts' which has become so fashionable in these last years, but without subscribing to the connotations it has sometimes been given.

From the first efforts made by Irish scribes in Ireland or in Bobbio to decorate their manuscripts, we have been able to deduce that already

[1] L. Bieler, 'Insular Palaeography, Recent State and Problems', *Scriptorium*, 1949, pp. 267 sqq.

[2] E. A. Lowe, *Codices Latini Antiquiores*.

[3] See: A. W. Clapham, 'Notes on the Origin of Hiberno-Saxon Art', *Antiquity*, 1934, C. F. Burkitt, 'Kells, Durrow and Lindisfarne', *Antiquity*, 1935; Lowe, *C.L.A.*, II (Great Britain and Ireland, 1935), *passim*; Masai, *Origines de la Miniature dite irlandaise* (1947); *E.Q.C. Lindisfarnensis*, II (1960), *passim*; on these last two publications, see: *Studies*, 1948, pp. 267 and 275 and: *Antiquity*, 1963, pp. 100 sqq.

distinctive features of Irish illumination were beginning to appear,[1] chiefly the tendency to turn initials into curvilinear patterns, whilst surrounding them with dots, and the adoption of the scheme which consists in putting in the beginning of each section of a book a decorative page on the left and an introductory page with large initial on the right – the ornamental page replacing the framed title page which Continental manuscripts of that time had inherited from their Antique prototypes. In these first examples of Irish book-art a majuscule script emerges, which has already become distinct both from the Antique script from which it derives and from the contemporary Continental scripts. All this reappears in a more elaborate form in the manuscripts of a later date.

These manuscripts are of very varied origins. A few of them remained until the end of the Middle Ages in the libraries of Irish monasteries,[2] such as the Book of Durrow, which belonged up to the time of its dissolution in the sixteenth century to the Abbey of Durrow (Offaly) founded by Saint Columba, the Book of Mulling, certainly originating from Tech Moling (Saint Mullins, Carlow), the Stowe Missal which was at Lorrha (Tipperary) in the eleventh century and the 'Book of Dimma' which nearly certainly comes from Roscrea. This is all that can be definitely localized in Ireland for this period.

However, as in the preceding period, the libraries of the Irish foundations abroad help us to reconstruct the picture of what was happening in Ireland itself. Part of the library of Lindisfarne was taken away by the monks when they had to flee in face of the increasing pressure of Scandinavian invasions in the ninth century.[3] After long years of wanderings and a stop at Chester-le-Street, they finally settled at Durham where the Cathedral Library still keeps some of their manuscripts, in particular Ms. A.II.10 and Ms. A.II.17 which may have been originally brought from Ireland to Lindisfarne or may be products of the local scriptorium. Another manuscript of the same origin, the

---

[1] See pp. 58 sqq.

[2] Dom Louis Gougaud, O.S.B., 'Remains of Ancient Irish Monastic Libraries', in *F.-S. M. Néill*, pp. 319 sqq.

[3] *Relics of St Cuthbert* pp. 26 sqq.

Book of Lindisfarne, is now in the British Museum where it came with the Cottonian Library.

Several other manuscripts in English libraries whose presence is attested fairly early in Britain may even so have originally come from Ireland : one of them, the Lichfield Gospels, was already in Wales towards the end of the eighth century, as is shown by several annotations in Welsh which it received at that time. Another, the Rushworth Gospels or Book of Mac Regol, was in the tenth century in the north of England where an interlinear Saxon translation was added to it, but its colophon, for once reliable, attributes it to an abbot of Birr (Offaly). Of the origin of a third, now in very bad condition, of which the fragments are divided between the British Museum and the Library of Corpus Christi College, Cambridge, and of another incomplete Gospel-book which is in Oxford, nothing is known.

Finally the manuscripts from the Library of the Abbey of Echternach, which are now in the Bibliothèque Nationale in Paris and in some German libraries, and some manuscripts from the Abbey of Saint Gall, still in the Cathedral Library, may help us in this effort to reconstruct the appearance of Irish illumination.

Besides these decorated books we shall have to call to witness occasionally a few others where ornament is scanty, such as the Antiphonary of Bangor (Milan, Ambr. Libr., Ms. C.5.inf.), and the copy of the *Vita Columbae* which is in the Town Library of Schaffhausen (Ms. 1). They will supply useful comparisons in regard to script and presentation.

The decorated manuscripts, except two of the Echternach ones, part of the Stowe manuscript and a manuscript in Cologne, are all copies of the Gospels. This in itself is proof of tremendous losses : psalters and hymn books must have been in great demand, but not a single one has reached us. Of these Gospel-books, some are sumptuous manuscripts made for the use of the altar and written in majestic script[1] (mostly majuscule, but in the case of the Echternach Gospels, minuscule).

---

[1] On this distinction, see : E. Lesne, 'Les livres, scriptoria et bibliothèques du commencement du VIIIe à la fin du XIe siècle', *Mémoires et travaux publiés par des professeurs de Facultés catholiques de Lille*, 1938.

Others are books made to be carried easily here and there and were intended for private reading; they are written in a small compressed cursive script involving so many abbreviations that they are often not easy to decipher for the modern reader.[1]

All the luxury Gospel-books have in common the imposing decoration of the first page of each of the Gospels, usually taken up by gigantic initials followed by a few lines of ornamental text and sometimes inscribed in a decorative frame. Even the pocket-books betray a marked effort to give some majesty to this first page.

The page on the left which faces this introductory page is in most cases decorated. Sometimes, as happened already in the Orosius manuscript of the Ambrosian (Pl. 58),[2] it is a 'carpet-page' completely covered with patterns. In addition to this, or instead of it, there is also in the beginning of each of the Gospels, a page with either the symbol of the Evangelist or his 'portrait'. In one manuscript (Durham, Ms. A.II.17), a representation of the Crucifixion replaces it. The beginning of the text following immediately the Genealogy of Christ in the Gospel of Saint Matthew (Matt. I.18) is increasingly treated as if it were the beginning of a book, the monogram of Christ (Chi-Rho) gradually invading the whole page, and a page of ornament sometimes accompanying it to the left.

Ms. A.II.10 of the Cathedral Library at Durham[3] is the most archaic in the style of its ornament of all the manuscripts we shall have to consider, even if it is not absolutely certainly the oldest in date; it has features in common both with the Bobbio manuscripts and with the Book of Durrow which we shall examine later.

[1] The Irish pocket-books have been studied by P. McGurk ('The Irish pocket Gospel Books', *Sacris Erudiri*, 1956, pp. 249 sqq.), see the discussion of some points of this study below; also: F. Henry, 'An Irish Manuscript in the British Museum', *J.R.S.A.I.*, 1957, pp. 147 sqq. These small Gospel-books have no parallels in the West, whilst Byzantine art offers several in the eleventh and twelfth centuries. Earlier examples may have existed and may have been the models of the Irish books.

[2] See pp. 62 sqq.

[3] Mynors, *Durham Manuscripts*, No. 6; Lowe, *C.L.A.*, II, No. 147; C. Nordenfalk, 'Before the Book of Durrow', *Acta Archaeologica*, 1947, pp. 141 sqq.; F. Henry, 'Les Débuts de la Miniature irlandaise', *G.B.A.*, 1950, pp. 5 sqq.

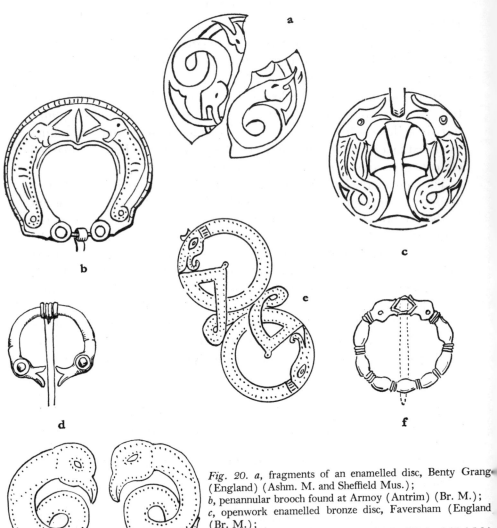

Fig. 20. a, fragments of an enamelled disc, Benty Grange (England) (Ashm. M. and Sheffield Mus.);
b, penannular brooch found at Armoy (Antrim) (Br. M.);
c, openwork enamelled bronze disc, Faversham (England) (Br. M.);
d, penannular brooch found in the North of Ireland (Bel. M.)
e, Durham, Ms. A.II.10, detail of initial (pl. 61);
f, Saxon penannular brooch, Faversham (Br. M.);
g, openwork silver object found in Lough Ravel crannog (Antrim) (Bel. M.).

It is a fragment of a Gospel-book of large size ($14\frac{1}{2}$ inches high), consisting now of only twelve pages (end of Saint Matthew–beginning of Saint Mark) scattered between several volumes (A.II.10, C.III.13, C.III.20; but the decorated pages belong to A.II.10). It is written in two columns, in Irish majuscule. The text is of the mixed Irish type, in which the Vulgate lessons are combined with older recensions, and it shows the erratic spelling characteristic of many Irish manuscripts; a glaring example of it meets the eye in the very first word of the Gospel of Saint Mark: INITITIUM instead of INITIUM.

The transition from one Gospel to the other is all that is left of the decoration. The end of Saint Matthew's Gospel is followed by three large loops of interlacing occupying all the column on the right of the page (Pl. 53),[1] in which are written in red ink, now very faded, the Explicit of Matthew and the Incipit of Mark followed by the Greek text of the Pater written in Latin characters. The text of Saint Mark begins with a decorated capital. All this decoration, which is on a very large scale, is brilliantly coloured. The plaits of ribbon are painted yellow with an overdotting of red. The knots between them and the jambs of the capital are both made of a mosaic of yellow-blue-red-green used so as to get a maximum of different juxtapositions of colours and to avoid repetition as much as possible. The decorative repertoire is very remarkable: there are in the initial the same groups of twin spirals as occurred in the same place in Ms. S.45.sup. of the Ambrosian (Pl. VI). In the corners of the loops, there are two groups of spirals with foliage pattern of the purest Irish type ('trumpet pattern'). The interlacings are not all made of wide ribbons; there are also in the capital twists of fine threads similar to those found in the capitals of the Orosius of Bobbio. The two snakes occupy the same place in the initial as do the fishes of S.45.sup. They are akin also to the animals on the enamelled disc from Benty Grange (Fig. 20). The other capitals in the manuscript are very simple with only a filling of colour and little terminal hooks;

---

[1] Their shape is very singular; given the fact that they mark the transition between the Gospels of Matthew and Mark, one may wonder if they are not meant for a half-uncial M written sideways as often happens in Irish manuscripts when a word is at the end of a line.

they are in the line of the Cathach initials, and like them they are not always surrounded with dots.

This manuscript clearly represents a stage in the decoration of Irish manuscripts later than the Bobbio manuscripts and the Cathach, where the three types of ornament which will form the staple repertoire of later illumination are for the first time found side by side: interlacings (of threads or ribbons), spirals and zoomorphic ornament.

From another aspect also, this manuscript is an important landmark: it shows the Irish majuscule script entering a new phase, very close to what we shall find in the Book of Durrow. In addition to this the end of the text of Matthew is written in a minuscule of which some letters (d, p, q) have strangely contorted shapes for which one could find parallels in some Echternach manuscripts. Two other manuscripts with very little decoration (chiefly initials with dots) supply other examples of seventh-century minuscule script. One is the collection of hymns written down in the middle of the century at Bangor, which was then sent to Bobbio and is known under the name of Antiphonary of Bangor;[1] the other is the copy of Adamnan's *Vita Columbae* made at Iona by Dorbene, no doubt shortly after the completion of the text, that is to say around 685–90 (Schaffhausen Town Libr., Ms. 1).[2] Both are written in a fairly regular rounded minuscule of which the letters are inclined to take on an ornamental appearance.

The Book of Durrow is a comparatively small manuscript of the Gospels (9½ by 6½ in)[3] which is known to have been kept in the monastery of Durrow, near Tullamore (Offaly). We know from an entry in the Martyrology of Donegal and from a mention in Conall Mac Geoghegan's translation of the Annals of Clonmacnois (1627) that in

---

[1] Ambr. Ms. C.5. inf.; Lowe, *C.L.A.*, III, No. 311; Warren, *Antiphonary of Bangor*; see for some foliage pattern in the initials: Henry, *Débuts min. irl.*, p. 23.

[2] Lowe, *C.L.A.*, VII, No. 998; for reproductions of some pages of the text, see: Anderson, *Adomnan*, four plates after p. 176; for reproductions of the initials: Reeves, *St Columba*, Pls. 1, 2.

[3] T. C. D. Library, No. 57 (A.IV.5); *E.Q.C. Durmachensis*; Lowe, *C.L.A.*, II, p. 43 and No. 273 (see corr. in Vol. VI); Zimmermann, III, Pls. 1–5; on the colours, see *E.Q.C. Lindisfarnensis*, II, p. 273 (Werner–Roosen–Runge).

the seventeenth century, after the dissolution of the monastery, it was kept near Durrow by a man who used it to cure sick cattle by dipping it in water which they were made to drink. In 1661, Henry Jones, who had been scoutmaster to Cromwell's army and had become Protestant Bishop of Meath and Vice-Chancellor of Trinity College, came into possession of it and gave it to the College, in whose Library it is still kept.

The text is a version of the Vulgate which includes some Old Latin readings.[1] This is a point which will have to be considered further on.

It is written in a beautiful Irish majuscule of a more evolved type than the script of the Cathach and very close to that of Ms. A.II.10 of Durham. It is already the formal majuscule of altar-books which will reappear, with only some differences, due to the individuality of the scribes and the habits of various scriptoria, in all the great Insular manuscripts.

The Book has a colophon, or better two successive colophons, which, since the re-binding done by Roger Powell, are restored to their original place, on the last page of the Book. The second: 'Ora pro me frater mi d$\overline{ns}$ tecum sit.,', seems to be by the hand of the scribe, and is in consequence the real colophon of the Book.[2] The first has probably been copied from an older manuscript and has been so thoroughly modified by erasures and rewritings that it has lost practically all value. All that can be said about it is that the alterations were made in an Irish and probably Columban milieu where the name of Columba has been arbitrarily added. As for the 'praesbiter Patricius' which it mentions, he has probably nothing in common with Saint Patrick.

The decoration is elaborate and its distribution is methodical. It is made more striking by the fact that few colours are used: a beautiful

---

[1] A. A. Luce in *E.Q.C. Durmachensis*, II; Lawlor, *Cathach*, pp. 259 sqq.; it is so far from being a pure Vulgate text that Wordsworth and White decided not to use it in their collection of Vulgate texts (*Novum Testamentum Latine*, I, p. 10).

[2] On the colophons, see *E.Q.C. Durmachensis*, II, pp. 17 sqq. On the occasion of the publication, that page was examined with all modern means of investigation, and there is very little hope that anything more will ever be known on the subject than what is summed up by Dr Luce.

deep green which is an acetate of copper, a bright yellow (orpiment) and a glowing red which is lead red. Another colour which has faded to a pale brown is used more sparingly. All this stands out sharply on a deep tone of black-brown or sometimes on the ivory colour of the vellum. As in the Durham manuscript and, earlier, in the Bobbio Orosius, dots are an essential part of the decoration, whether they soften the transition between a large initial and the vellum or form a shimmering background for a few lines of ornamented text.

The Book opens by a great double cross outlined against tightly knotted interlacings.[1] The next page bears the four symbols of the Evangelists, each in one of the compartments made by the arms of another cross set in a rectangular frame. The canons of concordance of the Gospels are framed by very narrow bands of interlacing or zig-zag patterns. Then starts a regular scheme of decoration consisting first of a page bearing the symbol of the Evangelist, then of an opening of text similar to that of the Orosius: a purely ornamental composition on the left facing the large initial on the right. The ornaments vary from page to page. On one page, wide ribbons, yellow, red and green, zig-zag and twist on a background of deep black (Pl. 55), on another they are knotted to form a series of circles, further on spirals swirl, whirl and curl and seem so many hanging-bowl discs placed side by side and connected by yet more spirals (Pl. 31). Finally a whole page is made of fantastic animals, sinuous bodies plaited and interwoven together, wan, worm-like heads seizing everything within reach in soft, prehensile jaws. Nearly every page is surrounded by a border of interlacings and these also frame the symbols, which float, isolated, in the middle of a vast field of vellum. The man (Pl. 57), the eagle, the calf and the lion (Col. pl. E), boldly drawn, speckled with dazzling spots of yellow, red and green, are more startling from the contrast with the plain

---

[1] As has been pointed out (op. cit., II (P. Meyer), p. 166, note 8), this recalls the beginnings of Coptic books; see Hyvernat, *Album de paléographie copte* (Paris, 1888), *passim*, and: *Bibliothecae Pierpont-Morgan Codices Coptici photographice expressi, passim*; the colours also (green, yellow, red) are those used in the earliest of the surviving Coptic manuscripts, which go back to the eighth, ninth, tenth centuries.

Opposite: Pl. E. Book of Durrow, symbol page at the beginning of the Gospel of St John

ꝛaluſ arthaʒ ꝼ cimulch indri ꝼ iudnerth. Declenciſ ꝑ Nobiſ epꝭ copuſ te
ſuid ꝼacerdoꝛ teilian· dubnuo. Eccuhelin fili epꝭ· ſaꝛnbiu cum ibien·· et ꝼulʒen
neſ q̄ h̃ fidele ꝛcnꝓꝓit· q̃ cuſtodient h̃ decneꝛ libꝛatꝝ bleidiud ꞁphꝓ ꝑe
q̃ h̃ ncuſtodient· ſit maledioꝭ a d̃o et a taralian· inꝯ euangelio ſcꝛiꝑ q̃ et
ꝛanuꝛ uþ eꝛꝭ fiat··)

surface of skin. All this decoration is ruled by a feeling for the value of reserved spaces, of simplified and easily legible shapes, combined paradoxically with a love of intricacies, of closely interwoven patterns. It achieves effect by a simplicity, a directness of means which is illustrated by the use of a small number of colours and the sharpness of their tones, by the large scale of the ornament, the feeling for balance between a motif and a plain surface. But this stately appearance covers a primitive audacity and the impetus of an art in full course of development, still at the stage of discovery and invention.

In this as in the choice of patterns, the decoration is in full accord with the late seventh-century carvings. The symbol of Saint Matthew on the second page of the Book is represented by a square-cut bust practically identical with the half-figure engraved on the Killeen Cormac pillar (Pl. IV), whilst his full-length figure (Pl. 57), at the beginning of the Gospel, with its square dress, uplifted hair, pointed shoes, is no less reminiscent of the Ballyvourney or Fahan Mura figures (Pls. 50, 54). The analogy of the interlacings is obvious, though it applies more to the ribbon itself than to its tracery proper : the interlace of the Book of Durrow is often loosely woven, with untied loops, sharp or square angles which suggest a comparison with Armenian interlacing. This inconsequent aspect of the interlacing has parallels only in the twists at the foot of one of the crosses on the Fahan slab, and in one of the knots between cross and frame at Carndonagh. Still, in spite of a few differences, the Donegal carvings are the monuments which come closest to the Book of Durrow for this element of the decoration.

It is indeed remarkable that in the Book these interlacings occur only on the carpet-pages or the frames of the Evangelists' symbols. In the initials, there are only spirals and very fine two-strand twists as in the Durham and Bobbio manuscripts. The spirals are often coiled around a patterned centre and are connected by curved triangles with the usual foliage motifs. This is nothing new. It is no more in fact than the stock-in-trade of the enamels transferred to the vellum page, as is shown clearly by the only carpet-page where spirals are used.

There remains to be examined an element which has been discussed ad nauseam, the page opposite the beginning of Saint John's Gospel,

Opposite: Pl.F. Lichfield Gospels, 'portrait' of St Luke

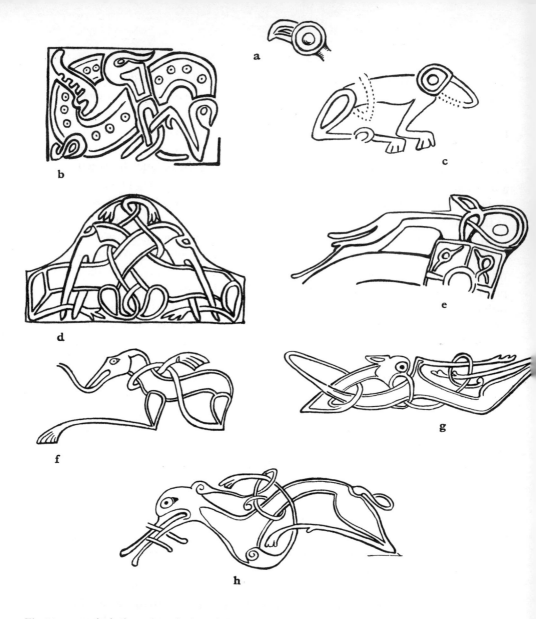

Fig. 21. a, terminal of a penannular brooch found in the North of Ireland (Br. M.);
    b, Scandinavian beast;
    c, animal from the Saxon disc found at Caenby (England) (Br. M.);
    d, Saxon sword pommel from Crundale Down (Br. M.);
    e, terminal of penannular brooch found in Lough Ravel crannog (Antrim)
    (Bel. M.; pl. 62);
    f, Book of Durrow (T.C.D.) detail of a carpet-page (pl. 60);
    g, Cathedral of Cologne, Ms. 213, detail (pl. 63);
    h, Durham, Ms. A.II.17, detail (pl. 62).

with its three different arrangements of the same type of beast. It has been repeatedly compared with the animals found on several Saxon objects, the Crundale Down sword pommel (Fig. 21) (British Museum), the silver disc from Caenby (Fig. 21) (id.), the Sutton Hoo buckle (id.),[1] etc. Recently, Bruce-Mitford has introduced into the debate some hitherto unpublished details of the Sutton Hoo drinking horns.[2] It all boils down to the fact that the 'Durrow animal' is derived from an animal of Bernhard Salin's style II, and more precisely from its Saxon version. So far everybody agrees. Granted that if one does not arrive at the study of illumination after a detailed study of Irish metalwork this Saxon intrusion might seem disconcerting. To some people the bewilderment has been such that they have seen there a reason to think that the Book of Durrow was written in Northumbria – in Lindisfarne probably – and that its decoration is entirely conditioned by Saxon work. It is too easily forgotten that Ireland in the seventh century was flooded by Saxon objects. We have seen what an important place the Saxon inspiration plays in the metalwork of that time and also how freely it is transcribed by Irish artists. We have in the Saint John page of the Book of Durrow just one of these free transcriptions.

Apart from this ornament, the text seemed to several historians to point, as the place of origin of the Book, to a monastery in the orbit of the Northumbrian scriptoria, such as Lindisfarne. It has often been said that its text is similar to that of the Codex Amiatinus and the Lindisfarne Gospels. But the latest research on the subject seems to define it as a version of the Vulgate belonging to a family of Vulgate manuscripts other than the Northumbrian and in no way devoid of pre-hieronymian

[1] To quote only a few landmarks: Salin, *Thierornamentik* (1904), pp. 322 sqq.; Baldwin Brown, *Arts in E. England*, V, Pl. XLII; Smith, *Guide Anglo-Saxon A.* (1923), p. 86; N. Åberg, *The Anglo-Saxons in England* (Uppsala, 1926), pp. 178–9; Henry, *Sc. irl.* (1932), p. 58; Kendrick, *A.-S. Art* (1938), pp. 100–1; Henry, *Irish Art* (1940), p. 198; E.Q.C. *Lindisfarnensis* (1961), II, pp. 111–12. It is to be noted that Åberg in *Occident–Orient* (1943) shows a tendency to stress the differences between the Durrow beasts and those of Salin style II; J. E. Forssänder (Irland–Oseberg), *Bulletin de la Société royâle des Lettres de Lund*, 1943, pp. 130 sqq.) tries to reverse the process, seeing in the Irish animals the origin of the Germanic ones.

[2] E.Q.C. *Lindisfarnensis*, II, pp. 111–12.

171

admixtures.[1] This in a way comes back to Lawlor's estimate that it is a text whose connection with the purest Vulgate texts is of the same order as that of the Cathach with the 'Gallican psalter' of Saint Jerome. Thus its text does not represent a great novelty and from the middle or the end of the sixth century, texts similar to that which was used as model for the Book of Durrow were probably to be found in a few places in Ireland.[2] A sentence from the letter of Saint Columbanus to Gregory the Great comes as a confirmation of this. With his usual violence, he states that: 'Anyone impugning the authority of Saint Jerome will be a heretic or reprobate in the eyes of the Western Churches [Irish, etc.], whoever that man may be; for at all points they repose an undoubted confidence in the Holy Scriptures.'[3] He speaks obviously of the 'Western Churches' as he had left them probably ten or eleven years earlier, at the time of his departure from Bangor in 590. The biblical quotations in the Antiphonary written in this same monastery of Bangor nearly half a century later (c. 650) are already of the 'mixed' Irish type,[4] a fact which points to a fairly long familiarity with the Vulgate text already at that time. The picture which A. A. Luce gives of the Book of Durrow as a Vulgate text surrounded by non-Vulgate elements – preliminaries of a type usually associated with Old Latin versions, symbols of the Evangelists in the Old Latin order (Matthew, John, Mark, Luke)[5] –

[1] A. A. Luce finds points in common with the fragments of an early Vulgate text in Ms. 1395 of Saint-Gall (*E.Q.C. Durmachensis*, II, p. 14), cf. C. H. Turner, *The Oldest Manuscript of the Vulgate Gospels* (Oxford, 1931).

[2] See pp. 26, 60.

[3] *Epistula*, I, Walker, *S. Columbani Op.*, pp. 8–9 (simpliciter enim ego tibi confiteor, quod contra sancti Hieronymi auctoritatem veniens apud occidentis ecclesias hereticus seu respuendus erit, quicumque ille fuerit; illae enim per omnia indubitatam in scripturis divinis accomodant fidem).

[4] The Biblical quotations in Cummian's letter (c. 633, see pp. 29–30) and in the Antiphonary of Bangor (c. 650, see p. 166) are of a 'mixed' type, with in some places a strong Vulgate element; Warren, *Antiphonary of Bangor*, pp. xxxi sqq.

[5] In the first edition of this book (1940), I proposed to see in this order the proof that the Book, perhaps written in a centre in close contact with Northumbria, was illuminated in Ireland by a painter who was familiar only with the Old Latin order of the Gospels (pp. 67–8). This now, after a complete re-evaluation of the problem, seems to me highly unlikely: the Book has to be taken as a whole, and, like the Echternach Gospels, though in a different way, shows the juxtaposition of

172

answers well to what one might expect at that time in Ireland where a centuries-old tradition of Gospel writing would allow for the existence of such fossils. It is in Ireland and not in England that the Vulgate and the earlier biblical translations have been incessantly juxtaposed and mixed from an early date, and the a priori notion that the Vulgate was introduced into Ireland through England in the time of Benedict Biscop is far from being true. This type of text could occur in Lindisfarne also insofar as the scriptorium of Lindisfarne was in fact an Irish scriptorium. But why look for a source abroad when the manuscript fits so perfectly in an Irish atmosphere and was found in an Irish monastery? The region where the monuments closest in style to the Book were carved may also be where it was illuminated. The Columban monastery of Derry, in the close neighbourhood of Fahan and Carndonagh, is a likely place of origin. The manuscript could easily have passed from there to another Columban monastery, that of Durrow. But in fact what do we know of the art which was practised in Durrow itself at that time? Or in Iona, the metropolis of the Columban monasteries?

The date of the manuscript may not be as easy to establish as has been often assumed. The presence on one page of Saxon ornament akin to objects buried in Sutton Hoo around 655, does not prove a great deal after what we have seen on some objects like the Moylough belt, for example. Saxon elements were long-lived in Irish metalwork and the same may well be true of illumination. There has been for a long time a tendency to look upon the Books of Durrow, Lindisfarne and Kells as landmarks in a continuous evolution of Irish painting. This view is probably far too systematic. There may be a Durrow style rather than a Durrow phase, a style developed in the Columban monasteries which were, through their missions in England, in especially close contact with Saxon art. This is made likely by the fact that the two manuscripts

the Vulgate and Old Latin tradition in Ireland. It is to be noted in this context, that the Gospel-Book from Sainte-Croix in Poitiers Library (Ms. 17), which has a Vulgate text, has also the Evangelists arranged around a cross in a non-Vulgate order. It comes from the North of France, probably from Corbie which had close contacts with Ireland. See: Dom. P. Minard, O.S.B., 'L'Evangéliaire oncial de l'abbaye Sainte Croix de Poitiers', *Revue Mabillon*, 1943, pp. 1 sqq. (Like the Maihingen Gospels, it has the poem of Aileran on the Canons.)

where the purest trend of this style is found – the Book of Durrow and Ms. A.II.10 – both belonged to libraries of Columban monasteries, Durrow and Lindisfarne. Quite possibly at the very time when they were being illuminated, in other scriptoria in Ireland, or in what Kenney terms 'greater Ireland', a slightly different style of book-painting was cultivated.

The study of animal-interlacing, or more specifically of the animal involved in it, points in this direction. In other manuscripts, such as the Lindisfarne and Lichfield Gospels, there are little animals of a very different type, usually accompanied by some birds. There exist inter-mediate forms, which would hardly explain the Lichfield animal as derived from that of Durrow. They appear much more as hybrids of two parallel types, in fact, up to a point, nothing more than muddles, as occasionally the animal borrows the long beak of the bird. A manuscript which may be of Insular origin or may have been written on the Continent by an Insular scribe (Cologne Cathedral Library, Ms. 213; *Collectio Canonum*)[1] supplies an example of these hesitations: on its first page (Pl. 63) there are several versions of an animal which has practically the head of the Caenby beasts (Fig. 21, *g*), combined with a body slightly more realistic in definition than that of the Durrow animal. The same manuscript has elsewhere birds which are more or less of the Lichfield–Lindisfarne type (Pl. 101). The aptness in an Irish context of beasts such as those on the first page is amply shown by the penannular brooch from Lough Ravel crannog in Belfast Museum (Pl. 62, Fig. 21, *e*) where they appear cast in bronze. Ms. A.II.17 of Durham supplies another version (Pl. 62), at times nearly bird-like, and variants of this appear in Ms. 197 of Corpus Christi College, Cambridge (Pl. 100), and even in the Gospel-book from the cathedral of Trier (Pl. VI) which originates from a scriptorium related to Echternach. These comparatively late forms (Fig. 21, *h*) show a survival of the Durrow beast more or less in a parallel line with the development of the animal-and-bird theme. It seems in consequence that the origin of the animal-and-bird type has to be sought elsewhere than in the milieu where the Durrow animal originated.

[1] Lowe, *C.L.A.*, VIII, No. 1163; Zimmermann, Pl. 252; Micheli, *Miniature*, p. 47.

Another remarkable feature of the Book of Durrow is the complete absence in its pages of real key-patterns. It has angular motifs, but of the kind which would be easily adapted from the cloisons of glass inlay or champlevé enamel. It lacks the diagonal angular patterns which most probably have an Oriental origin.

These comparisons may be a good introduction to the study of another group of manuscripts and especially of two books both of which have, like Durrow, symbols instead of Evangelists' portraits in the beginning of the Gospels and which are also linked by the very treatment of these symbols: the great Echternach Gospel-book (Paris, B.N., Ms. Lat. 9389),[1] and a Gospel-book of which only two fragments survive, one nearly completely charred in the fire of the Cottonian Library in the eighteenth century (Br. Mus., Cotton Ms. Otho.C.V.),[2] the other mercifully in a wonderful state of preservation (Cambridge, Corpus Christi College, Ms. 197).[3] They are both of mixed Irish text. There are differences between their scripts, though they have a strong family likeness: the Echternach manuscript is nearly entirely written in a large minuscule,[4] with only occasional use of majuscule, and some colophons in a cursive which foreshadows that of the pocket-books. The dismembered Gospel-book is written in a stately majuscule, distinguished from that of all the books we shall have to examine except the Echternach Gospels, by the use of uncial G instead of the characteristic Insular shape.[5] A colophon of the Echternach Gospels claims that the book was revised in 538 on a text which belonged to Eugipius (generally identified with an abbot of a monastery near Naples). This evidently

---

[1] Lowe, *C.L.A.*, V, No. 578; Zimmermann, IV, Pls. 255–8; McGurk, No. 59; Micheli, *Miniature*, pp. 21–3.

[2] Lowe, *C.L.A.*, II, No. 125; Zimmermann, IV, Pl. 266; McGurk, No. 2; Micheli, *Miniature*, pp. 22–3.

[3] Id. Lowe suggests that another fragment (Br. Mus., Roy. Ms. 7 C. XII, *C.L.A.*, II, No. 217; remains of canon tables) may have belonged to the same manuscript.

[4] This minuscule has a good deal in common with that of the Schaffhausen manuscript (see p. 166) written at Iona in the late seventh century.

[5] This occurs only in a few places in the Echternach Gospels.

concerns one of the archetypes of the Gospel-book. It has sometimes been assumed that this colophon shows a connection between our manuscript and the manuscripts brought from Italy by Benedict Biscop and Ceolfrid.[1] But in fact there is no reason why this archetype might not be one of the Vulgate texts which reached Ireland in the sixth century.

A comparison between the symbols in these two books and those of the Book of Durrow is instructive, especially if an anticipation of the study of the Lichfield Gospels is added to it. First of all in these books they are in the proper Vulgate order and not in the Old Latin sequence favoured by the painter of Durrow. *Homo* is only found in Durrow, where it occurs twice (Pl. 57), in Echternach and in Lichfield (Pl. 98) and there is no common feature between the figures reduced to square and rectangle of Durrow and the curious seated figure of Echternach or the flying angel of Lichfield. We can learn more from *Leo*. The two representations in the Book of Durrow remain isolated (Col. pl. E). But the same svelte bounding creature, shaking its golden locks, speeds, nearly identical, on the pages of the manuscripts from Echternach and Lichfield (Pl. 103) and on the burnt page of the Cotton manuscript (Pl. 97).[2] For *Vitulus*, Durrow and Echternach agree closely, while the Lichfield winged symbol (Pl. 105) is closer to that of the Lindisfarne Gospels. *Aquila* in the Book of Durrow and the symbol page of Lichfield (Pl. 98) is an Imperial eagle, standing upright, its body facing front, its head in profile and is completely different from the sitting birds of Echternach and Otho.C.V. (Pl. V, Col. pl. J).

Nothing is known of the history of the manuscript in the Cottonian collection[3] or of its other fragment. That in the Bibliothèque nationale

---

[1] It has also been suggested that the archetype could have been brought to Lindisfarne by Hadrian who had lived in Naples. On this colophon, see : J. Chapman, O.S.B., *Notes on the Early History of the Vulgate Gospels* (Oxford, 1908), p. 26, and Id., 'Cassiodorus and the Echternach Gospels', *Revue bénédictine*, 1911, p. 283; also the very guarded statement of Julian Brown in *E.Q.C. Lindisfarnensis*, II, pp. 49–50.

[2] The general outline of the bouncing lion found both in the Echternach Gospels and Cotton Ms. Otho C. V, may be inspired by an Oriental model; see : W. R. Hovey, 'Sources of the Irish Illuminated Art', *Art Studies*, 1928, pp. 118 sqq.

[3] Planta, *Catalogue of the Manuscripts in the Cottonian Library deposited in the British Museum* (London, 1802).

Fig. 22. Calendar of Echternach
(Paris, B.N.), initial.

was, until the late eighteenth century, in the library of the monastery at Echternach. It probably came there in the time of Willibrord. It has been suggested that the missionaries brought it with them when they arrived from Ireland. It has also been said that it was sent from Northumbria. Both hypotheses are acceptable from a historical point of view. But considering the Irish character of ornament and script Lindisfarne would be the only possible origin in the north of England, whilst an Irish origin remains perfectly possible.

The decoration of the Echternach Gospels is not without a certain geometrical stiffness. Animal ornament is totally absent. There is nothing but the most abstract decoration. The initials are covered with

Fig. 23. Book of the Prophets
(Paris, B.N.), initial.

N

a fine network of interwoven threads and end with incredibly finely coiled spirals. Even the symbols are partly drawn by geometric devices: this is specially striking in the case of the eagle, the head and the whole body being drawn by compass arcs (Pl. V and Fig. 33). The colours are of an extreme delicacy, each tone, red, purple and yellow, existing in a dark and a lighter shade. As in the Cotton manuscript, the symbols are not left floating in the middle of the page but are linked to the frame by a grid of coloured lines over which they sometimes encroach very slightly, very delicately.

A whole series of manuscripts originates from the scriptorium of Echternach or closely associated scriptoria: a Calendar and a Martyrology bound together probably since the ninth century,[1] a Book of the Prophets (Bibl. nat. Paris),[2] a Gospel-book in Maihingen,[3] another in Trier (Dombibl.).[4] In all this, there are quite a lot of spirals of most beautiful design, but practically no animal-interlacing proper, at most some birds and terminal heads of great diversity: heads of lions, of eagles, of birds with long beaks, of fantastic monsters, and only a few animals, hardly interlaced at all, in the Trier manuscript (Pl. VI).

These manuscripts are the work of a few scribes, Laurentius, Virgilius and a pupil of Laurentius, all belonging to the Echternach scriptorium,[5] and of another, Thomas, who may be a monk of a different monastery in close contact with Willibrord's abbey. These names are of course travesties of Saxon or Irish names, possibly taken at an important turn of an ecclesiastical career. Willibrord himself, when he was consecrated bishop in Rome, had become Clemens, or Clemens Willibrord. About

[1] Paris, B.N., Ms. Lat. 10837; Kenney, *Sources*, No. 69, pp. 233–4; H. A. Wilson, *The Calendar of St Willibrord* (London, 1918); Lowe, *C.L.A.*, V, No. 605.

[2] Ms. Lat. 9382; Lowe, *C.L.A.*, V, No. 577.

[3] Now at Schloss Harburg (*olim* at Maihingen) (Coll. Oettingen-Wallerstein); Lowe, *C.L.A.*, VIII, No. 1216; Zimmermann, IV, Pls. 260–6; McGurk, No. 72; Micheli, *Miniature*, pp. 44–5; M. Stokes, *Early Christian Art in Ireland* (London 1887, Dublin, 1928), p. 36 of 1928 ed.

[4] Trier, Domschatz, Ms. 61 (*olim* 134); Lowe, *C.L.A.*, VIII, No. 1368; Zimmermann, IV, Pls. 267–79; McGurk, No. 76; Kenney, *Sources*, No. 487, pp. 649–50; Micheli, *Miniature*, pp. 44–5; M. Stokes, op. cit., p. 41.

[5] C. Nordenfalk, 'On the Age of the earliest Echternach Manuscripts', *Acta Archaeologica*, 1932, pp. 60 sqq.

178

Laurentius, we are in the dark, but the name of Virgilius or Vergilius betrays an Irish origin and is a common adaptation of the Irish names Fergus or Ferghil; the Virgile who occupied the see of Salzburg in the eighth century was an Irishman.[1] So we are probably faced by a group of scribes who had come with Willibrord from Ireland and of whom some were Irish, some possibly Saxon. Nothing indeed could show better the futility of the Ireland–Northumbria controversies as the existence of such a mixed scriptorium.

The activity of Laurentius as a scribe can be traced in 704, then in 710, 718 and 721 or 722, all dates when he wrote charters for Willibrord.[2] He signed the Martyrologium, which has no more decoration than a large capital for each kalend; but the delicate work of the flourishes of these capitals shows him as a spirited draftsman. Virgilius also wrote charters: one in 709, and another which he signed with Laurentius in 721 or 722. He signed the Book of Prophets of which he wrote part of the text. His decorative work is more ambitious than that of Laurentius and is of a remarkably massive quality (Fig. 23). The Calendar was probably written in 717. As in the case of the Martyrologium, the decoration consists essentially of one decorated initial for each kalend; they are of the same lace-like tracery, but are drawn on a larger scale and with a more florid display of ornament (Fig. 22). Lowe is inclined to see in it the same hand as in the Gospels of Maihingen. This last manuscript, as Nordenfalk has shown, was written, judging from the acrostic it contains (Laurentius vivat senio[r]), by a pupil of Laurentius. Nordenfalk has suggested that he is no other than Virgilius. Perhaps, though the styles of the Book of Prophets (Fig. 23)

---

[1] His death is recorded in *A.F.M.*, at the year 784 (*recte* 789) thus: 'Ferghil, i.e. the Geometer, abbot of Aghaboe, died in Germany, in the thirteenth year of his bishopric. Father Grosjean has queried the identity of the Ferghil thus mentioned with Virgil of Salzburg (P. Grosjean, 'Virgile de Salzbourg en Irlande', *An. Boll.*, 1960, pp. 92 sqq.) This raises the problem of Irish abbots or bishops living abroad and the recording of their death in the Annals with their former Irish title. There are several examples of it in the eleventh century. See for example: *A.I.*, 1037, 4, and 1070, 4. In consequence I feel justified in accepting the entry relative to Virgil.

[2] C. Wampach, *Geschichte der Grundherrschaft Echternach in frühen Mittelalter* (Luxemburg, 1930), I, p. 76.

and the Maihingen Gospels (Pl. 106) are not so easy to reconcile. It might be better to postulate the existence of a third scribe, possibly Irish like Virgilius. The mentions of the feasts of Saint Brigid, Saint Patrick and Saint Columba in this Calendar which otherwise follows closely the 'hieronymian' series of names, shows at least some links with Ireland. The feast of Aidan, the founder of Lindisfarne, is not indicated in the primary text and only figures as an addition.

As for Thomas, the scribe of the Trier Gospel-book, it has been suggested that he might be the Irishman of that name who was abbot of the Irish monastery of Honau, on an island in the Rhine near Strasbourg, from 750 to 770.[1] In that case he may have belonged originally to the abbey of Echternach, as some features of his work proceed from a similar atmosphere to that which surrounds the Maihingen Gospels. Nordenfalk[2] suggested c. 730 as a possible date for the Maihingen Gospels. This seems somewhat late and they may be as early as 720, a date when we know that the Echternach scriptorium was active. In this case the Trier Gospels might belong to the following decade.

Both the Maihingen and Trier manuscripts are not purely Insular in their decoration. They have canon tables under arcadings supported by semi-classical columns and accompanied by very realistic birds and animals[3] which show clearly the imitation of an Oriental manuscript with decorative porticoes possibly similar to the Syriac Gospels of Rabbula written in the sixth century.[4] The birds on one of the cover pages of the Maihingen Gospels are of the same type (Pl. VII). Willibrord, like all his contemporaries, certainly took advantage of his stay in Rome to collect books. There may well have been among them the manuscript which inspired these violent departures from Insular style.[5] They are sometimes considered as being by a different hand, or

---

[1] See p. 40; Kenney, *Sources*, p. 650.   [2] Nordenfalk, op cit.

[3] Zimmermann, loc. cit.

[4] C. Cechelli, G. Furlani, M. Salmi, *Rabbula Gospels* (Olten-Lausanne, 1959).

[5] That manuscript might have remained in the neighbourhood of Trier-Lorsch, where, some fifty or sixty years later it would have been a source of inspiration for the painters of the early Carolingian manuscripts, and specially of the Alba Julia Gospels, which were written in Lorsch (see: Köhler, *Die Karolingische Miniaturen*, II, *Die Hofschule Karls des Grossen* (Berlin, 1938), Pls. 99–108).

even of very much later date than the bulk of the manuscript. But the interlaced bases of the columns in the Trier manuscript betray a hand used to Irish style, and the first page of the Trier Gospels where very Irish-looking symbols of the Evangelists surround a perfectly Byzantine bust of Christ come to reinforce the impression that everything is by the same hand. In fact such versatility would fit in very well with what one can guess of the exuberant character of the scribe who displays his signature here and there: 'Thomas', 'Thomas scripsit'. One may even wonder if the parts which are written in uncials and have Merovingian initials are not also due to his attempts at copying everything which came within his reach.[1] His Irish style, however, is energetic and occasionally weird, as when he combines the four symbols of the Evangelists in one monstrous figure.[2] Some of the frames of ribbon interlacing and Saint Luke's calf are practically identical with those of the Echternach Gospels and could have been copied from them. Only a few very inferior pages, such as the portraits of Mark and Luke, may be due to unskilled collaborators.

The Gospels of Maihingen are less chaotic in appearance. Apart from the canon arcadings their decoration consists mostly of not very elaborate and comparatively small initials. For simple, elegant design, nothing could be more delightful than the small Chi-Rho festooned with a delicate thread knotted at intervals, or the Quoniam whose ornaments seem to flow, like a wandering stream, interrupted by the tiny whirl-pools of the spirals (Pl. 106). We are here very near the Book of Durrow. In fact the Chi-Rho, the Quoniam, the M of the *Breves Causae* are practically identical in general shape with the same letters in the Durrow manuscript. But in the Maihingen Gospels, some bird inter-lacings are introduced. There is also a full page of ornament, an orgy of purples, greens and yellows dancing up and down the step-ladders of

---

[1] The uncial script has certainly here and there a strong Insular flavour.

[2] This representation is in fact based on the text of the Vision of Ezekiah, and has parallels both in Byzantine and Medieval art; see: R. Crozet, 'Les premières représentations anthropo-zoomorphiques des évangélistes (VIe–IXe siècles)', *Études mérov.*, p. 57. It may have also something to do with a pronouncement of S. Irenaeus on the Gospels: 'The Word . . . has given us the Tetramorphic Gospel, governed by one only Spirit' (*Adversus haereses*, III, 11).

an ever-recurring pattern to form a large cross in a frame. The Irish affinities of the Book are stressed by two facts : the presence in it of the poem of Aileran, probably lector of Clonard (who died in 664), on the Canons of the Gospels,[1] and the quite surprising similarity of the Chi-Rho of a manuscript illuminated in Bangor in the twelfth century with that of the Maihingen Gospels;[2] this is so striking that it can only be explained by the survival in Ireland of a prototype of the Maihingen Gospels, now lost, which was imitated by the twelfth-century scribe.

Such composite works as these two Gospel-books deserve careful study, not only because of what they tell us of a certain phase of Irish illumination, but also because they may explain the way in which certain Continental and Oriental elements are introduced into Irish work. The foundations of the Irish and Saxon-Irish missions may well have played their part in some of the transformations of the Irish style, and in any case, these two manuscripts show in a blatant way the imitation of elements which in Ireland probably became immediately integrated and are consequently harder to detect.

Wherever it was elaborated first, whether in some Continental Irish centre, in Ireland, in Iona, or in the north of England, a new repertoire appears, possibly at the end of the seventh century and certainly in the two first decades of the eighth. On the already accepted theme of animal bodies woven into a continuous pattern, is grafted the fascination of all those delicately sketched animals which enliven the margins of Oriental manuscripts. The shock of this new element determines the formation of a style and the appearance of agile little monsters sometimes reminiscent of greyhounds, combined with long-necked birds, both endowed with a wonderful array of claws and talons.

Though it is difficult to define its mode of transmission, the key-pattern, the grille made of hooked lines, which is ultimately of Oriental, probably Coptic, origin, is now completely adopted. It covers a whole page in the Maihingen Gospels. It will also zigzag along the frames of pages of the Lichfield Gospels.

The spiral, the oldest of the Irish patterns, still plays an essential part. In fact the way spiral-patterns are built, on a lay-out of compass-drawn

[1] Kenney, *Sources*, p. 634.   [2] Henry–Marsh-Micheli, *Illumination*, Pl. XXX.

Opposite: Pl.G. Book of Dimma, 'portrait' of St Mark

circles, is adapted to the construction of other patterns; it now supplies the frame-work in which they are inserted.[1]

All the painters of the eighth century will be satisfied with this fairly limited stock of ornament. Only later, in the Book of Kells, will foliage panels introduce a new complication. This repertoire appears already developed in the decoration of two manuscripts which have more than one point in common, though their styles are very different, the Book of Lichfield and the Book of Lindisfarne.

Nothing is known of the history of the Lichfield Gospels until the time when some notes in Welsh were inserted in it in the late eighth and ninth century.[2] One of them mentions that the Book was exchanged for 'a good horse' and given to Saint Teliau, that is to say the monastery of Llandaff, near the Bristol Channel, which he had founded. It seems to have remained there until the tenth century when it was transferred to the cathedral of Saint Chad in Lichfield, hence the name by which it is known 'Book of Saint Chad'.

It is at present $11\frac{1}{2}$ by $8\frac{3}{4}$ in, but was originally a good deal larger as it has been badly clipped. It was a luxury manuscript, of which only badly preserved fragments are left. It has lost the end of Saint Luke's Gospel and the whole of Saint John's. It seems that the first page of Matthew, now rubbed and worn, must have played for a very long time the part of first page of the Book, but it was obviously originally preceded by other pages,[3] how many, one cannot say, so that it is now impossible to know whether the usual preliminaries, prefaces, canons, etc., were present in the Book or not.

[1] See p. 223 and: *E.Q.C. Lindisfarnensis*, II, pp. 221 sqq.

[2] Lowe, *C.L.A.*, II, No. 159; Zimmermann, III, Pls. 245–6; McGurk, No. 16; Kenney, *Sources*, p. 639; Micheli, *Miniature*, pp. 18–19; H. E. Savage, 'The Story of the St Chad's Gospels', *Trans. Birmingham Arch. Soc.*, 1915. The Lichfield Gospels have been rebound in 1962 by Roger Powell. With the kind permission of the Dean of Lichfield, I was fortunate enough to be able to study them at leisure before the pages were sewn again, but after the vellum had been flattened – a process which always brings out the details of faded illumination –. They were also photographed in the same exceptionally favourable conditions (Col. Pls. 6, 8 and 9, Pls. 103, 105 and 107.)

[3] In any case by a page bearing an Evangelist portrait, as for the other Gospels.

Opposite: Pl.H. Lichfield Gospels, Chi-Rho

The text is of the 'mixed' Irish type, the pre-hieronymian elements going back to a text similar to that of the Codex Usserianus Secundus.[1] The script is a handsome majuscule not very different from what we have seen in the various manuscripts examined from the Book of Durrow on.

The colours, in their present state, have a very strange appearance. Some of them seem to have been prepared with a filler, probably lead white, meant to give them a thick consistency. These are mostly cracked and scaly. Others seem to have been washed away, whilst the ink remained unaffected. They seem to have consisted, as far as can be judged in the present state of the manuscript, of a light blue, a darker blue which was probably indigo, a red, a yellow, a purple and a white.[2]

It would be difficult now to reconstruct the original decorative scheme with absolute certainty. It involved in any case the use of the 'portrait' of the Evangelist accompanied by his symbol, as a decorative page facing the beginning of each Gospel text. In addition there is a folio with the four symbols on one side and a great ornamental cross on the other, which is at present at the beginning of Saint Luke's Gospel and may well have been there always.

We have already seen the relation of the symbols with those of the Echternach and Cotton manuscripts, but some of them have wings (Pl. 98), a sign, like the use of portraits, of the imitation of new models. They have a delightful simplicity of presentation: they are drawn in a few lines, embellished with a scatter of rosettes and touched up lightly with some colour which enhances the incisive continuity of the line.

The two surviving 'portraits' show the Evangelists in full face, seated on improbable thrones. The chair of Saint Mark (Pl. 103) is made of a cushion of Byzantine type installed between two spiky beasts with unending legs and arched, elongated bodies, whose tails blossom into interlacings, whilst their curled up heads emit a roar in a flourish of darting tongues. The staring Evangelist accommodated on such a

[1] Wordsworth and White, op. cit.; *Collected papers of Henry Bradshaw* (Cambridge, 1889), pp. 458 sqq.

[2] See the remarks on the pigments by Werner and Roosen-Runge, *E.Q.C. Lindisfarnensis*, II, pp. 275 sqq.

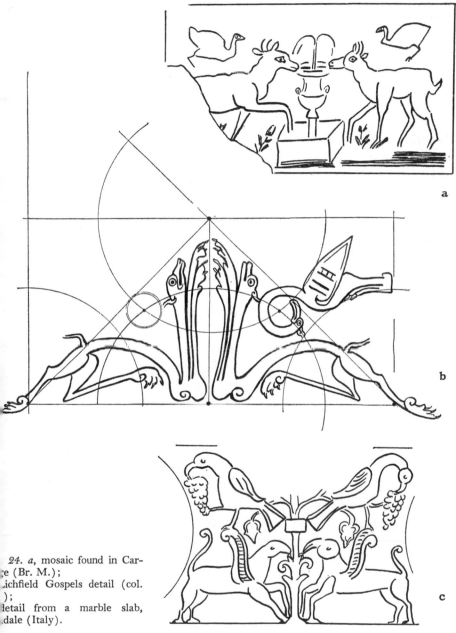

24. *a*, mosaic found in Car-
[th]e (Br. M.);
[*b*, L]ichfield Gospels detail (col.
[...]);
[*c*, d]etail from a marble slab,
[...]dale (Italy).

perilous seat, sits very stiffly, his draperies flung about him like bunting, absolutely unmoved by the leap over his head of the Echternach lion grasping a book in its claws. Luke is rather different (Col. pl. F). He dominates the page where throne and symbol are reduced to accessories. His face, much larger in proportion to the body than that of Saint Mark, is surmounted by a mop of variegated locks and his clothes have become a series of geometric patterns. He holds a cross in one hand and a flowering staff in the other in the traditional attitude of the Osiris-judge as represented in the Egyptian Book of the Dead,[1] the very attitude which will be that of Christ-Judge on the ninth- and tenth-century sculptured crosses.[2] Whether by way of paintings or textiles, the transmission is obvious. The whole portrait constitutes an extraordinary mosaic of colours enhanced by the nearly empty field of vellum on which it stands and by the unobtrusive thin frame. A subtle play of overlapping or just tangent lines connects in fact this border with the portrait; it is exactly the method of composition which we have found in the symbol pages of the Echternach Gospels.

The drawing of the ornamental pages is of a magnificent incisive and animated quality where everything is set in motion (Pl. 24). The letters suddenly turn into monsters which, with wild, protruding eyes, bite their own necks. The frames unexpectedly curl up into a pair of legs or develop a biting snout. There are some organized patterns of animals regularly combined and strictly framed. But other larger beasts disport themselves between the initials. White, pink, pale blue birds cover the whole surface of the Chi-Rho (Col. pl. H). They have thin curled-up necks, elongated wings and spindly legs, and vaguely suggest the appearance of herons or cranes. The way in which they are combined on the carpet-page may give the clue to the motif which is their ultimate inspiration: the well-known scheme of two animals face to face on both sides of a tree on which are perched two birds, their necks curved in an effort

[1] E. Naville, *Das Egyptische Todtenbuch der XVIII bis XX Dynastie aus verschiedenen Urkunden* (Berlin, 1886), *passim*.

[2] The same attitude is found in the Book of Kells (figure inside the door of the Temple, Temptation of Christ) and on the Alfred Jewel (J. Kirk, *The Alfred and Minster Lowel Jewells* (Oxford, 1948).

Opposite: Pl. I. Lichfield Gospels, ornamental page

imago aquilae

to reach some fruit (Fig. 24). This is a frequent theme on works of art of all kinds in the Mediterranean countries in the sixth and seventh centuries. We have learned from the Echternach scriptorium to expect the imitation of models from the south (Pl. VII). Where the adaptation which gave the Lichfield cross-page precisely did take place would be hard to say. Lindisfarne, whose scribes had access to the Northumbrian libraries, is a possibility. Echternach has offered us another. Less well-known Irish centres on the Continent may have indulged in similar experiments and have had an influence on art at home. But it is essential to remember that we know absolutely nothing of the books which were imported from Italy to Ireland at the time when Irish delegations went to Rome to find out the exact facts about the calculation of Easter. We must call to mind those 'Hebrew, Greek and Egyptian' Christians which some of them met,[1] and also the habit of the popes of the Early Middle Ages of sending such envoys home with armfuls of books. During all the late part of the seventh century we have proof of comings and goings between Italy and Ireland. It may be through such journeys that the Antiphonary of Bangor was brought to Bobbio and that the Usserianus Primus was brought from Bobbio to Ireland. Other books which have vanished certainly followed the same routes. Where did they arrive? Lismore appears more and more as one of the great centres of intellectual activity of that period,[2] and the works of exegesis which were written there presuppose the existence of an important library. Clonmacnois, Iona and Bangor are other possible centres. After the Antiphonary which was written in the middle of the seventh century, the activity of the scriptorium of Bangor escapes us. Except for the manuscript of the *Vita Columbae*, we know nothing of that of Iona. Both are ordinary reference books. What were the formal service books written in the same monasteries? And what foreign books were available at the end of the seventh century and at the beginning of

[1] See p. 30. In the case of Bangor there may have been contacts going back to the early seventh century, such as the meeting of Abbot Sinlan (d. 610) with 'a certain learned Greek' from whom he learned the computus (Kenney, *Sources*, p. 213). See also p. 127 for the possibility of the Greek inscription on the Fahan slab being copied from a Greek manuscript.

[2] See p. 30.

Opposite: Pl. J. Ms. 197, Corpus Christi College, Cambridge, symbol of St John

the eighth? What imported miniatures were before the eyes of their painters? About all this we are in complete ignorance. But what we have seen at Echternach, what we are going to see at Lindisfarne, shows borrowing from Mediterranean manuscripts. In Ireland itself, in the heart of an artistic milieu which had intensely original traditions, these borrowings had every chance of becoming from the start indiscernible and of appearing at once under a transposed and disguised aspect in which subsists no more than a deformed shadow of the model. The early carvings supply examples of such adaptations of imported paintings.

In fact, a few objects of engraved metal may preserve some of the intermediate stages leading to the Irish animal-interlacing. For example the pail found in the Swedish emporium of Birka (Fig. 25, a) shows a first step in adaptation:[1] caricatures of birds solemnly pace up and down desiccated branches of little straight trees – a bewildered version of some design of Oriental origin – or are caught in the scrolls of a 'rinceau'. A gilt bronze object from Fure (Bergen Museum)[1] has similarly preserved several episodes of the transformation of the animal, from the two affronted beasts on both sides of a tree down to animal-interlacing proper.

The next stage is represented by the pail found at Sondre (Norway), where the scroll has disappeared and only the birds are left (Fig. 25, c), linked to one another by an interlacement of the tail feathers passing through the two segments of their split neck. This evidently did not satisfy the artist: it was too obvious and straightforward. The censer in Bergen Museum and the fragment from Torshov (Norway)[2] introduce a more subtle solution; the artist suddenly finds a means of reconciling his love for abstract forms and distrust of the obvious with the fascination which the new patterns exercise upon him: that vegetable scroll with which he can do nothing satisfactory he will suggest without exactly describing. The body of the animal, coiled on itself, will take the place of the missing branch and there will be a continuous entwinement of scroll-shaped animal bodies (cf. Fig. 25, d).

Wherever that style originated, it does not seem to have received a great welcome from the sculptors, nor even, at first, from some of the metalworkers. This strengthens the hypothesis that it was elaborated

[1] *V. Ant.*, V, pp. 51–2 and Fig. 55.   [2] *V. Ant.*, V, p. 15 and Fig. 2.

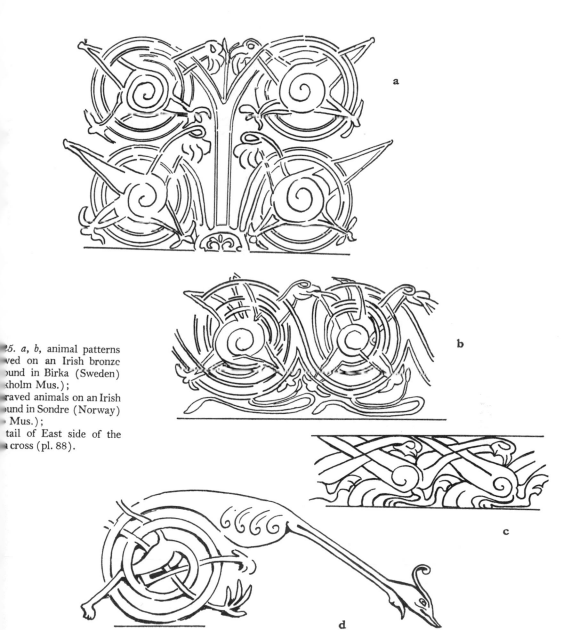

25. *a, b,* animal patterns
ved on an Irish bronze
ound in Birka (Sweden)
kholm Mus.);
raved animals on an Irish
ound in Sondre (Norway)
Mus.);
tail of East side of the
cross (pl. 88).

Fig. 26. Animal interlacing, Kilkieran cross
(Kilkenny) (pl. 78).

first on pages of vellum, with elements borrowed from pages of manuscripts of foreign origin. From the scriptorium it only gradually
spread to the other workshops. Its near total absence from the decoration of grave-slabs which are essentially routine work,[1] throws a good
deal of light on the confined atmosphere where it was elaborated. One
would be tempted to see in it a relaxation of erudite minds, a conceit, in
the same vein as the poem scrawled by one of these scholars in the margin
of a manuscript, about his cat, Pangur-the-white :

> 'I and my white Pangur
> Have each his special art :
> His mind is set on hunting mice,
> Mine is upon my special craft.
>
> .   .   .   .
>
> He rejoices with quick leaps
> When in his sharp claw sticks a mouse,
> I too rejoice when I have grasped
> A problem difficult and dearly loved[2]
>
> .   .   .   .'

In more ways than one the Book of Lichfield has an obvious kinship
with another luxury Gospel-book, the Lindisfarne Gospels, which is

[1] Lionard, *Grave-Slabs*, p. 144.   [2] Meyer, *A. Irish Poetry*, p. 83.

now in the British Museum (Cotton Ms. Nero D. IV).[1] It is a complete Gospel-book, with all the array of prefaces, canons, argumenta, etc., and is in a remarkable state of preservation which makes it, at a first glance, much more impressive than the Lichfield manuscript. It appears as the larger of the two, being 13¾ by 10 in, but this is chiefly because it has not been clipped. In actual fact, several of the frames of decorated pages are exactly of the same size, and a few times the surface covered is actually larger in Lichfield. The original association of the British Museum codex with Lindisfarne is as certain as such manuscript ascriptions can be. What is known of its early history is entirely based on a tenth-century colophon written, while the Lindisfarne community was at Chester-le-street before settling in Durham, by Aldred, the prior of the community, who had just completed his work of adding to it an interlinear translation into Anglo-Saxon. He tells us that 'Eadfrith, bishop of the Church of Lindisfarne, first wrote this book for God and Saint Cuthbert and all the saints in general who are in the island'. He then mentions the binding and probably the shrine in which the book was enclosed,[2] before coming to his own addition. Eadfrith, as we have seen, was Bishop of Lindisfarne from 698 to 721. In spite of the fact that Aldred made his translation more than two centuries later (around 970) the reliability of the colophon is generally accepted, as most historians are prepared to subscribe to Baldwin Brown's remark[3] that somebody making up a statement not based on a strong tradition would have ascribed the Book not to the relatively inconspicuous Eadfrith, but to Saint Cuthbert himself. To this may be added the fact that most of Eadfrith's activities seem to be connected with the fostering of the fame of Saint Cuthbert and the embellishing of his tomb and church.[4] The prose *Vita Cuthberti* of Bede, finished in 721, is dedicated

[1] E. G. Millar, *The Lindisfarne Gospels* (London, 1923); *E.Q.C. Lindisfarnensis* (1956, 1960); Lowe, *C.L.A.*, II, No. 187; Zimmermann, pp. 262–9, Pls. 223–44; McGurk, No. 22.

[2] It is likely to have been a 'cumdach' or metal box of the type which has survived for several Irish books; contra: *E.Q.C. Lindisfarnensis*, II, p. 84.

[3] Baldwin Brown, *Arts in E. England*, V, pp. 337–41.

[4] *E.Q.C. Lindisfarnensis*, II, pp. 17 sqq.; F. Henry, 'The Lindisfarne Gospels', *Antiquity*, 1963, pp. 100 sqq.

to him. The Gospel-book, meant to be displayed on the altar, would fit in well with this picture. So the colophon proposes facts which are eminently credible, but it is well not to lose sight completely of the fact that the lateness of the colophon remains a little worrying.

We shall accept its data however, not because they seem unassailable, but because they fit in fairly convincingly with what we have seen of the Echternach manuscripts and complete the picture in a way which is altogether plausible. But we shall not follow the joint authors of the latest monumental study on the Lindisfarne Gospels when they choose 698 as the date of completion of the manuscript.[1] Their chief reason for this seems to be that Eadfrith having become in 698 Bishop-Abbot of Lindisfarne would have had no more time to spare for such work after that date. This is a mistaken view of the occupations of a medieval abbot. Does not Adamnan show us Columba copying manuscripts to the very last day of his life, and what of Adamnan himself, who, at the request of his community, undertook the writing of the *Vita Columbae* shortly after becoming Abbot of Iona[2] and completed the task – however busy he might have been otherwise – in four or five years? The writing of the Gospels whilst Eadfrith was abbot is in fact very much more likely and there is no reason whatsoever why it would not have taken place in the latter part of his life. The book, as Bruce-Mitford has shown,[3] has remained unfinished, at least in some details of its decoration, which makes it likely that it was written and painted shortly before Eadfrith's death in 721.

The text is a very pure version of the Vulgate, of Italo-Northumbrian type, a fact which is in no way surprising if the Book was written at Lindisfarne at the time when the Codex Amiatinus was being completed in the scriptorium of Jarrow–Wearmouth (shortly before 716). The script has on the whole a family likeness to that of the other manuscripts we have examined, but if one puts together samples of the scripts of Lichfield, Otho C.V. and Durham A.II.17, their close relation, in spite of individual habits of the pen, will appear obvious. They are the work of scribes trained in the same principles and working in the same atmos-

---

[1] *E.Q.C. Lindisfarnensis*, pp. 11 sqq.   [2] *Vit. Col.*, preface.
[3] *E.Q.C. Lindisfarnensis*, II, pp. 122–3.

phere.[1] To add to this series a sample of the writing of Lindisfarne does not mean introducing a completely discordant note, but, clearly, the unity is broken. The difference – not very considerable, really – would be more or less the same as that between the closely-knit group of manuscripts just mentioned and the Maihingen Gospels.

Bruce-Mitford thinks that he can prove that in the Book of Lindisfarne scribe and painter are one and the same man.[2] It may be so. In fact there is something very tempting in the view that Eadfrith was actually the painter of the Book, as he fulfills all the conditions which would make its special characteristics really intelligible. He had probably spent six years of studies in Ireland, coming back some time before 690.[3] It is likely that he learned there a style of writing to which he remained attached all his life, and which was anyway not very different from the type of writing which had been taught in Lindisfarne by generations of Irish teachers. This he may have altered slightly as the years passed. He had also probably learnt there some principles of illumination. One of the remarkable discoveries made by Bruce-Mitford during his meticulous study of the manuscript relates to the still visible imprints of the grilles and the compass designs which the painter used to build the decoration of the large ornamental pages.[4] This method proceeds exactly from what we have seen of the construction of spiral patterns such as those on the Lough Crew bones and the Bann disc,[5] and the grilles are to be found beside more elaborate patterns on some of the Irish carved bones. It was probably elaborated at the time in Irish scriptoria, the painters taking advantage of the experiments made over centuries by the metalworkers. Either Eadfrith learned this method while in Ireland or it was taught to him by a scribe who came from Ireland at a later date. Lindisfarne was certainly not cut off from Iona and Ireland by the departure of Colman. In 686–7 and 688–9,

---

[1] J. Brown goes as far as suggesting that the Echternach Gospels and Ms. A.II.17 of Durham are by the same hand (*E.Q.C. Lindisfarnensis*, II, p. 102 (2nd col.)) certainly his comparison of scripts is very striking (Pls. 2 and 3), but the similarities may only amount to those due to a common training. The illuminations can hardly be by the same hand as he claims (Pls. 8 and 9).

[2] *E.Q.C. Lindisfarnensis*, II, pp. 5–11, 123–5. [3] See p. 35.

[4] See Fig. 34 and op. cit., pp. 221 sqq. [5] See p. 15.

Adamnan came to visit his former pupil, King Aldfrid,[1] on one occasion presenting him with his book *De Locis Sanctis* which was given by Aldfrid to Jarrow. Rather unexpected perspectives are opened by the fact that Ceolfrid's own brother was a hermit in Ireland.[2] If Jarrow had such contacts with Ireland, what of Lindisfarne itself? Up to his death in 704, the family links of Aldfrid with Ireland[3] would be sure to make for fairly close relations which Eadfrith, if he was a pupil of the Irish schools, would make a point of cultivating to the maximum. In fact such a background may account for the links between the Books of Lindisfarne and Lichfield though we are at a loss to grasp the exact circumstances which would make the connection clear.

The treatment of colours is very complex in the Lindisfarne Gospels. For each tone there are several pigments: three blues (lapis lazuli, indigo, folium sapphireum), three yellows, two reds,[4] etc. Gold is used in a few places, an element of decoration which is absent from all the large manuscripts which we have examined so far, except the Trier Gospels, where it is also the result of contacts with non-Insular milieus.

The Book being practically intact, its plan of decoration can be studied easily. It starts with a large ornamental cross. Then come, after the prefaces, canon-tables framed by arcades like those of the Maihingen and Trier manuscripts. But here these have only retained from semi-classical models the general shape of the arches which are covered by animal and bird interlacing. Each Gospel is heralded by a portrait page, and then an ornamental page, on a cruciform plan, faces the decorated beginning of the text.

The portraits reveal immediately contacts with Mediterranean models, which are emphasized by the presence of slightly debased Greek inscriptions identifying each Evangelist. The rest of the decoration is on the contrary Insular in style and includes all the patterns which are used in the Lichfield Gospels: the same elongated fauna, brilliantly coloured, woven into elaborate ornaments, the same birds, though stouter and with variegated feathers. A certain monotony which does not exist in the Lichfield Gospels slightly mars the skilful arrangements, the over-

[1] *Vit. Col.*, II, 46.   [2] See p. 35.   [3] See p. 37.
[4] *E.Q.C. Lindisfarnensis*, II, pp. 275 sqq. (Werner and Roosen-Runge).

Opposite: Pl.K. Add. Ms. 40.618, 'portrait' of St Luke

exact symmetry. The frames still end sometimes in the head or the legs of an animal, but in an inert and tame way. The whole decoration is permeated by a sort of frozen perfection. Still, dressed in all the original brilliance of its colours, the Book has a majestic impact which reveals more of the quality of Insular work than anything we can laboriously deduce from the aspect of the water-stained, torn and charred books which have been part of our study so far.

Its position in regard to the Lichfield Gospels is difficult to define. They have in common not only an ornamental repertoire, but the general plan of several of the decorative pages as well as the disposition and use of the animal and bird interlacing on one of the large crosses (Saint Matthew in Lindisfarne, Saint Luke in Lichfield). Given the constant surges of invention in Lichfield and the slightly bored atmosphere of Lindisfarne, it would be much more satisfactory to envisage Lichfield as the prototype, especially as some of its Evangelists' symbols have archaic features lacking in Lindisfarne. It would remain, however, to explain the presence in the Lichfield Gospels of some winged symbols very similar to those of Lindisfarne and which one might be tempted to consider as imitated from them, though they may in fact go back to a common prototype.[1]

We may never know the real explanation. But in any case the Book of Lindisfarne only takes its full significance when considered as one of those offshoots of Irish art in the foundations of the missions from Ireland, similar to the Echternach manuscripts and the Trier Gospels. This style spread through the whole of England, though with a greater and greater admixture of heterogeneous elements. The 'Codex Aureus' in Stockholm Library,[2] a manuscript from Canterbury, is a good example of this: beside very handsome spiral patterns its decoration includes a whole fauna of small animals treated in a humoristic mood

[1] Here intervenes also the problem of the relation of the symbols with those on the wooden sarcophagus of Saint Cuthbert studied by E. Kitzinger (*Relics of St Cuthbert*, pp. 202 sqq.), and in the 'Majestas' page of the Amiatinus (*E.Q.C. Lindisfarnensis*, II, Pl. 24). It is impossible to deal here in detail with the subject, especially as I have strong doubts about the date of 698 generally ascribed to the coffin decoration, doubts which could only be justified by a lengthy exposition.

[2] Stockholm, Royal Library, Ms. A. 135; Zimmermann, IV, Pls. 289–92.

Opposite: Pl. L. Book of Dimma, symbol of St John

which have little in common with the Lichfield beasts, and the lavish use of gold belongs to a different world. In the north of England, this style will live on until the ninth century and we shall have to invoke it in comparisons with the Book of Kells.

The continuation of the style of Lichfield in Ireland is represented by a fragment of manuscript preserved in Oxford and by a Gospel-book in the Library of the cathedral of Saint-Gall.

The Oxford fragment (Bodleian Libr., Rawlinson Ms. G.167)[1] is an incomplete Gospel-book of which only the greatest part of the text of Saint Luke and part of that of Saint John have survived. It is about 13 by 10 in, which brings it near the size of the Lindisfarne Gospels and the original size of the Lichfield Gospels. The text is of the 'mixed Irish' type, with all sorts of peculiarities of script and spelling which are essentially Irish. All that remains of its decoration is one page badly damaged by damp. Still this is enough to show that it was a magnificent volume whose ornamental frames were of roughly the same size as those of the Lichfield Gospels. This page – the first of St Luke's Gospel – is occupied by a large initial similar in general lay-out to that of the corresponding page of the Lindisfarne Gospels. The colours are very faded, but it is still possible to identify red and yellow and a purple which seems to have had a lead white filler like some of the colours of Lichfield. In addition to flourishes of spirals there were certainly animal and bird interlacings, now practically impossible to disentangle.

The Saint-Gall Gospel-book (Ms. 51)[2] was probably written in Ireland about the middle of the eighth century, and brought to Saint-Gall, perhaps with some stops on the Continent, by a wandering monk of the ninth century. Though it is certainly somewhat later than the Lichfield Gospels, it has many points in common with it: the setting on

[1] Lowe, *C.L.A.*, II, No. 256; *New Pal. Soc.*, II, pl. 81; McGurk, No. 35; *Catal. Bodl.* No. 14890.

[2] *The Irish Miniatures in the Cathedral Library of St Gall* (Berne–Olten–Lausanne, 1954), text by J. Duft and P. Meyer; Lowe, *C.L.A.*, VII, No. 901; Zimmermann, p. 240, III, Pls. 185–92; McGurk, No. 117; G. L. Micheli, 'Recherches sur les manuscrits décorés de Saint Gall et de Reichenau', *R.A.*, 1936, I, p. 189 sqq., II, p. 54 sqq.

Opposite: Pl.M. St Gall Gospels, the Last Judgment

the page of the large initials and of the lines of ornamental letters which follow them, the analogy of two of the Evangelists' portraits with the Saint Luke of Lichfield, etc. Still, to pass from these imposing volumes about 13 inches high such as Lichfield, Lindisfarne and the Rawlinson fragment, and from their incredibly assured drawing, to this $11\frac{1}{4}$ inch volume whose drawing is sometimes slightly crude, means going down a peg in the scale of manuscript values.

The Saint-Gall manuscript has the four Gospels, without any of the preliminary texts, in the 'mixed Irish' version. The script is a rather compressed Irish majuscule. The decoration follows a perfectly clear plan: each Gospel begins by an Evangelist portrait facing a page of ornamental writing (Pls. 108–109). The Chi-Rho monogram at the beginning of Matthew I, 18 is treated in the same way as the beginnings of Gospels. Instead of a portrait, a carpet-page balances there the page with ornamental writing. The symbols of the Evangelists do not occupy a whole page, as in the Lichfield Gospels, but are grudgingly accommodated in the four corners of the frame around the portrait of Saint Mark. In contrast to this rather economical programme, two pages, at the end of the volume, are devoted to illustrations of the Crucifixion and the Last Judgment (Col. pl. M).

The drawing is somewhat heavy but is capable of a great energy. The figures are summed up in impressive masses. The animals forming the ornament of the carpet-page are flung across the compartments in a few bold curves. The colours are one of the most attractive features of the Book; there are delightful light blues and golden yellows and everywhere variations and mixed tones are obtained by a play of coloured dots on letters, patterns and draperies. If there is nothing here of the alertness of the Lichfield Gospels this is compensated for by a great sense of the dramatic value of the figures. The Evangelists all have the same haunting presence as the Saint Luke of Lichfield. Like him they look as if they were standing in front of their seats, and they are wrapped in draperies which are no more than a series of geometric patterns edged by a coloured border. Each has his own well-defined individuality: Matthew holding a large book, his golden hair gathered up to a point, dwarfed by his symbol, Mark with large staring eyes framed by the

197

stylized locks of his hair and his beard, Luke so commanding, so tall
that he overlaps the whole border (Pl. 109), and John with his intense
blue wig outlined on a purple halo.

This arbitrary play of the colours reaches its maximum in the
Crucifixion, where it assumes a savagely tragic accent, while the
Judgment (Col. pl. M) is variegated by endless combinations of coloured
dots which conjure up delicate shades of mauve, orange and green on
the draperies of the apostles, whose heads are all sharply bent in an
effort to look at the bust of Christ–Judge and at the trumpet-blowing
angels.

Something of the massive and simple presentation of the Saint-Gall
Book is to be found also in a charming little Gospel-book in the Chapter
Library of Hereford,[1] whose decoration is confined to large ornamental letters. Something also of its lack of finesse in the treatment
of details is to be found in another, dateable to the end of the eighth
century at least, the Book of Mac Regol or Rushworth Gospels, which
belongs to the Bodleian Library (Ms. Auct.D.II.19).[2] The colophon
written on the last page inside a frame of interlacings proclaims that
'Mac Regol depincxit hoc evangelium' and adds 'quicumque legerit et
intellegerit istam narrationem orat pro mac reguil scriptori', so that
in this special case we have reason to think that painter and scribe are
one and the same man; in addition he can be identified as an Abbot of
Birr (Offaly) who died in 822.[3] Given the striking analogies of some of
the ornamental letters with those of the Saint-Gall manuscript, one
feels tempted to think that Mac Regol painted this book at the onset of
a long career, so that it might date between 770 and 790.

Mac Regol gives the impression of having had a vehement personality.

[1] Hereford, Cathedral Library, Ms. P. I. 2; Lowe, *C.L.A.*, II, No. 157; Zimmermann, IV, Pl. 328; McGurk, No. 15.

[2] Bodl. Libr., Ms. Auct. D. II. 19 (catalogue, No. 3946); Lowe, *C.L.A.*, II, No.
231; Zimmermann, pp. 247–8, III, Pls. 199–204; McGurk, No. 33; S. Hemphill,
'The Gospels of Mac Regol of Birr: a Study in Celtic Illumination', *P.R.I.A.*,
1911 (C), pp. 1 sqq.

[3] The *Annals of Ulster* mention at the year 822 the death of Mac Riaghoil ua
Magleni, scribe and bishop, Abbot of Birr. As the name is an uncommon one, the
identification seems satisfactory.

Opposite: Pl.N. Book of Mac Regol

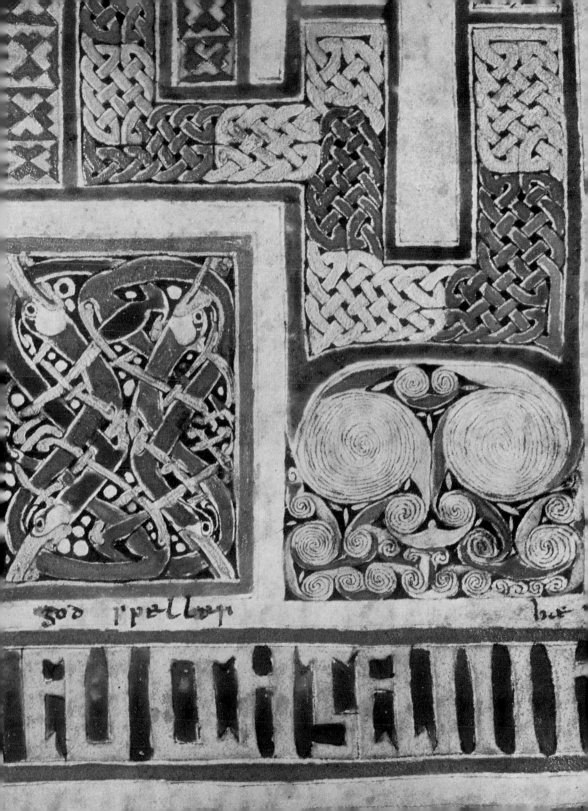

god rpellun   hir

His book is very large (13½ by 10 in). He uses colours of an incredible intensity: deep violet, bright red, apple green, golden yellow. His drawing is irregular and slap-dash; he certainly does not seem to have any use for compasses. But he is endowed with a sort of disarming eloquence. We are at the opposite pole to the delicate patterns of Lichfield. Nonetheless, some interlacings made of enormous birds with powerful talons are surprisingly vigorous and however harsh his colour may be it has a sort of brutal splendour (Col. pl. N). There are here and there in his ornament human figures similar to those on the Banagher shaft; sometimes they appear in bust at the top of the page like puppets, gesticulating, holding their hair in their hands. Portraits and symbols are surrounded by a double frame and indicated by a few streaks of violent colour. The strangest thing is that this painter who leaves everything to improvisation is a remarkable scribe, much more skilful than the scribe of the Saint-Gall Gospels. As one might expect, his script is of a large size, but it has a simple majesty which makes of each page of text a work of art (Pl. 110).

Beside these large luxury Gospel-books made mainly to be used on the altar, several 'pocket-books' have survived. They are of a much smaller size, are written in a minuscule or cursive which is full of abbreviations and which is cramped so as to accommodate as much text as possible on each page and to keep the book small and light to carry. Four decorated ones can be attributed to the time we are dealing with: the Book of Mulling,[1] the Book of Dimma, a much disfigured manuscript in the British Museum and the Stowe Manuscript which is made up of a Gospel of Saint John bound up with a missal.[2] They belong to a

[1] A few pages of another Gospel-Book are bound with the Book of Mulling.

[2] To this one could add a manuscript at Fulda which has four identical Evangelists. But it is rather uncouth compared with the other books. The history of the manuscript is confused, but the name of the scribe, Cadmug, is clearly Irish. See: Henry, *An Irish Manuscript*, pp. 154–5. The pocket Irish Gospel-Book in Bern has practically no ornament (McGurk, *Pocket-Books*). In the ninth century, the Gospels in the Book of Armagh, and the Book of Mac Durnan belong to the same type. It lives on in the twelfth century in two Gospel-Books in the British Museum (Harley, 1023 and 1802) and a Gospel-Book in the Bodleian (Corpus Christi Coll. Ms. 122); see Henry–Marsh-Micheli, *Illumination*. It is not absolutely exact, as

199

type of book which will remain in great favour for obvious practical reasons and whose development can be followed right into the twelfth century. Their decoration consists generally in portraits or symbols and in a first page of text whose ornament is occasionally reduced to a small capital.

The Book of Mulling has been sometimes attributed to the seventh century, because of its colophon which mentions Saint Moling who died between 692 and 697.[1] But the colophon seems to have been copied from an older book and the manuscript belongs probably to the eighth century. It comes from Tech Moling, the monastery founded by Saint Moling on the banks of the Barrow (Carlow). Prefaces and canons have probably been added slightly later than the time when the main text was written.[2] The three portraits which are now bound at the end of the volume (Pl. 111 did most probably originally occupy their usual place at the beginning of each of the Gospels.[3] They belong to the same type of Evangelists' figures as those in the Saint-Gall Gospels and their frames which are divided into several panels indicate similar affinities.

McGurk has stated (op. cit. and *Latin Gospel-Books*, p. 11) that the early pocket Gospels never have preliminaries; in this he has been misled (*a*) by the fact that he considers the main text of the Book of Mulling as seventh century, and consequently the preliminaries as a much later addition, (*b*) that he has not included the Armagh Gospels in his study. The Twelfth century ones have preliminaries.

[1] T. C. D. Libr. Ms. 60 (A.I.15); H. J. Lawlor, *Chapters on the Book of Mulling* (Edinburgh, 1897); Lowe, *C.L.A.*, II, No. 276; Zimmermann, pp. 244–5, III, Pls. 194, 196*a*; McGurk, No. 89. A fragment of the Book is preserved in the British Museum.

[2] Lawlor (op. cit., p. 13 sqq.) was of the opinion that the colophon mentioning Moling or Mulling was copied with the text by the scribe. He considered the Book as belonging to the eighth century and of the Introductory matter he says: 'the hand appears to be the same as that in which the Gospels are written' (op. cit., p. 8). In fact there seem to be several scribes. Lowe considers the Introductory matter as 'later, perhaps much later' than the rest of the manuscript; but this probably because he dates the manuscript to the seventh century. The capitals in the introductory part of the Book are very similar to those in the Stowe Missal which is generally ascribed to around 800.

[3] Lawlor wondered if these 'portraits' belonged to the Book or perhaps to the fragment bound with it. The very slight differences in size he mentions would

Additional manuscript 40.618 of the British Museum was probably a very similar book, judging by the only portrait which has survived a drastic restoration done in England in the eleventh century.[1] This is a delightful little figure standing jauntily between four delicately drawn animal-interlacing panels (Col. pl. K).

The Book of Dimma's colophons were falsified so as to ascribe its writing to a scribe contemporary with Saint Cronan, the founder of the monastery of Roscrea (Tipperary).[2] This faking would have been meaningless anywhere other than Roscrea, so that the book, which anyway was found not very far away, nearly certainly comes from there. But its date can not be fixed with any precision. It was written by several scribes and lacks unity, as the eagle (Col. pl. L) and the large initial which marks the beginning of Saint John's Gospel are very close to the style of the Book of Saint-Gall, while the portraits in the beginning of the three other Gospels (Col. pl. G) are nearer to the violent ornamental simplifications of the symbol of Saint Matthew in the Echternah Gospels.

The Stowe Manuscript in the Library of the Royal Irish Academy[3] is clearly a product of the reform of Tallaght, but it is difficult to say whether it was written in Tallaght, in Terryglass or in Lorrha. In any case, it was at Lorrha (Tipperary) in the beginning of the eleventh century, and it dates from the end of the eighth. It continues the style

---

hardly matter with a book whose pages are very worn; McGurk (*Pocket-Books*) assumed first that they were at the end of the Book; in *Latin Gospel-Books* (p. 83) he wonders if they were originally at the beginning or at the end as they do not seem to fit into the quire system as indicated by Lawlor; but illuminated pages are often additions to the quire. So there is no difficulty in assuming that they were originally at the beginning of each Gospel, in the same position as the surviving evangelist of very similar type of Br. Mus. Add. Ms. 40.618.

[1] Henry, *An Irish Manuscript*; Lowe, *C.L.A.*, II, No. 179; McGurk, No. 20.

[2] T.C.D. Libr. Ms. 59 (A.IV.23); R. J. Best, 'On the *Subscriptiones* in the Book of Dimma', *Hermathena*, 1930, pp. 84 sqq.; Lowe, *C.L.A.*, II, No. 275; Zimmermann, pp. 245–6, III, Pls. 195–6; Henry, *An Irish Manuscript*, pp. 151 and 153.

[3] G. F. Warner, *The Stowe Missal* (London, 1915–16); T. F. O'Rahilly, 'The History of the Stowe Missal', *Eriu*, 1926–8, pp. 95 sqq.; Henry, *An Irish Manuscript*.

of the preceding manuscripts in delicate harmonies of pink and yellow (Pl. 112).

These humbler volumes complete, up to a point, the picture of Irish illumination which can be conjured up from the study of the luxury manuscripts. But to tell the truth they should be examined anew. Irish cursive script has hardly been studied at all since Lindsay's time. This leaves us without any elements of chronology or classification, apart from the late date of the Stowe manuscripts and what can be deduced from comparisons with the Book of Armagh which dates from 807. It remains possible that the Book of Mulling may belong to a comparatively early date in the eighth century, and that the Book of Dimma would be contemporary with the Saint-Gall Gospels. But all this has to remain vague in the present state of things.

Chronology is not the essential point in a study of Irish illumination. In fact it is wise, given the fact that we can only reach vestiges of an abundant production, to leave to it as much elasticity and even vagueness as possible. This means that the suggestions – often very remote from current theories – which have been made in this chapter, can only be summed up with the utmost prudence. The story would start, towards the end of the seventh century or the beginning of the eighth, with two styles more or less parallel to each other, that 'of Durrow', perhaps closely linked with the monasteries of Saint Columba, and that 'of Lichfield', developed in a great centre rich in imported manuscripts. The modifications of the Irish style in Lindisfarne and in Echternach during the first twenty or thirty years of the eighth century help us to understand but probably do not explain directly its elaboration. For the later phases of the middle or late eighth century, we have at our disposal chiefly manuscripts of a lesser quality, whether altar-books or reference-books. This does not mean in fact that no great luxury books existed at that tme, as otherwise the sudden appearance in the beginning of the ninth century, or even slightly earlier, of a volume of such technical perfection as the Book of Kells would hardly be understandable.

8. Conclusions

WE HAVE followed in its main episodes the complex evolution of an art which at all its various stages remains disconcerting and so foreign to the conceptions of art which dominated western Europe for centuries that we are in danger of misunderstanding its meaning, its aims and methods. To try and grasp its real significance, one has to keep in mind the fact that it still embodies in the Early Middle Ages a persistent prehistoric tradition. It is a Christian art with a strong pre-Christian background, and an Early Medieval art to which the points of view of the Iron Age are still familiar. Enriching its rather meagre initial repertory with various borrowings from Oriental or Germanic patterns, it went on using principles of composition and methods of drawing which went back to its early past, and so evolved one of the most successful abstract arts which the world has ever known. It will perhaps be useful at this stage to look back upon indications which have appeared so far scattered along the various phases of a historical evolution, and to try to wrest their meaning from them.

In Ireland as everywhere else, Christian art was in its beginning based on the existing art of the country. This is no isolated phenomenon. In the same way the catacomb paintings, the carvings of early sarcophagi, were only at first slightly inadequate adaptations to a new purpose of the current Roman decoration. The same blending and adaptation took place with even more ease in Ireland because of the absence of violent conflict at the time when Christianity was introduced. The pagan Irish had their own sculpture and ornament which they retained, making such transformations as they found necessary and the whole repertoire of curvilinear decoration was adopted, much in the same way as the stories of Cúchulainn or Finn and the fabulous voyages overseas.

The result of this easy blending is strange. To a certain extent in its

203

early phase Irish Christian art lived on false pretences. It was a pagan decoration masquerading under the guise of an ecclesiastical art. The ornaments which were used for croziers, shrines, church lamps, which covered cruciform slabs and standing crosses, or were intertwined around the initials of Gospel-books were none other than the old La Tene spiral, Germanic animals and half-disguised representations of Celtic gods.

But this is only an obvious and in a way superficial aspect. In an even more subtle and deeper way, Irish Christian art belongs to a very ancient past. The attitude of the artist towards an object or a monument, his use or arrangement of ornament, his sources of inspiration, and his reaction in face of the world, all proceed from a long tradition. Preserved and fortified during centuries of seclusion and independence, this tradition became codified into a system of rules so firm that every borrowed element had to be assimilated and bent to its rigid, uncompromising discipline.

Just as the sculptor of New Grange and the man who carved the Turoe stone interfered as little as possible with the shape of the boulders they were covering with spirals, so the monastic artists long hesitated to deprive their pillars of their natural irregularities. They decorated the surface and no more : an engraved line was often enough for them, or at most a very light relief, without modelling, a work on two planes, which seems a sort of embroidery thrown on the stone. The Reask pillar or those of Carndonagh plainly reveal their hesitancy.

Their notion of human representation proceeded from the same point of view. Certain powers connected with the human shape or with an entity thought of as having a human shape, had to be transferred to the stone or the bronze. To achieve this, some identifying features of a human being – a head, arms, feet – were given to a block of stone or to a lump of bronze; as long as they were there, it was enough, and no indication of the structure of the body need intervene. The attitude of mind which had led to the making of such monuments as the Stuttgart and Boa Island statues survived into Christian times and it is to that tendency to see a figure as the symbol of an idea instead of being concerned with its purely plastic appearance that are due such strange

204

representations as the Athlone Crucifixion, the Inishkea and Fahan Mura slabs and the figures on the Moone cross.

In the same way, though we have now lost the exact meaning of the patterns used in Irish art, there can be little doubt that spiral, interlacing, step-patterns, and stylized foliage are no mere 'ornaments' in the modern meaning of the word. All of them, for centuries, had been carefully spread over objects and on the surface of walls for the sake of their protective virtues and hidden symbols. The interlacing seems to arise in Chaldaea from a stylized representation of running water as is clear from the ducks which are sometimes figured swimming on it.[1] This often carried with it the idea of fertility, but it could lend itself also to the notion of purification. Several explanations have been suggested for the spiral. To the solar origin often proposed, one feels inclined to oppose its close and constant associations with vegetal patterns. As the derivation of curvilinear devices from foliage scrolls was still taking place in the seventh and eighth centuries, we are entitled to assume that its vegetal origin was still felt even when most leaves had dropped from the coiled and desiccated stems, so that the Irish artist could use it as any Early Christian artist would have used the vine. The conspicuous spiral pattern which covers the breast of Christ in the Athlone Crucifixion tends to confirm this. As for the step and key patterns, which derive from combinations of the swastika, they probably keep something of its solar connotation, being sometimes associated with fire and then perhaps with the spirit.

Ornamentation conceived in such a way is a sort of sacred riddle. From a pagan cryptogram it insensibly merged into a Christian one. And there is a possibility that, with the newly awakened interest in Christian symbolism of which the Stowe Missal is a proof at the beginning of the ninth century, these hidden values underlying the weavings of interlacings and spirals became even more subtle and elaborate. Some pages of the Book of Kells will raise the question.

This age-old training to see in a pattern the visible sign of an idea, as decorative words of a mystical language, seems to have prepared the Irish, when they came to draw figurative scenes, to see them instinctively

[1] *Syria*, 1925, pp. 205 sqq.

as, first and foremost, symbols of some abstraction. This is probably why they so readily accepted the Early Christian series of symbols of the Help of God and worked them out into a more elaborate system, also why the mysterious hunting scene, probably charged with a wealth of symbolic meaning, enjoyed such a vogue among Irish sculptors or their patrons.

But if the Irish shared with many other people the habit of making ornaments the essential texture of their art, they had their own method of defining these ornaments. And they organized them according to rules of their own where the love of intricacy, an inner regularity of structure often hidden under a casual appearance and the fear of too symmetrical compositions, were essential motives. Here we are no longer in the international realm of prehistoric art. We touch the special preferences of Celtic artists, inventors of one of the most fastidious and subtle systems of decoration ever seen.

The way the Celts[1] handled their ornament is extremely original. Celtic art throughout its history is dominated by a constant desire to escape from two threatening dangers; it shrinks as violently from the exact and literal imitation of living shapes as from the complete assimilation of an ornament to the rigidity of an obvious geometric figure. Between these two pit-falls it proceeds in a sort of zigzag course, recoiling from one only to be frightened by the other. These perpetual oscillations are the essential cause of its fluidity and elusiveness.

The shrinking from the imitation of real shapes is a fundamental principle of Celtic art from its beginning. For centuries it fed periodically on highly organized and semi-realistic vegetal patterns – palmette in the first period of La Tène, running scroll in the second period, and palmette again when Roman art began to be known in England. Each time the Celtic artist deduced from these classical models abstract and

[1] It is hardly necessary to stress the fact that the word 'Celt' has no racial connotation. There are Celtic languages, there is a Celtic civilization. But the Celts from the time they start emerging into history in the sixth or fifth century B.C., were already an aggregate of people of very different origins. This may be partly the reason why they absorbed newcomers so easily.

fantastic motifs of curves. The same thing happened when the Gauls copied Greek coins. A human profile, the shape of a horse, a flying Victory, were soon transformed into a series of interlocked spirals.

Some of the other abstract arts, in their fear of reality, took refuge in the safe rigidity of geometrical figures. This tendency, latent in Coptic and early Armenian decoration, triumphed in Arab art. But more subtle artists like the early Chinese and the Celts know the monotony and dryness which comes of the acceptance of rigidly abstract figures, and do their best to avoid them.

The most permanent danger threatening Celtic decoration was the assimilation into regularly and dryly coiled spirals of the curves derived from vegetal patterns. At this the Celt would have been just as pained as at a photographic imitation of nature. Hence he found himself engaged in a constant struggle to free his design from turning into closely wound coils connected by bare, thread-like curves. He avoided this menace by an amazing variety of solutions. Either, as in the case of Welsh, Cornish and Irish art of the first century A.D., the scrolls remained very open, and the emphasis was placed on the connecting lines which were bent into every possible variety of curves. Or a little leaf motif was introduced into the pattern – a method already used on the Turoe and Killycluggin stones, and which became general in the seventh and eighth centuries. Various means of turning the centre of the spiral into an ornamental motif were also found. Little secondary spirals and interlacings filled the middle of the coil (Fig. 29). Imagination in this regard rose to its greatest height in the Book of Kells, but the system is already well developed at an earlier period. One of the most frequent means of evading the threat of geometrical regularity is to turn the end of the coil into an animal or bird's head. This is a trick which reappears all through Celtic art and one can find countless examples of it, from the Gaulish scabbard of Cernon-sur-Coole (second century B.C.) to the Petrie crown, the Dublin Museum latchet and the Ahenny crosses, passing by several British objects of the first century A.D. and the Scottish mask from Torrs. The process is very strange when examined closely : a vegetal pattern turned into a combination of curves is saved from becoming a stiff spiral by being transformed into a half-animal motif.

207

Here, we plainly have that oscillation between life and geometry which is the essential rule of Celtic decoration. The final proof of the importance of this principle is given by the sudden disappearance of the spiral about A.D. 1000. In the tenth century, the Irish sculptor, absorbed by many new interests, relaxed in his constant struggle and allowed the curvilinear pattern to curl at last into perfectly regular spirals. As soon as it has thus become a dead motif, deprived of any possibilities of evolution and transformation, it was abandoned so suddenly that it is found only occasionally in eleventh- or twelfth-century decoration.

Strange as it may seem, the fear of imitation of real shapes and the fear of geometry are only two aspects of the same attitude of mind. Geometrical figures are, as much as the shape of an animal or a plant, universal realities which escape individual control, only they are realities of the human mind. They are permanent and unchangeable, purely objective truths which have to be accepted as such. The magical conception of the world rests on a notion of man as not subject to scientific laws. Obedient to it, the Irish artist, rather than submit to that immutable tyranny of facts, took refuge in a universe free of limitations. It is a world in many ways parallel to the real one and it has a fauna, a flora, a human population of its own. Its animals, its plants are not usually those we know, but though never seen, they are to our minds possible, they have a sort of liveable appearance. They are as convincing as beasts of legend and fairy-tale. But their anatomy is strange and allows them to perform astounding feats of decorative agility, and we are expected to believe in this unusual order of things.

These animals and plants are not only of unheard-of species, they are also subjected to a strange transformism. All the parts of this fantastic universe are interchangeable and can suddenly alter their form and merge into each other. Each being seems at once perfectly coherent, a finished individuality, and also able to partake of the nature of other beings or even of inanimate shapes. The animal of some interlacings is half-plant: it is twisted to suggest to the eye the appearance of a scroll and has often a tail ending in a little bunch of leaves. An interlacing, the frame of an illuminated page, suddenly develops head, legs and tail. The plant suggests a spiral. Letters devour each other or fight together.

This multiform and changing world where nothing is what it appears to be is but the plastic equivalent of that country of all wonders which haunts the mind of the Irish poets, and in which all those impossible fancies seem to come true to which the real world does not lend itself.

The theme of the Voyage to the world of eternal youth, to the Happy Islands, or to a country which lies hidden somewhere in the Western Ocean is the subject of one of the most enchanting series of Irish sagas.[1] Bran, son of Febal, Maelduin, and their holy imitator Brendan, all sail in quest of this fantastic vision. This theme was originally the story of a voyage to the Other World which the Celts placed beyond the western horizon, and it remained in the imagination of the Christian Irish as a vision of wonders sometimes sanctified into the quest of a Promised Land or coloured by the memories of seafaring tales. Everything the travellers see has the same shifting and elusive quality as has a page of the Lichfield Gospels or the decoration of the Saint-Germain objects. Manannan, riding across the sea towards the coracle of Bran sings to him:

'What is clear sea
For the prowed skiff in which Bran is
That to me in my chariot of two wheels
Is a delightful plain with a wealth of flowers.

Bran sees
A mass of waves beating across the clear sea;
I see myself in the Plain of Sports
Red-headed flowers that have no flaw.

Speckled salmon leap from the womb
Out of the white sea on which thou lookest:
They are calves, they are lambs of fair hue,
With truce, without mutual slaughter.'[2]

In the same way, in the voyage of Maelduin:

'They went to an island where a strange thing was shown to them, a great stream that rose up out of the strand, and that went like a bow

---

[1] A. G. Van Hamel, *Immrama* (Dublin, 1941).   [2] Meyer, *A. Irish Poetry*, p. 7.

P

of heaven over the whole of the island and came down into the strand on the other side. And they were going under the stream without getting any wet, and they were piercing the stream above, and very large salmon were falling from the stream above on to the ground of the island. . . . And from the evening of Sunday until the full light of the Monday that stream did not move, but stopped in its silence where it was in the sea.'[1]

They meet animals which have a disconcerting appearance :

'A great beast leaped up and went racing about the island and it seemed to Maelduin to be going quicker than the wind. And it went then to the high part of the island, and it did the straightening of the body feat, that is, its head below, its feet above; and this is the way it used to be: it turned in its skin, the flesh and the bones going around but the skin outside without moving. And at another time the skin outside would turn like a mill, and the flesh and the bones not stirring.'[2]

These tales, with the half-faded memories of gods and heroes and the shreds of mythology which linger through them, still enchanted the Irish poet of Christian times, not only because they allude in fantastic terms to a familiar seafaring life, but also because, like the decoration of the stone crosses and the manuscripts, they obey a primitive logic from which he had not yet freed himself. He had not fully accepted the world as something distinct from himself, to be treated objectively. He longed for a country where the rules he had evolved in his mind would be true, where he could mould things to his own will. He dreamed of approximations and impossibilities which would come true at his bidding, of a world where streams could be bent to the shape of a rainbow, where animals would tie themselves into knots, where men would have open-work bodies and pliant skeletons.

His conceptions are all of the same order as the fundamental principles of magic; he establishes certain relations between things, regardless of

---

[1] *Revue celtique*, 1889, p. 59.   [2] Ibid., p. 471.

the normal sequence of cause and effect, and believes that man can alter the normal course of things, reverse it to his will. For an Irishman of the eighth century there were relations between the different parts of the world, between living beings of all kinds and even inanimate things which we, with our scientific categories, are no longer able to understand. The saying still popular on the coasts of Connemara and Mayo, that 'everything which exists on land exists also in the sea', and the consequent close relation between the dog who lives on earth and the 'sea-dog' or otter was more obvious to them than our modern way of seeing a relation between the carnivorous mammal dog and the carnivorous mammal cat. In the same way there is no difficulty for the painter to see as equivalent a spiral-shaped vegetable scroll and a spiral-shaped animal body.

The theme of magical metamorphosis derives from the same attitude of mind. The passing from one shape to the other, from man to animal, from animal to plant is a common feat of wizardry. Poems like those of Amergin and Tuan Mac Cairill preserve it vividly. With Christianity, God was substituted for the wizard of old times, but the notion of perpetual transmutations remained unchanged.

Tuan, telling his protean life to Saint Finan, exclaims :

> 'A hawk to-day, a boar yesterday,
> Wonderful instability!
> Dearer to me every day
> God, the friend who chooses my shape. . . .
>
> . . . Among herds of boars I was,
> Though to-day I am among bird-flocks;
> I know what will come of it :
> I shall still be in another shape.'[1]

In the handling of these fantastic and half-abstract ornaments – animals, plants, curves, interlacings – the Irish artist has very peculiar methods and very often obeys age-old precepts of Celtic decoration.

[1] Kuno Meyer–A. Nutt, *The Voyage of Bran, Son of Febal, to the Land of the Living* (London, 1895), II, p. 290.

Here again his mind works in a disconcerting way. He shows himself infinitely subtle and gifted with such a fastidious taste that he is always afraid of the obvious.

His essential principle of composition is to give an impression of intricacy and complexity by the subtle combination of perfectly clear and highly organized elements. The most elaborate combinations of patterns are never a mere confusion. Every motif, however small, is worked out with all its details and has a perfectly well-defined outline. The animals, however fantastic, whatever their contortions and distortions, keep a coherent shape. In that lies the essential difference between Celtic and Germanic decoration. The Germans, having taken from the classical world figures of well-articulated, more or less naturalistic animals, turned them into ornaments not only by changing their proportions as the Irish did, but also by breaking their bodies and evolving incomplete, disconnected monsters. The animal brought by the Saxons into England was still at an early stage of disintegration, but the different parts of its body were already beginning to break loose from each other. When that fragmentary beast with its detached legs and isolated eyes came into the hands of the Irish artists, they at once proceeded to unite the vagrant pieces, in so doing bringing it back to life, and the broken creature of the Caenby disc or the Crundale sword became the lively little animal of the Book of Durrow. Through all the existence of animal-interlacing in Ireland, from the seventh to the twelfth century, this essential logic of each animal was maintained as a contrast to the growing incoherence of the Germanic animal of the eighth and ninth centuries. In the same way, the curvilinear motifs of early Celtic art kept a sort of internal cohesion, however meandering and disconnected they may look at first sight.

But to achieve an appearance of baffling complexity by the combination of perfectly clear patterns is not the only resource of the inventive minds of the Irish artists when they want to surprise us. More elaborate problems of composition worry them. Their difficulty has been that of the Celtic artist for centuries. The semi-classical motifs of foliage on which he based his system of curves brought into his world, each time he came into close contact with them, a too rigid and obvious symmetry.

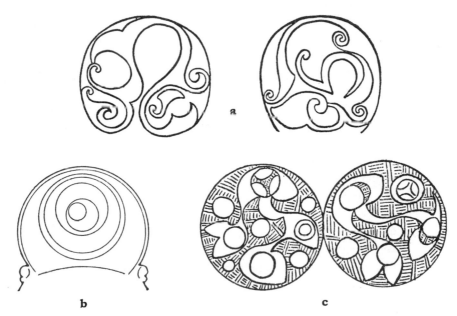

Fig. 27. a, handles of 'spoons' from Weston, near Bath (N.M.E.);
b, handle of 'spoon' found in Ireland (N.M.D.);
c, Trelan Bahow mirror, detail (Br. M.).

They were built around an axis, identical or reversed patterns exactly balancing each other on both sides of a central line. For a while the Celt may let this method rule his own work. But soon the internal logic of his art gets to work again and turns these regularly disposed patterns into new combinations governed by infinitely more subtle laws. It is not exactly the dislike of symmetry which rules the new disposition, but the dislike of an exact and rigid symmetry – the parallel, applied to a problem of composition, to the fear of geometry in the definition of a pattern. It is as if one of these 'geasa' or magical taboos, which bind the actions of all the heroes of the sagas acted constantly in forbidding the Irish artist to balance two exactly similar designs. Equality is generally replaced by equivalence. At an early date, there are a few examples of complete asymmetry – as the decoration of the British Museum helmet – and the use of alternating motifs or alternately coloured

213

patterns is frequent. But these are not quite satisfactory solutions. A reversed symmetry is still symmetry and complete asymmetry is a negative recognition of symmetry. The mind of the Irish decorator, left to itself, has shrewder and more elaborate ways of evading regularity. One, which flourishes especially in Ireland and in the Welsh–Cornish area around the first century A.D., consists in the use of deceptively similar curves disposed inside identical frames. The back of the mirror of Trelan Bahow, the handles of the Bath spoons, and those of the spoons in Dublin Museum (Fig. 27), are decorated according to this method. Later (Fig. 14), the Inishkea South slab with its angular patterns balancing curves on both sides of the handle, the panels of animals in the Saint-Gall Gospels with their infinite variations, all represent applications of the same principle. In all cases there is not an obvious asymmetry. The frames – or in the case of the slab, the centres of the coils and their disposition – are symmetrical. They give a reassuring impression of regularity to the eye. It is only after a moment that the feeling creeps into the onlooker's mind that, though there may be the same quantity of curves on both sides, and in similar frames or a similar disposition, there is something odd about the curves themselves, that their identity is only apparent, and does not stand a careful examination.

This tendency can be, at times, developed into a real method for cheating the eye, deceiving it into an appearance of geometry or of regular composition, when it is really given an extraordinary assortment of irregularities to look at. The circle interlacings with their suggestion of a discoid shape are the most elementary instance of that process. But the Celts have more subtle resources at their disposal. A Welsh shield of the first century A.D. found at Mael Hirradug is a good example of their virtuosity (Fig. 30). On it a square, a circle and a threefold pattern are combined in such a way that the fundamental discordance between the four sides of the square and the three-fold rhythm of the inner pattern is disguised in an appearance of perfect balance. This type of composition is long-lived. The tripartite motif within a square frame is current in the manuscripts. One of the obvious examples occurs in the Book of Lindisfarne and we will soon meet it again.

214

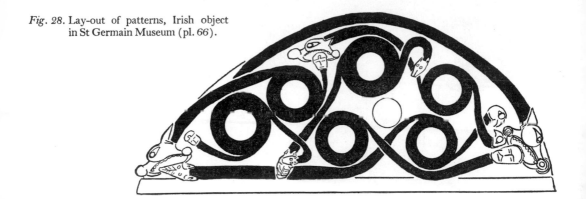

Fig. 28. Lay-out of patterns, Irish object in St Germain Museum (pl. 66).

The two bronze objects preserved in the Musée des Antiquités nationales, at Saint-Germain, show the persistence, in a more elaborate form, of the same method (Fig. 28). Along the slightly irregular curve and the straight line which constitute their outline, runs an illusion of continuous border given by the crossing of four snakes' bodies. In this deceptive frame, six discs of uneven sizes – very slightly uneven, so that one would hardly notice their disparity at first – are irregularly disposed. A kind of rhythm is given to the whole composition by the repetition of the heads of devouring beasts and the four times repeated crossings of the snakes, but the rigidity which might ensue is abolished by the bending upwards of the stem with the human head. As for the discs, their spirals have three threads, as they come from three centres, but from one of them only start three serpent-like stems. The others have only two or even one, whilst the idle threads disappear in the interlacings of the background. Still the illusion of three stems is preserved by the passing close by of one or two stems coming from another disc.

Many other jewels and pages of manuscripts reveal the same astounding combinations. That deliberate cheating coming of a refinement of subtlety, of a virtuosity which likes to hide itself, calls to mind the 'syllogism of deceit' which Benedict of Aniane accused the Irish scholastics of practising,[1] probably an equivalent feat in terms of verbal virtuosity, the masterpiece of a twisted logic.

[1] Kenney, *Sources*, p. 537.

215

Fig. 29. Details of spirals from Irish
manuscripts.

During the seventh and eighth centuries, however, close contacts with
foreign arts bring in a conflicting sense of regularity. The composition
of crosses, jewels, pages of illumination, obey alternately the old subtle
methods and the more straightforward foreign ways. Nevertheless the
tendency to asymmetry and equivalence remained so strongly part
and parcel of the Celtic mind that it produced some time later in Irish
poetry one of the most elaborate systems of metres, rhymes and asson-
ances ever invented.[1]

If now we turn to the physical method, the practical means by which
all this is produced, we will find that, by an ultimate twist, it is very
often the result of an incredibly clever play of compasses, or that it is
based, as if on a scaffolding, on tiny grilles and regular networks of lines
or circles. Since the study of Bruce-Mitford on the Lindisfarne Gospels,
actual proofs of this exist as far as manuscripts are concerned : centres
of compass-drawn circles or arcs and lines scratched on the surface of

[1] Kuno Meyer, *A Primer of Irish Metrics* (Dublin, 1909); Gerard Murphy,
Early Irish Metrics (Dublin, 1961).

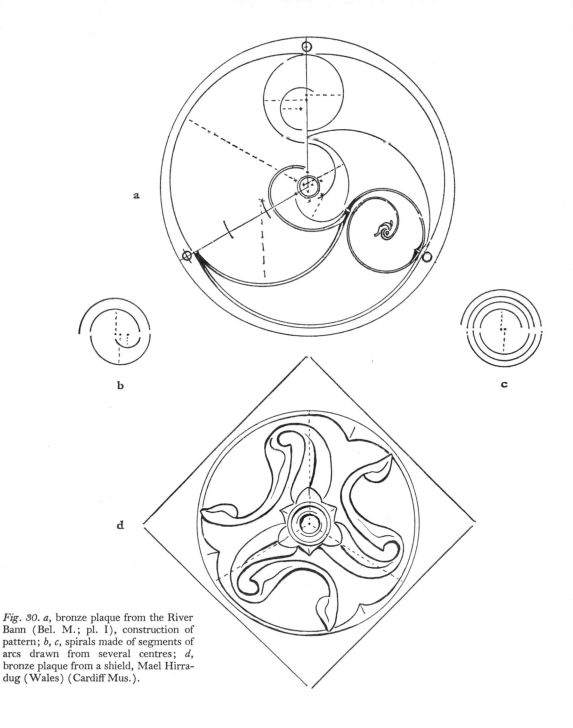

Fig. 30. a, bronze plaque from the River Bann (Bel. M.; pl. I), construction of pattern; *b, c,* spirals made of segments of arcs drawn from several centres; *d,* bronze plaque from a shield, Mael Hirradug (Wales) (Cardiff Mus.).

the vellum have been photographed or plotted. These are mechanical aids which one would expect in the execution of any overall pattern. But perhaps their use goes further and shows a reliance on the compass-drawn curve which would seem, at first sight, to come as a contradiction to that fear of geometry which has been stressed above. In fact it is something much more complex: the use of geometrical instruments perversely turned to the construction of asymmetrical or irregular patterns. In some cases only, and chiefly in the Lindisfarne Gospels where it is overdone and perhaps not fully understood, does this use of compasses result in stiffness and rigid balance.

It goes back very far. We have seen a striking example of it in the box from the Somerset hoard (Pl. 5). There, its outcome is the most incredible sleight of hand where all symmetry is eluded. A very simple play of circles drawn from points nearly all on one line gives the less bewildering arrangement on the handles of the Dublin 'spoons', still unexpected in its juggling of rings (Fig. 27). In both these examples most of the centres from which the circles or arcs were drawn are still visible. In the case of the Bann disc they have been obliterated by the artist. But there can be no doubt that these perfect segments of curves were drawn with compasses (Pl. I and Fig. 30). E. M. Jope has reconstructed very convincingly the method. It would consist in drawing from the centre of a bronze disc three equidistant radii. These were apparently divided in three segments. From the farther of these dividing points, half-circles were drawn, which combine with other half-circles to give a spiral curve. The other dividing points serve to mark the places where other arcs meet, completing the design. Then for fear that the pattern would be too regular, some of the lines are thickened and worked in slight relief and the centres of the spirals are given the appearance of little animal heads.

This is already pretty complicated as a pattern revolving around a centre and gives the initial principle of building spirals by means of half-circle arcs drawn alternatively from two centres (Fig. 30). The proof of a later use of this method is to be found on a page of the Lichfield Gospels where the centres are perfectly visible (Pl. 102). Another type of composition appears on some of the Lough Crew bone-slips and there the centres are nearly all perfectly marked so that it is easy to

218

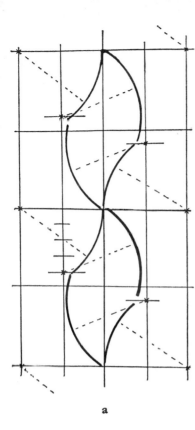

a

Fig. 31. Geometrical construction of pattern on one of the bone slips from Lough Crew (pl. 8): *a*, squared framework used to determine the centres from which are drawn the segments of arc forming the main structure of the pattern; *b*, complement of the pattern.

b

reconstruct the way in which the pattern was built. Some are of the off-centre circles type, emphasized by stippling as on the Somerset box. Another has a flowing garland pattern which has a deceptive appearance of free-hand drawing (Pl. 8). In actual fact, to reconstruct it, one must establish a grille (Fig. 31) on which all the chief centres are found and which is based on the use of a definite unit of measurement. Most of the radii of the arcs drawn from these centres are also based on this unit. Still, probably again to avoid a deadly regularity, a few radii are of different length and a few accessory centres are placed off the network of the grille. Actually the grille is not indicated on the surface of the bone and one has to assume that a drawing previously made on a scrap of vellum or on a slate served as a first basis for the composition. It is likely that the patterns on the best of the engraved scabbards from the Bann valley were drawn by a similar method.[1]

Some of the patterns of the Lichfield–Lindisfarne group of manuscripts are made in practically the same way as those we have examined. For example the square which Bruce-Mitford has studied and where compass-centres can be seen (Fig. 32 and Pl. 102), reveals a method of construction which pertains both to that of the Bann disc and of the Lough Crew bone-slip, and which is close also to the Mael Hirradug shield-piece in its method of composition (Fig. 31). Inside a square a circle was drawn from the intersecting point of the diagonals. On the four segments of diagonals outside it, four small circles were drawn, stressing the four-fold aspect of the pattern. From that the artist had to pass to a rhythm of three. He did it by drawing two diameters and keeping one of the diagonals, so that the circle was divided into six equal segments. Then, as in the case of the Bann disc, each radius was divided into three equal sections by two points, one of which was used to draw arcs of circles forming a part of the pattern, while the other determined the

---

[1] A possible method of establishing the patterns is indicated in a passage of a story relating to Cúchulainn: '[Mac Enge] saw a man coming over the outer wall to him, with a fork in his hand, and two prongs projecting from it; he planted one of the prongs in the ashes and with the other described the devices that were to be engraved on Cúchulainn's shield' (T.C.D., Ms. 1336 (H.3.17); see: H. S. Crawford, 'The engraved bone objects found at Lough Crew', *J.R.S.A.I.*, 1925, pp. 15 sqq.).

a

Fig. 32. Geometrical construction of a pattern of spirals in the Lindisfarne Gospels (Pl. 102) : *a*, main lines of construction; *b*, position of the centres from which are drawn the segments of arcs forming the pattern.

b

point of contact of the hooked patterns which constitute the final design. There again there are centres off this general scheme. The finished pattern has an added irregularity in the fact that the small circles are finally turned into spirals connected by the usual leaf motifs which are of necessity put sideways in the spandrels.

This elaborate method of disciplined drawing was applied to the new patterns which enriched the Irish repertoire. One of the most striking examples of this is the symbol of Saint John in the Echternach Gospels which is all drawn by arcs of circles from various centres (Pl. V and Fig. 33). The same method of elaborate composition governs the arrangement of animal-interlacings, especially when they are turned into a regular weaving of beasts' bodies. There, compass-drawn arcs are less often used in the actual definition of the pattern. They are more often aids to the lay-out and, together with diagonals, they determine the space allotted to each animal or the curve of part of its body (Figs. 24, 34). Still some careful probing would probably reveal more use of arcs in the definition of the body itself than one would expect, so natural a means of expression had it become.

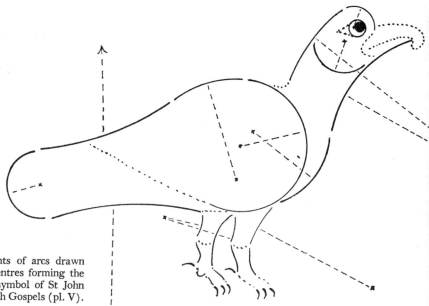

Fig. 33. Segments of arcs drawn from various centres forming the outline of the symbol of St John in the Echternach Gospels (pl. V).

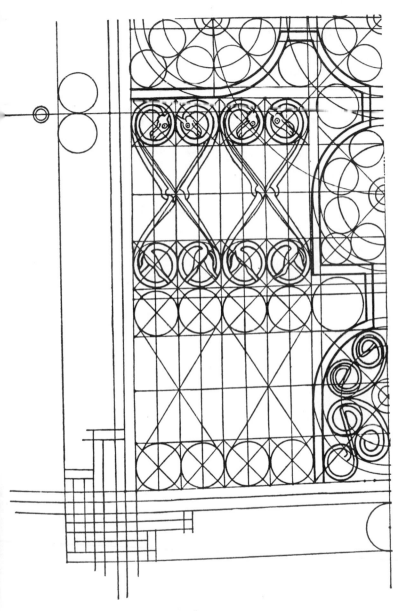

Fig. 34. Geometrical construction of the patterns
on a page of the Lindisfarne Gospels (pl.
104), from the pricks and lines found on
the reverse of the page by R. Bruce-
Mitford (after *E.Q.C. Lindisfarnensis*).

For the interlacings, Bruce-Mitford has supplied the proof that they were built on a fine grid, lightly marked on the surface of the vellum. The same applies to step-patterns.

All these mechanical aids do not, of course, minimize, as Bruce-Mitford seems to think, the part of the artist in the elaboration of his decor. They are tools to be used to the best effect, his role being to combine the patterns which they help him to produce and make a work of art out of that inert material. Of these tools, his mind must remain master, as the architect keeps under control all the mechanical aids which have to be used in the making of the blue-print, or as the musician uses the formidable array of carefully measured and stretched wires which fill the sound-box of the piano. In fact, these comparisons with those of the arts which are based on mathematical combinations are only approximate. These geometrical means of building a pattern are not used absolutely constantly; and the total dependence on them of the artist of the Lindisfarne Gospels does not speak very highly for the way in which he had mastered the elements of his training. It is not impossible that a really original artist of that time was expected to outgrow to a certain extent all these props which were probably used rigidly during his training. The Lichfield Gospels are perhaps less fiercely submitted to that iron discipline.

Here, a study of the 'trial-pieces' could be of interest (Pls. 13, 37), though there is certainly not enough material available to yield very definite results. Still, they would provide grilles very similar to those found by Bruce-Mitford, and arrangements of compass-drawn circles which fall within the same construction system.

A question remains, that of knowing how far the study of this art which is nearly constantly 'non representational' – or at least wanders from the representation of real things, even if it likes to show under a precise guise the creatures of its fancies and dreams – how far the example of this abstract art based on subtle geometrical combinations, may be rich in teachings for the modern artist obsessed by similar problems. This it will remain the part of the artists themselves to decide.

Bibliographical Abbreviations

AA. SS. Boll. – *Aeta Sanctorum,* edited by the Bollandists.

Åberg, *Occident-Orient* – Nils Åberg, *The Occident and the Orient in the Art of the Seventh Century;* I, *The British Isles,* Stockholm, 1943; II, *Lombard Italy,* Stockholm, 1945; III, *The Merovingian Empire,* Stockholm, 1947.

A.F.M. – *Annals of the Kingdom of Ireland by the Four Masters,* ed. John O'Donovan, Dublin, vol. I, 1851.

Allen, *Celtic Art* – J. Romilly Allen, *Celtic Art in Pagan and Christian Times,* London, 1904.

Allen–Anderson – *The Early Christian Monuments of Scotland. A classified, illustrated, descriptive list of the monuments, with an analysis of their Symbolism and Ornamentation,* by J. Romilly Allen, *with an Introduction* by Joseph Anderson, Edinburgh, 1903.

An. Boll. – *Analecta Bollandiana.*

Ancient Laws of Ir. – *Ancient Laws of Ireland, Senchus Mór,* Dublin, 5 vol., 1865–1901.

Anderson, *Adomnan* – A. O. and M. O. Anderson, *Adomnan's Life of Columba,* London, 1961.

Anglo-Saxon Chr. – Dorothy Whitelock, with D. C. Douglas and S. I. Tucker, *The Anglo-Saxon Chronicle,* London, 1961.

Ant. J. – *The Antiquaries Journal* (Journal of the Society of Antiquaries of London).

A.U. – *Annals of Ulster, otherwise Annals of Senat. A Chronicle of Irish Affairs from A.D. 431 to A.D. 1540,* vol. I, ed. by William M. Hennessy, Dublin, 1887.

Baldwin Brown, *Arts in E. England* – G. Baldwin Brown, *The Arts in Early England,* London, 1903–1930.

Bede, *H. abb.* – *Historia abbatum auctore Baeda* (see Plummer).

Bede, *H. E.* – *Baedae Historia Ecclesiastica Gentis Anglorum* (see Plummer).

Bieler, *Ireland* – Ludwig Bieler, *Ireland, Harbinger of the Middle Ages,* London, New York, Toronto, 1963.

Brash, *Eccles. Arch.* – R. R. Brash, *The Ecclesiastical Architecture of Ireland, to the close of the Twelfth Century,* Dublin, 1875.

C.A.A.I. – *Christian Art in Ancient Ireland,* Dublin, vol. I, ed. by Adolf Mahr, 1932, vol. II, ed. by Joseph Raftery, 1941.

Cabrol-Leclercq – Rme Dom Fernand Cabrol – R. P. Dom H. Leclercq, *Dictionnaire d'Archéologie chrétienne et de Liturgie,* Paris, 1907 sqq.

C. de la Croix, *Hypogée-Martyrium* – Camille de la Croix, S.J., *Hypogée-Martyrium de Poitiers,* Paris, 1883.

Champneys, *Ir. Eccl. Arch.* – Arthur Charles Champneys, *Irish Ecclesiastical Architecture, with some notice of similar or related work in England, Scotland and elsewhere,* London, 1910.

Coffey, *Guide* – George Coffey, *Guide to the Celtic Antiquities of the Christian Period preserved in the National Museum, Dublin,* Dublin, 1909, 1910.

Colgan, *Tr. Thaum.* – J. Colgan, O.F.M., *Triadis Thaumaturgae,* Louvain, 1647.

Colgan, *AA. SS. Hib.* – J. Colgan, O.F.M., *Acta Sanctorum veteris et majoris Scotiae, seu Hiberniae sanctorum Insulae,* Louvain, 1645 (only vol. I published) see : *The Acta Sanctorum Hiberniae,* (Irish Manuscripts Commission), Dublin, 1947.

Collingwood, *Northumbrian Crosses* – W. G. Collingwood, *Northumbrian Crosses of the Pre-Norman Age,* London, 1927.

Dark Age Britain – *Dark Age Britain, Studies presented to E. T. Leeds,* ed. by D. B. Harden, London, 1956.

Dunraven, *Notes* – The Earl of Dunraven, *Notes on Irish Architecture,* (ed. by Margaret Stokes), 2 vol., London, 1875, 1877.

Ehwald, *Aldhelmi Opera* – R. Ehwald, *Aldhelmi Opera, M.G.H., Auct. Ant.,* XV (1919).

E.Q.C. Durmachensis – *Evangeliorum Quattuor Codex Durmachensis,* Olten-Lausanne-Fribourg, 1960, vol. I : facsimile, vol. II : text by A. A. Luce, G. O. Simms, P. Meyer, L. Bieler.

E.Q.C. Lindisfarnensis – *Evangeliorum Quattuor Codex Lindisfarnensis,* Olten-Lausanne-Fribourg, vol. I, 1956: facsimile; vol. II, 1960: text by T. D. Kendrick, T. J. Brown, R. L. S. Bruce-Mitford, H. Rosen-Runge, A. S. C. Ross, E. G. Stanley, A. E. A. Werner.

Etudes mérov. – *Etudes mérovingiennes, Actes des journées de Poitiers, 1er-3 mai 1952,* Paris, 1953.

Flower, *The Two Eyes of Ireland* – Robin Flower, 'The Two Eyes of Ireland, Religion and Literature in Ireland in the eighth and ninth centuries', *Report of the Church of Ireland Conference held in Dublin, 11th–14th October, 1932,* pp. 66 sqq, Dublin, 1932.

F.-S. M. Néill – *Féil-sgríbhinn Eóin Mhic Néill, Essays and Studies presented to Professor Eoin Mac Neill,* ed. by J. Ryan, S.J., Dublin, 1940. *G.B.A.* – *Gazette des Beaux-Arts.*

Gougaud, *Christianity* – Dom Louis Gougaud, O.S.B., *Christianity in Celtic Lands; a History of the Churches of the Celts, their development, influence and mutual relations,* London, 1932.

H. abb. a. – *Historia Abbatum auctore Anonymo* (see Plummer).

Hencken, *Cahercommaun* – Hugh O'Neill-Hencken, *Cahercommaun: a Stone Fort in County Clare,* Dublin (*J.R.S.A.I.*), 1938.

Hencken, *Lagore* – Hugh Hencken, 'Lagore Crannog, an Irish Royal Residence of the 7th to 10th centuries A.D.', *P.R.I.A.,* 1950 (C), pp. 1 sqq, including (pp. 18–34): Liam Price, 'The History of Lagore, from Annals and other Sources'.

H.B.S. – Henry Bradshaw Society.

Henry, *Débuts min. irl.* – Françoise Henry, 'Les débuts de la miniature irlandaise, *G.B.A.,* 1950, pp. 5 sqq.

Henry, *An Irish Manuscript* – F. Henry, 'An Irish Manuscript in the British Museum', *J.R.S.A.I.,* 1957, pp. 147 sqq.

Henry, *Early Monasteries* – F. Henry, 'Early Monasteries, Beehive Huts and Dry-Stone Houses in the neighbourhood of Caherciveen and Waterville (Co. Kerry)', *P.R.I.A.,* 1957 (C), pp. 45 sqq.

Henry, *Em. Occ.* – F. Henry, 'Emailleurs d'Occident', *Préhistoire,* II, 1, pp. 65 sqq.

Henry, *Inishkea* – F. Henry, 'Remains of the Early Christian Period on Inishkea North, Co. Mayo', *J.R.S.A.I.,* 1945, pp. 127 sqq.

Henry, *Ir. Enam.* – F. Henry, 'Irish Enamels of the Dark Ages and their Relation to the Cloisonné Techniques, *Dark Age Britain*, pp. 71 sqq.

Henry, *Sc. irl.* – F. Henry, *La sculpture irlandaise pendant les douze premiers siècles de l'ère chrétienne*, Paris, 1932.

Henry, *Slabs and Pillars* – F. Henry, 'Early Christian Slabs and Pillar-Stones in the West of Ireland', *J.R.S.A.I.*, 1937, pp. 265 sqq.

Henry – Marsh-Micheli, *Illumination* – F. Henry – G. L. Marsh-Micheli, 'A Century of Irish Illumination (1070–1170)', *P.R.I.A.*, 1962(C), pp. 101 sqq.

I.H.S. – *Irish Historical Studies.*

Jackson, *Nature Poetry* – Kenneth Jackson, *Studies in Early Celtic Nature Poetry*, Cambridge, 1955.

Jacobsthal, *C.A.* – Paul Jacobsthal, *Early Celtic Art*, Oxford, 1944.

J.C.H.A.S. – *Journal of the Cork Historical and Archaeological Society.*

J.G.A.H.S. – *Journal of the Galway Historical and Archaeological Society.*

Jonas, *Vita Columbani* – B. Krusch, *Ionae Vita Columbani*, *M.G.H. Script. Rer. Merov.*, IV (1902); *separatim*: 1905.

J.R.S.A.I. – *Journal of the Royal Society of Antiquaries of Ireland.*

Kendrick, *A. S. Art* – T. D. Kendrick, *Anglo-Saxon Art to A.D. 900*, London, 1938.

Kenney, *Sources* – James F. Kenney, *The Sources of the Early History of Ireland, an Introduction and Guide*, vol. I: *Ecclesiastical* (the only volume published), New York, 1929.

Kilbride-Jones, *Brooches* – H. E. Kilbride-Jones, 'The Evolution of the Penannular Brooches with Zoomorphic Terminals in Great Britain and Ireland', *P.R.I.A.*, 1937 (C), pp. 379 sqq.

Lawlor, *Cathach* – H. J. Lawlor, 'The Cathach of St Columba', *P.R.I.A.*, 1916 (C), pp. 241 sqq.

Lawlor, *Mulling* – H. J. Lawlor, *Chapters on the Book of Mulling*, Edinburgh, 1897.

Leask, *Ir. Churches* – Harold G. Leask, *Irish Churches and Monastic Buildings*, I: *The First Phases and the Romanesque Period*, Dundalk, 1955.

Lionard, *Grave-Slabs* – P. Lionard, C.S.Sp., 'Early Irish Grave-Slabs', *P.R.I.A.*, 1961(C), pp. 95 sqq.

Lowe, *C. L. A.* – Elias Avery Lowe, *Codices Latini Antiquiores*, I, Vatican City, Oxford, 1935; II, Great Britain and Ireland, 1935; III, Italy (Ancona-Novara), 1938; IV, Italy (Perugia-Verona), 1947; V, France (Paris), 1950; VI, France (Abbeville-Valenciennes), 1953; VII, Switzerland, 1956; VIII, Germany (Altenburg-Leipzig), 1959; IX, Germany (Maria Laach-Würzburg), 1959.

McGurk – Patrick McGurk, *Latin Gospel-Books from A.D. 400 to A.D. 800*, Paris-Brussels-Antwerp-Amsterdam, 1961.

McGurk, *Pocket-Books* – P. McGurk 'The Irish Pocket Gospel-Books', *Sacris Erudiri*, 1956, pp. 249 sqq.

MacNeill, *Phases* – Eoin MacNeill, *Phases of Irish History*, Dublin, 1920.

Mahr – see : *C.A.A.I.*

Masai, *Origines*, F. Masai, *Essai sur les Origines de la Miniature dite irlandaise*, Brussels, 1947.

Macalister, *Arch. Ir.* – R. A. S. Macalister, *The Archaeology of Ireland*, 1st ed., London, 1928.

Macalister, *Clonmacnois* – R. A. S. Macalister, *The Memorial Slabs at Clonmacnois, King's County*, Dublin (*J.R.S.A.I.*), 1909.

Macalister, *Corpus* – R. A. S. Macalister, *Corpus Inscriptionum Insularum Celticarum*, 2 vol., Dublin, 1945, 1949.

Med. Arch. – *Medieval Archaeology.*

Meyer, *E. Irish Poetry* – Kuno Meyer, *Selections from Early Irish Poetry*, London, 1911.

M.G.H. – *Monumenta Germaniae Historica.*

Micheli, *Miniature* – G. L. Micheli, *La Miniature du Haut Moyen-Age et les Influences irlandaises*, Brussels, 1939.

Micheli – see : Henry – Marsh-Micheli.

Migne, *P. L.* – J. P. Migne, *Patrologiae cursus completus, series latina*, Paris, 1878 sqq.

Morey, *E. C. Art* – C. R. Morey, *Early Christian Art*, Princeton, New Jersey, 1953.

Mynors, *Durham Manuscripts* – R. A. B. Mynors, *Durham Cathedral Manuscripts to the End of the Twelfth Century*, Oxford, 1939.

Nash-Williams – E. Nash-Williams, *Early Christian Monuments of Wales*, Cardiff, 1950.

Nordenfalk, *Before the B. of Durrow* – Carl Nordenfalk, 'Before the Book of Durrow', *Acta Archaeologica*, 1947, pp. 141 sqq.

O'Rahilly, *Hist and Myth.* – T. F. O'Rahilly, *Early Irish History and Mythology*, Dublin, 1946.

Ó Ríordáin, *Antiquities* – Seán P. Ó Ríordáin, *Antiquities of the Irish Countryside*, Cork, 1942, London, 1953.

Paor, *E. C. Ireland* – Maire and Liam de Paor, *Early Christian Ireland*, London, 1958.

Petrie, *Round Towers* – George Petrie, *The Ecclesiastical Architecture of Ireland anterior to the Anglo-Norman Invasion, comprising an Essay on the Origin and Uses of the Round Towers of Ireland*, Dublin, 1845.

Plummer – C. Plummer, *Venerabilis Bedae Opera Historica*, Oxford, 1896; *Historia Ecclesiastica Gentis Anglorum*, vol. I, pp. 1 sqq.; *Historia Abbatum auctore Beda*, vol. I, pp. 364 sqq.; *Historia Abbatum auctore Anonymo*, vol. I, pp. 388 sqq.

Plummer, *VV.SS.Hib.* – C. Plummer, *Vitae Sanctorum Hiberniae*, Oxford, 1910.

P.P.S. – *Proceedings of the Prehistoric Society.*

P.R.I.A. – *Proceedings of the Royal Irish Academy.*

P.S.A.Sc. – *Proceedings of the Society of Antiquaries of Scotland.*

R.A. – *Revue archeologique.*

Raftery, *Preh. Ir.* – Joseph Raftery, *Prehistoric Ireland*, London, 1951.

Raftery – see : *C.A.A.I.*

Reeves, *St Columba* – William Reeves, *The Life of St Columba, Founder of Hy, written by Adamnan*, Dublin, 1857.

Relics of St Cuthbert – *The Relics of Saint Cuthbert, Studies by various authors*, ed. C. F. Battiscombe, Oxford, 1956.

Roe, *Western Ossory* – Helen M. Roe, *The High Crosses of Western Ossory*, Kilkenny, 1958, 1962.

Ryan, *Monasticism* – John Ryan, S.J., *Irish Monasticism, Origins and early Development*, Dublin, 1931.

Salin, *C. M.* – Edouard Salin, *La civilisation mérovingienne d'après les sépultures, les textes et le laboratoire*, Paris, 4 vol., 1950–59.

230

Salin, *Thierornamentik* – Bernhard Salin, *Die altgermanische Thierorna-mentik*, Stockholm, 1904.

Smith, *Guide Anglo-Saxon A.* – Reginald Smith, *British Museum Guide to Anglo-Saxon Antiquities*, London, 1923.

Smith, *Guide Iron Age* – Reginald Smith, *British Museum Guide to Early Iron Age Antiquities*, London, 1925.

Stokes, *Early Christian Arch.* – Margaret Stokes, *Early Christian Architecture in Ireland*, London, 1878.

Stokes, *Martyr. Oengus* – Whitley Stokes, *The Martyrology of Oengus the Culdee* London (*H.B.S.*), 1905.

Thurneysen, *Helden und Königsage* – R. Thurneysen, *Die Irische Helden und Königsage*, Halle, 1900.

Traube, *Perrona Scottorum*, L. Traube, 'Perrona Scottorum, ein Beitrag zur Veberlieferungsgeschichte und zur Paleographie des Mittelalters', *Sitzungsberichte der philos., philol., und der hist. Klasse der königlig. bayerische Akademie d. Wissenschaft*, 1900, pp. 469–538.

U.J.A. – *Ulster Journal of Archaeology*.

Ussher, *Sylloge* – J. Ussher, *The whole Works*, vol. IV, Dublin, 1631.

Varagnac – Fabre, *Art gaulois* – André Varagnac – Gabrielle Fabre, *L'Art gaulois*, col. Zodiaque, 1956.

Vit. Col. – *Vita Columbae*; see : Reeves.

V. Ant. – *Viking Antiquities in Great Britain and Ireland*, vol. II : Sigurd Grieg, *Viking Antiquities in Scotland*; vol. V : Jan Petersen, *British Antiquities of the Viking Period found in Norway*; Oslo, 1940.

Wakeman, *Inismurray* – W. F. Wakeman, *A Survey of the Antiquarian Remains on the Island of Inismurray*, London-Edinburgh, 1867.

Walker, *S. Columbani Op.* – C. S. M. Walker, *Sancti Columbani Opera*, Dublin, 1957.

Ward-Perkins, *Sc. of Visigothic France* – J. B. Ward-Perkins, 'The Sculpture of Visigothic France', *Archaeologia*, 1937, pp. 79 sqq.

Warren, *Antiphonary of Bangor* – F. E. Warren, *The Antiphonary of Bangor*, London (*H.B.S.*), 2 vol., 1893, 1895.

Wilpert, *R. Mosaiken* – J. Wilpert, *Dir Römischen Mosaiken und Male-reien der kirchlischen Bauten vom IV bis XIII Jahrhundert*, Freiburg-am-Brisgau, 1916.

Wordsworth and White – J. Wordsworth – H. J. White, *Novum Testamentum Latine secundum editionem sancti Hieronymi*, Oxford, 1911.

Wood-Martin, *Lake Dwellings* – W. G. Wood-Martin, *The Lake-Dwellings of Ireland*, Dublin, London, 1886.

Z.C.P. – *Zeitschrift für celtische Philologie*.

Zimmermann – E. Heinrich Zimmermann, *Vorkarolingische Miniaturen* (1 vol. text, 4 vol. plates), Berlin, 1916.

General Index

Figures in brackets refer to footnotes (pages).
Figures in square brackets refer to relevant
pages where the word is not mentioned.
Figures in italics refer to line illustrations (pages).

235

List of Monochrome Plates

All monochrome photographs without indication of origin are by P. Belzeaux–Zodiaque.
The others, except two which are by J. Dieuzaide–Zodiaque, are from the Photographic Archives of the Department of Archaeology, University College, Dublin, and for these the origin of each negative has been indicated.

1. Tumulus of New Grange, Meath, detail of carved stone
2. Statue, Boa Island, Fermanagh (*Ph. F. Henry*)
3. Statue, formerly at Tanderagee, Armagh, now in Armagh Cathedral (*Ph. F. Henry*)
4. Details of horse-trappings found at Attymon, Galway (N.M.D.) (*Ph. N.M.D.*)
5. Bronze box, Somerset hoard, Galway (N.M.D.)
6. Engraved scabbard, Lisnacroghera, Antrim (Br. M.)
7. Engraved bone depicting a stag hunt, Lough Crew, Meath (N.M.D.); detail of scabbard from Lisnacroghera, Antrim (Bel.M.) (*Ph. F. Henry*)
8. Engraved bone slips, Lough Crew, Meath (N.M.D.)
9. Initials from the Cathach (R.I.A.)
10. Embossed bronze disc found in Ireland (Br.M.); Ardakillin Brooch, Roscommon (N.M.D.)
11. Detail of the Petrie Crown (N.M.D.)
12. Initials from the Cathach (R.I.A.)
13. Enamelled bronze brooch and latchet, Ireland (N.M.D.); carved bone, Dooey (N.M.D.)
14. Stone pillar with engraved cross and ogham inscription from Aglish, Kerry (N.M.D.)
15. Kilfountain Pillar, Kerry (*Ph. I. Crozier*); Reask Pillar, Kerry (*Ph. F. Henry*)

16. Loher Pillar, Kerry (*Ph. F. Henry*)
17. Skellig Michael, Kerry, stairs leading to the monastery (*Ph. F. Henry*)
18. Skellig Michael, Kerry, monastic settlement (*Ph. F. Henry*)
19. Oratory of Temple Cashel, Kerry (*Ph. F. Henry*); Skellig Michael, Kerry, monastic cells (*Ph. F. Henry*)
20. Portable reliquaries, one found in Lough Erne, Fermanagh (N.M.D.); and the other in a Norwegian tomb (Copenhagen Museum) (*Ph. Copenh. M.*)
21. Carved slab at Glendalough, Wicklow (*Ph. F. Henry*)
22. Doorway of church, Clonamery, Kilkenny
23. Doorway of church, Fore, Westmeath (*Ph. F. Henry*)
24. Large penannular brooch found in crannog No. 2, Ballinderry, Westmeath, and two hand-pins (N.M.D.)
25. Enamelled plaque from the large hanging-bowl found at Sutton Hoo, England (Br.M.)
26. Lullingstone hanging-bowl, England (Br.M.); enamelled bird head found in the north of Ireland (Ashmolean Museum, Oxford)
27. Detail from the Lullingstone bowl (Br.M.)
28. Enamelled disc and bronze belt buckle found at Lagore, Meath (N.M.D.); detail of the Tara Brooch (N.M.D.)
29. Enamelled hanging-bowl escutcheon found at Clonmacnois, Offaly (N.M.D.)
30. Enamelled disc from the hanging-bowl found at Winchester, England (N.M.D.)
31. Book of Durrow, ornamental page (T.C.D.)
32. West front of the Cathedral of Glendalough, Wicklow
33. Disc of gilt bronze with gold filigree on the foot of the chalice found at Ardagh, Limerick (N.M.D.)
34. Belt Reliquary found at Moylough, Sligo, detail (N.M.D.)
35. Belt Reliquary found at Moylough, Sligo, detail (N.M.D.)
36. Glass stud with its clay mould from Lagore, Meath (N.M.D.); Killamery Brooch, Kilkenny (N.M.D.)
37. Engraved and carved bone from Lagore, Meath (N.M.D.)

251

Durham Libr.); detail of an annular brooch found in the crannog of Lough Ravel, Antrim (Bel.M.) (*Ph. F. Henry*)

63. Ms. 213, Cathedral Library, Cologne (Collectio canonum), beginning of text (*Ph. G. L. Marsh-Micheli*)
64. Slab at Gallen Priory, Offaly
65. Slab excavated at Gallen Priory, Offaly
66. Detail of an Irish gilt bronze object (Saint-Germain Museum) (*Ph. St G.M.*)
67. Detail of the Killamery Cross, Kilkenny
68. Moone Cross, Kildare
69. Crozier found at Ekerö, Sweden (Stockholm Museum) (*Ph. Stockh. M.*); bronze gilt plaque found at Marykyate, England (Br.M.)
70. Moone Cross, Kildare, the Three Children in the fiery Furnace; St Paul and St Anthony the hermits
71. Moone Cross, Kildare, the Twelve Apostles
72. Moone Cross, Kildare, Flight into Egypt; the Temptation of St Anthony
73. Old Kilcullen Cross, Kildare; carved panel
74. Cross at Old Kilcullen, Kildare
75. Cross of Kilrea, Kilkenny, west side
76. South Cross, Ahenny, Tipperary
77. South Cross, Ahenny, Tipperary, detail
78. Kilkieran Cross, Kilkenny
79. North Cross, Ahenny, Tipperary, north and west sides of the base
80. North Cross, Ahenny, Tipperary, south side of the base; base of cross, Mona Incha, Tipperary
81. Details of the pillar at Tibberaghny, Kilkenny, and of the cross at Moone, Kildare
82. Cross at Dromiskin, Louth
83. North Cross, Ahenny, Tipperary, east side of the base
84. South Cross, Clonmacnois, Offaly
85. South Cross at Clonmacnois, Offaly; St Martin's Cross at Iona, Scotland (*Ph. L. de Paor*)
86. North Cross, Lorrha, Tipperary (*Ph. H. S. Crawford*)

253

87. Bucket from Hoprekstad, Norway (Bergen Museum) (*Ph. F. Henry*)
88. Bealin Cross, Offaly (*Ph. H. S. Crawford*); detail from Ahenny Cross, Tipperary
89. Lichfield Gospels (Lichfield Cathedral), detail of the Chi-Rho
90. Top of bell-shine (N.M.D.), gilt bronze plaque found at Romføejellen, Norway (Oslo Museum) (*Ph. Oslo M.*)
91. North Cross, Clonmacnois, Offaly, detail; applied enamelled plaque from the Oseberg bucket (Bygdö Museum, Oslo) (*Ph. Oslo M.*)
92. Shaft of Banagher Cross, Offaly (N.M.D.)
93. Shaft of Banagher Cross, Offaly; reverse (N.M.D.)
94. Detail of the Banagher Cross (N.M.D.)
95. Pillar at Clonmacnois, Offaly
96. Cross at Iona, Scotland (*Ph. I. Crozier*); cross at Kilrea, Kilkenny
97. Cotton Ms. Otho. C.V., British Museum, symbol of St Mark
98. Lichfield Gospels (Lichfield Cathedral), the four symbols of the Evangelists
99. Ms. A.II.17, Cathedral Library, Durham, detail of Crucifixion (*Ph. Durham Libr.*)
100. Ms. 197, Corpus Christi College, Cambridge, beginning of the Gospel of St John
101. Ms. 213, Cathedral Library, Cologne (Collectio canonum), initial letter (*Ph. G. L. Marsh-Micheli*)
102. Lichfield Gospels (Lichfield Cathedral), detail; Lindisfarne Gospels (Br.M.); detail (*Ph. Br.M.*)
103. Lichfield Gospels (Lichfield Cathedral), portrait of St Mark
104. Lindisfarne Gospels (Br.M.), ornamental page (*Ph. Br.M.*)
105. Lichfield Gospels (Lichfield Cathedral), symbol of St Luke
106. Maihingen Gospels (Schloss Harburg, Germany), beginning of the Gospel of St Luke (*Ph. G. L. Marsh-Micheli*); Kilrea Cross, Kilkenny, detail
107. Lichfield Gospels (Lichfield Cathedral), beginning of the Gospel of St Mark, detail

List of Documentary Plates

I. Bronze disc from the Bann and enamelled bronze object from Lisnacroghera (Bel.M.) (*Ph. F. Henry*)

II. Irish bronze object found in a Viking grave in Norway (Trondheim Mus.; see Pl. 12) (*Ph. F. Henry*); filigree panel from the Tara Brooch compared during cleaning to a Saxon belt buckle decorated with filigree (Br.M.) (*Ph. F. Henry*)

III. Reverse of the Duvillaun Slab (Mayo; see Pl. 51) (*Ph. F. Henry*); slab found near Whithorn, Scotland (Whithorn Museum) (*Ph. I. Crozier*)

IV. Cross-slab on Caher Island, Mayo; engraved bust on the Killeen Cormac Pillar, Kildare; Killaghtee Slab, Donegal (*all Ph. F. Henry*)

V. Echternach Gospels (Bibliothèque nationale, Paris), symbol of St John (*Ph. B.N.*)

VI. Trier Gospels (Treasury of the Cathedral of Trier), initial letter (*Ph. G. L. Marsh-Micheli*); Ms. S.45.sup., Ambrosian Library, Milan, initial letter (*Ph. F. Henry*)

VII. Two birds on the fly-leaf of the Maihingen Gospels (Schloss Harburg, Germany) (*Ph. G. L. Marsh-Micheli*); birds on each side of a vase and birds perched on a vase, two details from the Syriac manuscript of Rabbula (Laurentian Library, Florence) (*Ph. Laur. Libr.*); Greek inscription on the Fahan Mura Slab, Donegal (*Ph. F. Henry*); Greek text of the Lord's Prayer on the last page of the manuscript of the *Vita Columbae* (Ms. 1, Municipal Library, Schaffhausen, Switzerland)

VIII. Ms. Rawlinson, G.167 (Bodleian Library, Oxford), illuminated initial page of the Gospel of St Luke (*Ph. O.U.Pr.*)

256

3

4

Innomine

& : in

DS extuidio

aunibur pencipeuen

POSC

qu

&

bo

9

II

emul
neq: zelau
quoniamtamqu
Et quemadmodumho
spena
Et inhubra
Reuelad nou

13

19

23

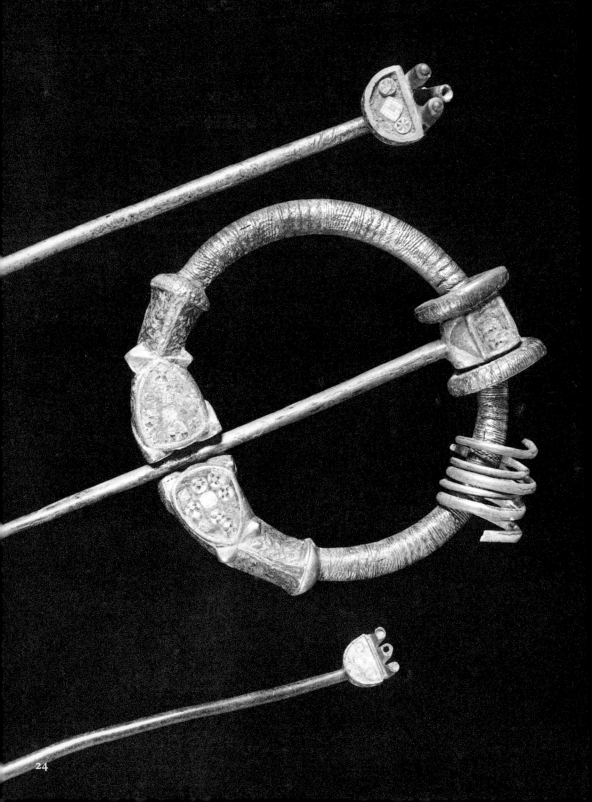

31

33

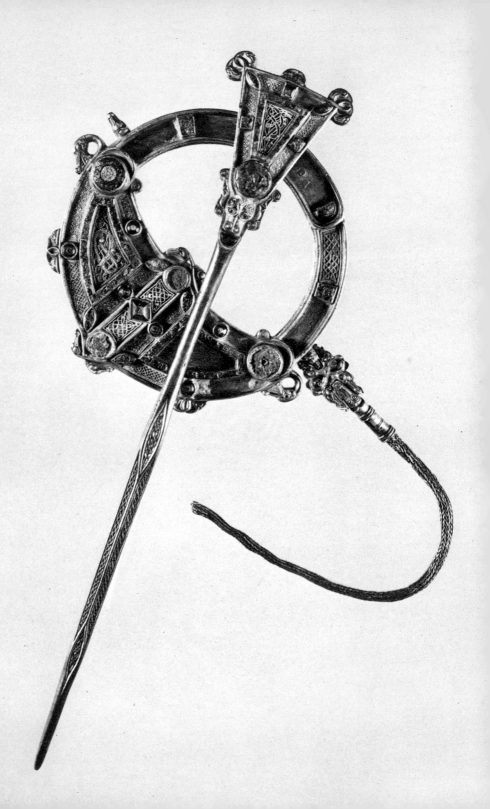

39

41

42

44

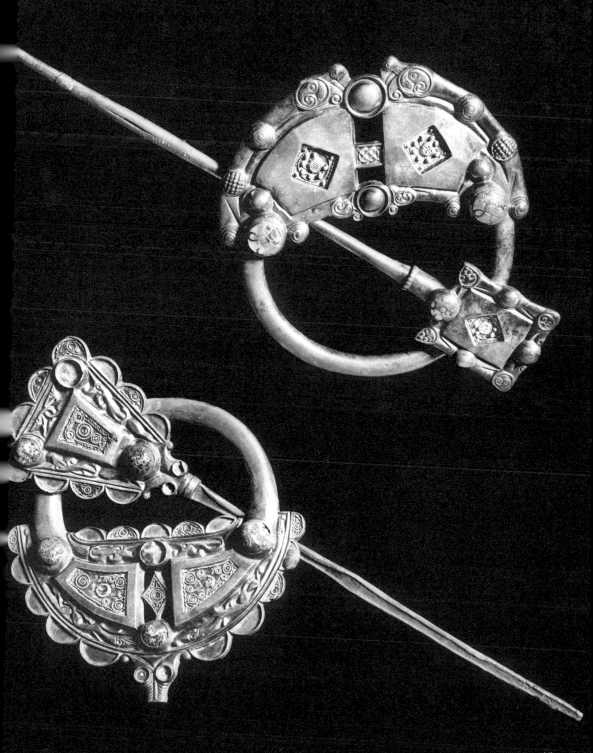

45

46

47

51

57

explicit
secundum
lucam

incipit
secundum
marcum

58

59

Incipit euangelium
secundum marcum

Nitium
euange
liihuxpi
fiui di sicut sc
riptum ines ea
pnofeta
gelum meum
uiam qui pne
Uox clamā
to panate u
tas factes et
fuit iohann
babtizans
babtismum
Inremisione

(inset, comparison manuscript)

Marci
caput I

Gū
euan
eli ihuxpi fili
di sicut scribtu
e in esaia
pnopheta ec
ce mitto ang
elum meum ante faciem
tuam qui pnaepanabitu
antuam. Uox clama
tis indeserto panate uiā
dni rectas facite semitas
eus. fuit iohannis
in deserto baptizans
pnaedicans baptismum
paenitentiae enemissi
em peccatonum egredie
batur adillum omnis iudeae
nego ethienusolymite uniuensi
baptizabantun abillo in ionda

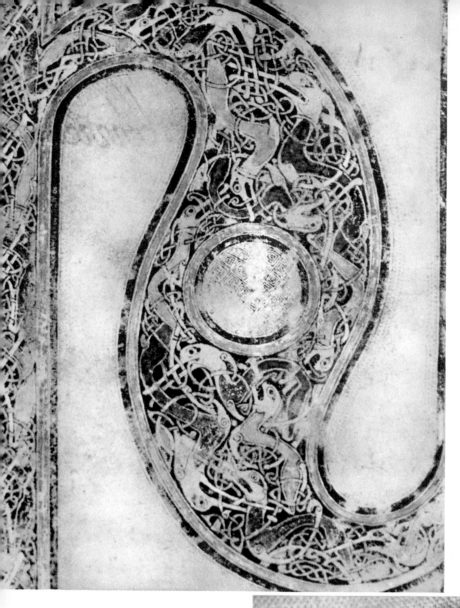

66

69

70

73

80

81

82

84

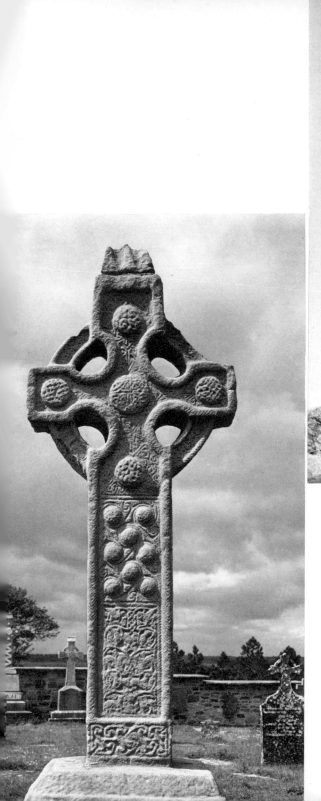

85

86

87

88

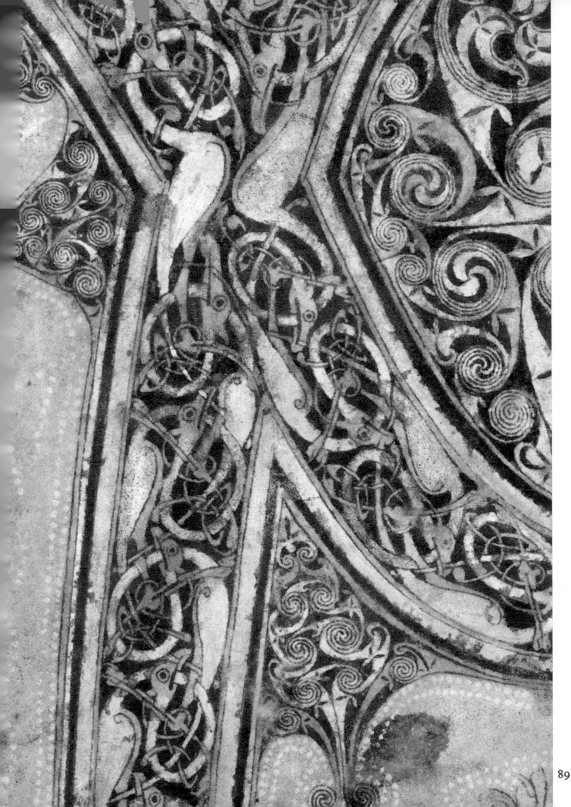

89

91

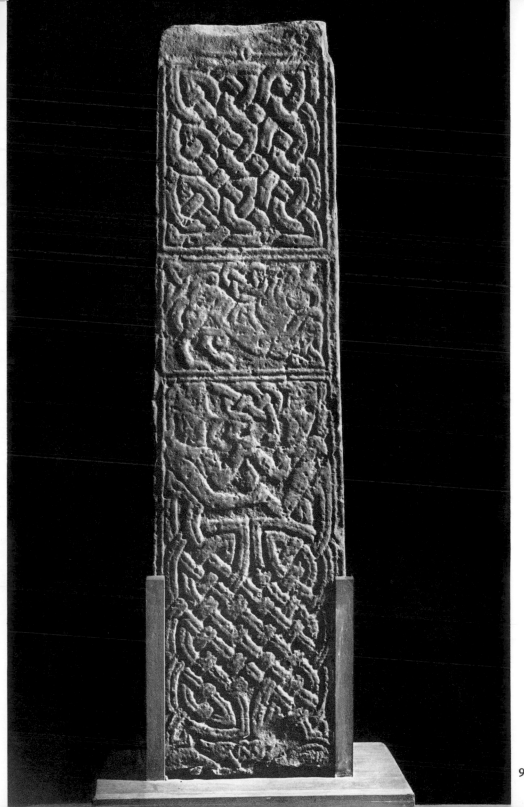

93

94

96

97

98

QNIAM
QUI
DEM
ᗺER et ueᖇ

anusque ka conf
se uideamur

capitul

eordi

eort

terii

Hihil

ter q

offer

quae species aclatu

102

103

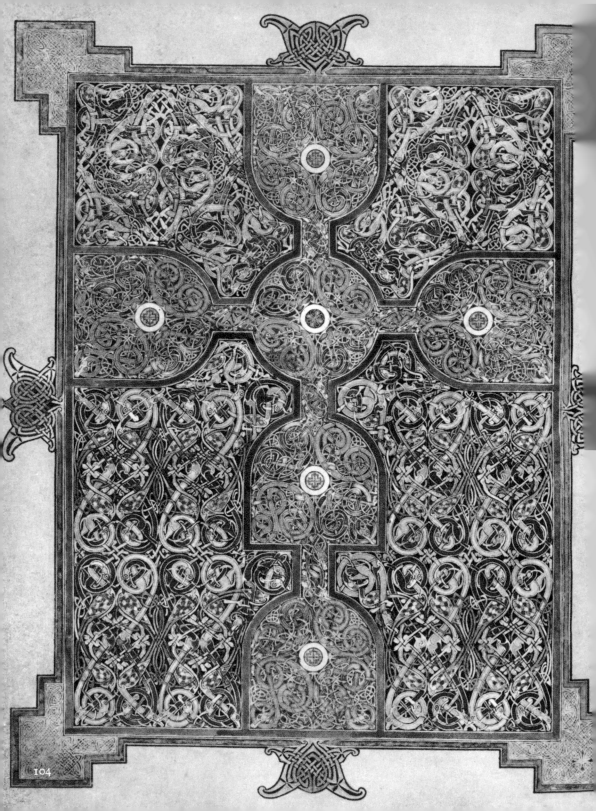

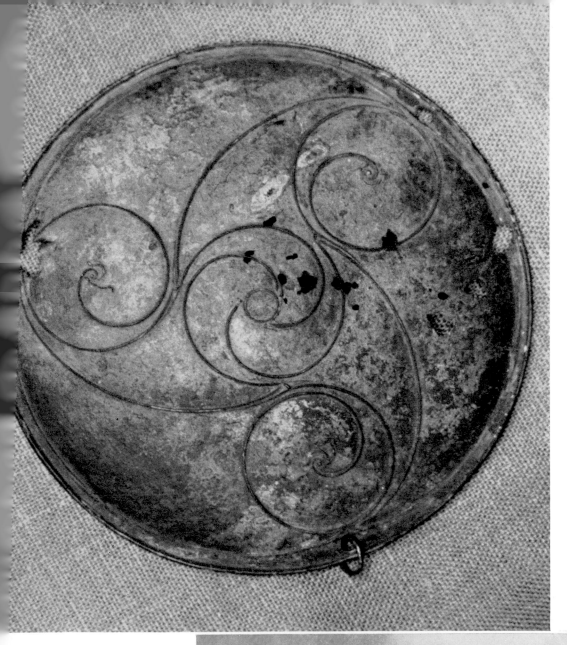

I

II

III

IV

IMAGO AQUILE

VI

VII

ΠΑΤΗΡ ΗΜΩΝ Ο ΕΙ ΕΝΤΟΙC ΥΡΑΝΟΙC · ΑΓΙΑC
ΘΗΤΩ ΤΟ ΟΝΟΜΑ COΥ · ΗΛΘΑΤΩ Η ΒΑCΙΛΕΙΑ COΥ ··
ΓΕΝΗΘΗΤΩ ΤΟ ΘΕΛΗΜΑ COΥ · ΩC ΕΝΟΥΡΑΝΩ ΚΑΙ
ΕΠΙ ΓΗC · ΤΟΝ ΑΡΤΟΝ ΗΜΩΝ ΤΟΝ ΕΠΙΟΥCΙΟΝ ΔΟC
ΗΜΙΝ CΗΜΕΡΟΝ · ΚΑΙ ΑΦΕC ΗΜΙΝ ΤΑ ΟΦΙΛΗΜΑΤΑ
ΗΜΩΝ · ΩC ΚΑΙ ΗΜΙC ΑΦΙΟΜΕΝ ΤΟΙC ΑΦΙΛΗΤΑΙC
ΗΜΩΝ · ΚΑΙΜΗ ΕΙC · ΕΝΕΓΚΗC ΗΜΑC ΕΙC ΠΙΡΑCΜΩΝ ·
ΑΛΛΑ ΡΥCΑΙ ΗΜΑC ΑΠΟΤΟΥ ΠΟΝΗΡΟΥ ·